11-11-18

TO DOLORES

CHARLES KING

BY James Fisher

UNBELIEVABLE

Unbelievable

Charles King

To order additional copies of this book, contact:
Xlibris
1-888-795-4274
www.Xlibris.com
Orders@Xlibris.com
774352

CONTENTS

May 22, 2008

On this particular night, Jake was entering in his journal what happened to him at work that day. To him, it was out of the ordinary; he thought it was very important. He did not know how important; he just had a hunch. Jake took the disk out, went into the garage, and made sure all his equipment was in his trunk. He then backed out of his garage very slowly, driving away. Jake and his friends had a system they thought was foolproof, where nobody could really find out what they were up to.

Jake drove around, looking for a phone booth. He was always very careful to make sure he was not followed. When he found the phone booth, he thought it all right for him to still drive around to make sure no strange car had parked there in the last few minutes. They all decided to try to use different phone booths at different times. Jake always did it at night. He found out that nobody was around trying to use the phone as much.

Jake finally parked his Ford Tempo beside the phone booth. He had to find a booth that was no more than ten feet from the car. He liked the Tempo mainly because of the passenger seat folding all the way back. Jake then got out of his car, opened his trunk, and carried the box in the passenger seat.

There inside the box was a computer with a modem. Jake and his friends even made a device that they thought would make sure the phone lines could not be traced. They even used change to make the call. When the operator told Jake it would be three dollars for the first three minutes, he then put in enough change for twelve minutes. The call came through. He quickly went to his car and placed the phone in his computer. They made a special battery pack so the computer would work in their cars. Jake turned on his disk drive. Whatever was on the disk was relayed to the home computer as they called it. Jake had that idea. He figured that if nobody knew where the main computer was, if they get caught, no one would ruin their work. This whole setup only took nine minutes.

Jake then decided to make sure his dad knew what he did, so he called. The answering machine kicked on. Jake said, "Damn it, Dad, just one time, you would be there to answer." Jake's dad never liked the machine, so it was in another room, where he would not be bothered with it. "Dad, you were right. Look at the computer. You have to check this out. I think they might be on to us. See you soon." Jake then hung up.

On the way back to his house, he had this machine in his car where he put the disk in, and it chopped the disk up in little pieces. Jake threw the pieces out the window a few blocks from his house and then pulled into his driveway.

The second he entered his house from the garage, he knew something was wrong. He yelled for Amanda; he thought she might have come early. She worked the three-to-eleven shift and usually arrived at Jake's at around eleven forty-five. It was only eleven o'clock. Nobody answered his yell. He started to turn on the light, and out of nowhere, he was hit on the back of the head.

Jake woke up with his hands and feet tied to a chair. One of the men grabbed him by his hair. The man just said, "Tell us who the rest of your friends are."

Jake stared at him and told him, "Go to hell."

The other man was ransacking the house. He found some computer disk and asked Jake, "Are these it?"

Jake just said, "Take anything you want. I do not know nothing."

The man grabbed him by his hair again. He said, "Jake, your buddy in Kansas messed up. We caught him. We killed him. In his belongings, your name came up. We put it all together and figured that you met him eight years ago. He has the same computer equipment you have. We want to know the rest of your group." Jake told them to go to hell again.

One of the men made a phone call. Jake could not hear what was said, but he knew it was not good. The man just said, "Kill him."

The other man said, "Any particular way?"

"Yes, make an example on this one."

The man grabbed Jake's hair and raised his neck high. Then with a smile on his face, he cut Jake's throat, not enough to kill him fast but enough for him to know he would die soon. The man then kicked him a few times. They untied Jake's weak body from the chair. While Jake was crawling, they took a nightstick and hit his legs with it. You could hear the knee break with his legs too. The men left out of the front door, which did not shut all the way because the chain caught it; they just kept walking slowly, not to disturb anyone. In less than thirty minutes, Jake's life was taken out of him; the only thing was the men still did not know no more than they did.

Amanda was running a little late after work; she stopped to get some food and gas. She arrived at around eleven fifty-eight. She knew something was wrong right off the bat. The front light was not on, which Jake always had on for her. The garage door was open. She knew Jake always kept the door closed, just a habit he had. When she walked to the door, it was not shut all the way; she had seen the chain in the door. She remembered telling Jake several times that the chain was too long.

Part of her told her not to go in; then the other part told her she had to see if Jake was all right. When she opened the door, she could tell that the house had been ransacked just with the little light from the other room. Amanda turned the light on, which was by the corner of the wall, just a few feet from the door. When the light went on, she could see Jake's body on the floor with blood all over the carpet. She let out a scream and took off running.

Jake's neighbor was outside, letting his dog out, about the same time Amanda screamed. He ran across the yard and caught Amanda. He asked, "What is wrong, Amanda?" He did not know Amanda real well, but through the last thirteen months Jake and Amanda were seeing each other, they did meet.

Amanda just said, "Jake has been murdered and passed away." Mr. Henderson carried her in his house and called the police.

It seemed like an hour. But then when you want someone fast, it seems like they never get there. Amanda awakened and started to scream. Mrs. Henderson tried to calm her down, but Amanda just continued crying and muttering, "What happened?"

Two police officers blocked off the house. Two more came over to Mr. Henderson's house to talk to Amanda and Jake's neighbors. Then this lieutenant, Ciara Steel, arrived at the same time the officers walked into the house. The lieutenant seemed charming and did not ask Amanda too many questions, just the time she and then Mr. Henderson arrived. They both said around midnight. Then Amanda told the lieutenant that Jake's father was still alive in Illinois. Someone should call him. The lieutenant said they would take care of it.

The lieutenant looked all through Jake's house. She could not really tell if anything was stolen, but by just looking at the body, it looked like they tortured or beaten him up severely.

Coal City, Illinois, 1:50 a.m.

Tom Parkes and Charles Appel were having a good time at the local bar. They had been golfing that day. They were celebrating their golf game. They always had their nineteenth hole at this tavern. Today was a special one. It was the first time they both shot in the low eighties. Tom shot an eighty-two, and Charles shot an eighty-three. They both knew they had their limit to drink, so they would have one more on last call, and then Charles would take Tom home.

They left the tavern at two ten. Tom just lived less than a quarter of a mile from the tavern. Tom asked Charles, "Do you want a snack before you go home?"

Charles said, "No, I will take you home and then go home myself." Tom said OK, so they started toward Tom's house.

Charles noticed the city police car driving by him, going toward the tavern. He stopped at the stop sign. He noticed the police car was turning around. Charles told Tom, "Well, I believe I am going to get my first DUI."

Tom said, "Surely not. You were not speeding, and you stopped at the stop sign."

Charles went straight just two blocks from Tom's house. Sure enough, the police car turned on its red lights. So Charles turned alongside the road. To Tom and Charles's dismay, Kate was in the police car. She ran up to the car crying. Tom jumped out of the car and asked Kate, "What is wrong?"

Then Burt walked up on Charles's side of the car. Charles looked at Burt and just muttered, "Is it Jake?" He remembered Burt's look when Burt had to tell him about his wife, daughter-in-law, and grandson Jeramy getting killed in a car wreck. Burt must have had the same look then as he did this night.

Burt told Charles to come with him. "Kate will drive your car to your house."

As Charles was getting in Burt's car, Charles asked, "Well, what happened?"

Burt, looking at Charles, said, "I am very sorry to tell you this, but your son has been murdered. Jake's girlfriend found him at his house dead."

Charles was in shock by the time they got to his house, which only took two minutes. He was just staring up at the sky with tears streaming out of his eyes. Then Charles just said, "Why me, Lord? Why take all my family?"

As they all went in the house, Kate was trying her best to calm Charles, but even she was crying. Through the last five years, Tom and Kate had become very close to him. Charles was just staring at the wall like he was in a daze. He looked right at Burt's eyes and asked, "Are they sure it is Jake?"

Burt looked at Charles and told him, "Wish I could lie to you. This police lieutenant, Ciara Steel, told me that Jake's girlfriend definitely made a positive identification."

Charles looked at all of them. "I am going to Newark as fast as we can make it." Then he asked Tom, "You will go with me, won't you?"

Without even hesitating, Tom looked at Charles and said, "If that is what you want to do, I will go with you."

Charles looked at Kate. "Could you stay in town to handle anything that I might need done while we go to Newark?"

Kate was just crying and then told Charles, "Tom and I will do whatever you ask."

Charles looked at Burt and said, "I need this policeman's full name and to know how to get in touch with the police out there."

Burt just told Charles, "You get your flight. Kate can call me to tell me your flight times, and the police will meet you at the airport."

Charles thanked Burt for helping him out. Burt just said, "I am very sorry to have to tell you. Even the Newark police thought so. They tried to call your house, and then they kept on getting your answering machine. This lieutenant did not believe that was how you should get bad news. So the Newark police called me."

Kate then said, "Well, Burt, when we work out the details, I will call you."

Burt said, "Good luck." And then he left.

Charles went to his kitchen cabinet right when the door shut. He reached for his whiskey bottle. He went to his other cabinet for two tall water glasses. Then he poured the glasses half full of whiskey. Charles walked to the refrigerator, reached in the icebox, and grabbed some ice. The whiskey splashed out some but not enough to bother him. He handed Tom one glass and just stared at him, and then he said, "I think I am going to get as plastered as I can. Then tomorrow I hope this is all a dream."

While they were at the table drinking and talking about Jake and what might have been, Charles handed Tom his car key. "I will be all right. Just take my car so you and Kate can get home. If you'll be back here tomorrow morning, say around nine o'clock or so, we will see if this is a nightmare or not."

Charles poured another glass of whiskey. By this time, he was well intoxicated. He walked to his living room chair, sat down, and passed out. The glass of whiskey spilled on the floor. While Kate picked the glass up, Tom told her to go home and get some sleep. "I will stay here with Charles." Tom started to lie on the couch and said, "Just be here in the morning."

Kate told Tom, "For once, you make sense." And she went home.

The next morning, Kate arrived back in Charles's house. She noticed, looking through the window, that the kitchen light was still on. Even the back porch door was not locked. So Kate walked in. Tom was still on the couch, asleep. Charles was still in his chair. Kate did not think Charles had moved even an inch since she left last night.

Kate shook Tom. He jumped up and said, "What are you doing here?"

"It is nine o'clock. We have to wake Charles up."

Tom looked at Kate; they must have had the same wish. "Do we have to wake him to tell him last night was not a dream?"

Kate shook Charles very lightly. He woke up, just stared at both of them, and said, "It was not a dream, was it? Jake is dead." Kate started to cry and just shook her head.

Charles stood up; he was shaking and, in a shaking voice, said, "We have some decision to make this morning. Will you help me?"

Tom just stared at Charles. "You know we will."

Charles started to take his shower. In the meantime, Tom went home to get cleaned up. Kate was making a list of things she felt should be done.

Charles, Tom, and Kate were sitting at the table. They all made their decision on how to handle everything. Kate made the plane reservations, called the Newark Police Department, and even called the funeral home to tell them that Tom and Charles were going to Newark. They would call back and make final arrangements. Tom left to fill the car with gas and went to the bank to cash a check that Charles filled out.

Charles and Tom were in Springfield on a plane headed for Saint Louis to make a transfer. They arrived in Saint Louis and caught their flight headed for Newark. Tom could not believe it; he had not flown too often, and this was one of the few times the airlines was only ten minutes behind schedule.

On the flight, neither one said too much. Charles was staring out the window like he still was in a dream. Tom decided to try to get Charles to be more of himself. Charles did not even notice that Tom stopped the stewardess to buy some drinks. Tom handed him a glass. "Here, you need this." Charles looked at Tom and just said, "I do not know what I would do without a good friend as you."

Tom just looked at Charles and started to drink his. Then he said, "To friends."

Just about fifteen minutes to land, the stewardess walked up to Tom since he had an aisle seat. Charles always liked to fly, but he always took a window seat. She asked if one of them was Mr. Appel. Charles told her, "I am."

She said, "The pilot received a radio message to tell you that a lieutenant, Ciara Steel, will be at the airline gate when we land."

Charles looked at Tom and said, "I knew if anyone can get something done, it'd be Kate."

Tom laughed. "Well, you know Kate. They would speak to either us or her. You know they did not want Kate to be here and give them hell." Charles even laughed on that one. That was the first time he smiled since they got the bad news.

After they landed and as he was walking to the terminal, Charles noticed this woman staring at the people while they were walking past her. Tom even noticed the woman. She had nice long black hair, a beautiful face, and a real nice-looking body. As they were walking closer to her, she was walking toward them. She said, "Excuse me, are you Mr. Appel?"

Charles told her, "Yes, I am Mr. Appel."

She then shocked him. "I am Lt. Ciara Steel. Then she said, "And you must be Tom." Tom stared at her and said yes. They all shook hands.

The lieutenant said, "Your wife, Kate, described you guys to a tee."

They started to leave the terminal. Tom told the lieutenant, "What about our luggage?"

She turned around. "My partner, George, is getting it for you." They were leaving the airport in a matter of minutes. The lieutenant introduced them to George.

They were having small talk, and then Charles thought, *If I am going to get my answers, I might as well start asking questions.* It then just came out. "I want to see my boy's body."

Ciara looked at her partner; they had this "well, what to do now" look. She pulled off the road onto the shoulder. She stopped the car, and then she got out to open Charles's door. She said, "Get out. We have to talk."

He said, "What you have to say, you say in front of all of us."

She just said, "Get out. I want to talk to you. You can tell your friend Tom whatever you want." So Charles got out.

As they were walking toward the back, the lieutenant said, "Mr. Appel—"

He then interrupted, "Just call me Charles, OK?"

She said, "Sure, Charles. I do not think it is a good idea to see your son's body."

"I want to see him," I explained in a stressed voice.

The lieutenant just looked at me with her beautiful eyes, but in these eyes, I could see fear. "Well, Charles, your son was treated very cruelly. He was murdered. I just feel that no father should see his son like that."

Charles looked at her right in the eye. "I am going to see my son's body. If it is that bad, I like to get it over with as soon as possible."

She just looked at Charles. "OK, we will do it right now."

"Good." They walked back to the car; as she started it, Charles began to cry as he told Tom what she said.

They arrived at the morgue. Charles had never been in one and had only seen it on television. There was not much difference. They walked in a room. The lieutenant knew the person who was working there. She arranged it so that it was just her, Tom, and Charles in the room. When she pulled the sheet off Jake's face, Charles started to yell. You could tell that they beat on it like a punching bag. Then the two grabbed Charles and started to force him out of the room. He just told Tom, "I want a few minutes with Jake by myself." They all calmed down, and Lieutenant Steel gave in.

Charles was terrified of seeing Jake's face like this. He was shocked that someone could do this to his son. He knew, though, or had this feeling that he had to see the rest of his body. As he pulled the sheet past the shoulders and then to his chest, all Charles could do was scream.

Tom ran in the room and grabbed him. He yelled at Charles so he could get a hold of himself. Charles could tell that, as he was yelling, Tom looked at Jake's arms and chest. Tom, all of a sudden, let go of Charles. He just said, "Oh my god." Jake's arms was so mangled that you could tell that they were broken. His chest was beaten with a club. His ribs were bruised; even one rib was sticking out.

George was shaking Charles so hard that when he did get his senses back, he took a swing at him. Luckily, he ducked. The lieutenant was talking to Tom. They were led out of the room. This all seemed like it took hours. But when Charles looked at the clock, he was only in the room less than five minutes or less by himself. Charles would never forget that horrible beating Jake was given. He made a promise to himself that he would find out who did it and why someone would do this to his son.

Lieutenant Steel took them to her office, where they had a cup of coffee. Charles never drank coffee; then again, he never would have dreamed seeing his son's body in a morgue. She apologized for letting Charles see Jake. He told her it was very shocking to him. "I will probably never forget it in my life. I would never forgive myself if I did not take a look at my son either."

Charles explained to Lieutenant Steel that he had to make funeral arrangements. "Could this be done?"

Lieutenant Steel said, "Sure, I believe so." She then grabbed her phone and asked her boss or someone.

When she hung up the phone, she said, "Mr. Appel, go ahead and make your arrangements." She even let him use her phone. Charles called Kate and asked her to call the funeral home. Lieutenant Steel passed Charles a note with the phone number to give to Kate. He could hardly speak, so he just handed the phone to Tom. Tom talked to Kate, gave her the information, and then hung up.

Charles was finally getting his senses back. His voice was still shaking. He told everybody in the room, "I want to see Jake's house and his girlfriend, Amanda, before we go back home."

Lieutenant Steel then went to her phone. She must be talking to her boss again. She asked if she could stay with the two until they went back to their hometown. After she hung up, Lieutenant Steel said, "Well, it is all taken care of. I will take you wherever you want to go until you leave our city." Charles was pleased that Lieutenant Steel could be with them. It just seemed good to have a woman around, not to mention a policewoman.

They arrived at Jake's at around 5:30 p.m. The police still had the place blocked off. Lieutenant Steel did not have to show her badge; the policeman there just let them through. Lieutenant Steel explained to Charles that if he had seen anything missing or unusual, he should let her know. He told her he would cooperate as much as he can.

Tom had never been at Jake's house before. He knew Jake was a computer person though. He asked the lieutenant if all his computer equipment was in order. She did not know for sure; she thought Charles could help them. Charles browsed through the computer equipment. He told her there was something strange. She looked at him excitedly and said, "What is it?"

"Jake had his own way of using disks. All his disks have been ransacked. I even notice some are missing."

She asked, "How do you know that?"

"Well, I taught him my system. And through the years, he used the same way I keep my disks. We number them. Then if we have something important on a certain one, we write the first five letters of that file beside that number. To me, it just seems weird that, out of all these disks, there is not one with letters on it, just numbers." Charles showed her. "Here is disk number 10, and then it goes to number 14. Probably 11 through 13 had letters on it."

Lieutenant Steel looked at him funny and then asked him how well he knew computers. He started to tell her, and then Tom started to laugh. As he was laughing, he said, "Charles taught Jake all he knows until Jake went to college in computers and law. Then old Dad was learning from the son."

Charles told Lieutenant Steel, "I know computers, but I have not kept up with them for the last few years."

Lieutenant Steel showed Charles all the equipment in Jake's car. She told him, "The police computer people said, with all this equipment, your son could reach any computer he wanted to." At that moment, Charles realized he might just know more about Jake's murder than he thought. After a few more minutes, he told her he had seen enough.

Charles noticed Lieutenant Steel looked at her watch. He asked her if she had a meeting with someone. She just said, "Even a policewoman gets hungry."

Tom looked at Charles and then said, "Well, I am hungry too."

Charles said, "Well, if we are going to think right, our bodies have to have energy." He asked Lieutenant Steel if she could take them to their hotel, where they can eat and she can go wherever she wanted.

She looked at him in a funny way. Out of the blue, she said, "Are you trying to get rid of me?"

Charles explained to her that she had been a great help in helping him with the loss of his son. "I just figured you have your job to do, not to mention your private life."

Lieutenant Steel just gave him that look again and then said, "You worry about your plans. I will worry about mine. I will be glad to have dinner with you and your friend."

In bewilderment, Charles said, "I will be glad to have you with us."

They were at the hotel in no time to Charles's dismay. Tom did not know how they got there; neither did Charles. When you have the police doing the driving, it does not take long. They all went to the lobby. Tom said he would check them in and meet them in the dining room. While Tom was gone, Charles ordered some drinks, two beers for Tom and him. Lieutenant Steel ordered a screwdriver. She gave Charles that look and then said, "I am off duty."

He looked back at her, and out of the blue, he mumbled, "In that case, do not forget to call me Charles and my friend Tom."

She started to smile. "Well, you can call me Ciara."

Charles smiled and then said, "Well, let's drink to new friends."

Tom showed up just as they were drinking. Charles told Tom, "Well, Lieutenant Steel has a first name. We can call this fine lieutenant of Newark Ciara."

Tom grinned and then said, "To new friends." Ciara started to laugh. Tom looked at Charles. "You did not do what I think you did."

"I did."

"You thief, that is my line. You've stolen that from me again."

Charles explained to Ciara that, through the years, Tom and he had met a lot of strangers. One time, Tom said that line. "I just borrow it now and again."

Tom was laughing. "Now and again? You say it more than I do."

"Well, it is a good one, so I use it a lot."

After they ate, they went to the hotel bar to have one more drink. Ciara had to go. She told them she had a big day tomorrow. Charles asked her if it would be possible if she could give him Amanda's phone number and address. "I would like to talk to her before we leave." Ciara did not hesitate. She went through her purse and pulled out a notebook. She copied down the number and address and then gave it to Charles. On this paper was her number at home and the police number and her extension.

Ciara said, "If you are ever back, call me."

He told her, "I most certainly will."

Tom and Charles had a few drinks and then went to their room. As they walked in, Tom immediately opened the little bar that was in the hotel room. He said, "They make it awfully easy to get drunk here." Charles agreed, and then they opened their beers.

Charles told Tom, "We make two phone calls."

Tom asked, "Who the hell are we going to call?"

Tom hardly got it out when Charles said, "You call Kate to check out the funeral arrangements."

Tom called Kate; after a few minutes, he said, "Hell, Charles, you talk to her."

Kate told Charles Jake's body would be in Coal City sometime tomorrow. He said, "Good. Tell Nate that I want visitation before the funeral and no church service. I will speak to Nate tomorrow, but tell him the service will be on the twenty-fifth or twenty-sixth."

Kate asked if he was all right. He told her, "With good friends, I have to be all right."

Charles gave the phone back to Tom. They talked just for a few minutes more and then hung up. Without even taking a breath, Tom asked, "Well, are you going to call Amanda?"

"You're damn right. I believe something is funny about this whole mess." Tom gave Charles his funny look. He told Tom, "Trust me until we get on the plane."

Tom, the good friend that he was, just said, "OK, no questions until we are on the plane."

Charles dialed the number Ciara gave him. The phone rang several times. Then a nice young voice answered. He asked if it was Amanda. She said, "Yes, who is this? Do I know you?"

He told her, "Sort of. I am Jake's father. I want to talk with you in person before we have to go back home tomorrow."

She was crying. Amanda said, "Sure, Mr. Appel. I would be glad to."

He explained their plane would leave at one thirty in the afternoon. "How about eight thirty in the morning?" Amanda told him she would be off. "That would be great." He apologized for not seeing her today because of the police and funeral arrangements.

Amanda started to cry again, and so did Charles. While Amanda was crying, she said, "I will be glad to see you in the morning." Then she hung up.

Tom asked if Charles was all right. He told Tom, "Yes, but I think it is all hitting me now. I will never see Jake again." And he threw the beer can against the wall. The beer went everywhere.

Tom walked up to Charles, hugged him, and said, "Get it out."

May 24, 7:00 a.m.

Tom woke Charles up. Charles still had on his clothes from yesterday. He asked Tom, "What happened?" Tom told him he passed out, so he left him that way. Tom already went down to the lobby to check out where Amanda lived. "The hotel clerk said it is around thirty minutes by cab, so I woke you up." Charles thanked Tom, took a shower, and got dressed.

Charles called down the lobby to get them a cab. The hotel clerk said, "No problem." As they entered the lobby, the cab was already waiting for them.

They jumped in the cab, and Charles told the driver the address. Charles asked him, "How far was it?"

The cabdriver replied, "About twenty to thirty minutes, depends on traffic."

"That is what I told you," Tom said in a distrusting voice.

Charles laughed and told Tom, "I believe you. I just wanted to know if the cabdriver is going to tell us the truth."

Charles could not believe how people could live in the big cities. He was very surprised that Jake liked it so much since all his immediate family always lived in a very small town. He thought about it for a second. He thought if he were only in Coal City, he probably never would have been murdered.

Tom was looking out the window. He turned around. "You know, Charles, I do not know how people could live in the big cities."

"That is exactly what I was thinking."

The cabdriver pulled alongside the street. He said, "There is your building."

Charles was very nervous. In fact, he was so nervous that he was already twenty feet from the cab. Tom yelled, "Wait for me!"

Charles did not realize that someone had to pay for the cab. Tom took care of it, just smiled, and said, "You owe me one."

"I won't forget."

"I know you won't. I won't let you."

As they were walking toward the apartment building, they thought it looked very nice. There was a three-car garage attached to the building. There were three mailboxes. So they assumed there must be three apartments in the building. When they entered the main door, there was a hallway about twenty long. The door on the right had a number 1 with the person's name on it. It was not Amanda. Down a few feet, there was a door on the left. This one was Amanda's. They assumed the stairs toward the end led to the third apartment.

The first thing Charles noticed even before he knocked on the door was a box beside the door. He noticed the red light was on. He told Tom, "This is the same box that Jake fixed in my house and he had in his house."

When Charles knocked on the door, Tom asked, "When the red light is on is when someone opens the door?"

"Yes, you are right, just depends on what door."

No one answered the door. Naturally, as they were from a small town, Charles tried the door. It was unlocked; in fact, it seemed that the door was not even latched. The door came open without any force all. Tom and Charles looked at each other like, "Should we go in or not?" Charles yelled for Amanda and got no answer. Tom yelled too, with no reply either. By this time, they already were eight feet in her apartment.

Amanda had a nice big living room. The kitchen was connected to the living room. There was on the left side of the kitchen another door on the back wall. Charles opened it. What he had seen he could not believe. There was a girl's naked body on the bed. She had been tied up, with her hands on the front of the bed. Her legs were tied spread apart, one ankle tied on each side of the bed.

You could tell Amanda had been beaten up very bad. Her eyes were black and blue. Big bruises were on her rib cage. Her breasts even looked like they had been tortured in some manner. Charles could tell she suffered a lot before she died. He did not know how long he was in the room. Tom grabbed him and asked, "What should we do?"

"Well, in the dumb movies, you do not touch nothing and call the police." So that was what they did. Charles shut Amanda's bedroom door and told Tom to call Lieutenant Steel.

Tom noticed Charles was walking toward the other door. Tom yelled, "What the hell are you doing?"

"I have to look in this room before the police gets here."

Tom started to the phone and said, "Do not do nothing stupid."

"Call the police. Let's get this over with."

Charles then went to the other room; the door was already partially open. He just took his foot and pushed it a little more. *There it is. I knew it would be here.* There was a nice computer just like Jake's; in fact, it was like the one Jake brought him. He knew right then that whatever Jake was working on, Amanda knew something about it.

He looked through her desk. He found a lot of disks. He knew he would find that. He did see that Amanda did not have a modem though. The computer was on the main screen, and there was nothing about e-mail. Jake had one; he also had all that equipment in his car.

Charles looked in an open drawer in the desk. He could tell someone ransacked through it. In fact, this room was a mess. Then he had this feeling that whoever did this terrible thing knew what they were looking for.

He could not get in any other drawer without being noticed. So he just looked around. Charles could not find nothing else that looked out of place, so he walked back in the living room. Tom just stared at him and said, "I hope the hell we do not end up in jail."

"I believe I know something. I won't be sure until we get home."

Tom had been waiting patiently. "Well, what is it?"

"I will tell you everything on the plane. Right now, I do not trust anyone in this city."

Tom just gave Charles this look and then mumbled, "You've been watching too many movies."

By this time, two police officers walked in. Charles explained where the body was. The police made them sit down. They made sure they would not touch anything. One officer asked what they touched before they arrived. Tom and Charles told them but not that Charles went in the other room.

Lieutenant Steel arrived; this whole thing seemed to happen like an hour or so, but really, it was only a few minutes. Charles looked at the clock on the wall. The time was eight forty. The lieutenant spoke to Tom and Charles just for a few seconds. She went in the bedroom and told the police to make sure they looked for any evidence and make sure nothing was moved from the crime scene.

Ciara came over to Charles. He could tell she was shook up herself. Then she said, "This girl has been tortured more or less like your son."

He then said, "More so. It is obvious she was raped as well, not just beaten up."

More police came in with so much equipment. Lieutenant Steel and her partner took the men to their hotel. Tom and Charles told them everything they did. They did not tell anybody that Charles went in the other room. Lieutenant Steel asked Charles if he noticed that little box by the apartment door. He told her he did. She then told him she noticed the computer system was similar to Jake's. Charles looked right at her eyes. "I did not see that." She told them it was in the other room.

Tom gave Charles his funny look when he lied to Lieutenant Steel. Tom did not say anything at all. Charles knew he would not because of their friendship. Charles told himself then, *I have to tell Tom as soon as we get out of this town.*

Charles explained that their flight was leaving soon. He asked if it was all right to leave. Lieutenant Steel looked at her partner and then said, "Sure, we will take you. We might have to get in touch with you for some questions."

He told them, "I will be more than glad to come back after my son's funeral. In fact, I know I will be back to see what you find out."

CHAPTER 1

The Funeral

On the way to their hotel room, there was not a word said by the lieutenant and her partner. Neither the police nor Charles knew who Amanda's family was. They knew they would find out by the time they would arrive at the police station. Tom and Charles went to the room to pick up their luggage and pay the bill. They were not gone fifteen minutes. The lieutenant told them that the police officer at Amanda's apartment found out where Amanda's family was. Charles asked the lieutenant if he could have their names and address. Lieutenant Steel said, "Sure, I'll be glad to. Sure you do not know something?"

He told her, "After Jake's funeral, I am going to visit Amanda's family. If between both of us if I find out anything, I will make sure I tell you."

Lieutenant Steel then grabbed a scratch pad and wrote their names and address on it. "Please do not call them until the police has. I will get in trouble. I am doing this more as a friend, not as a cop." He thanked Ciara and promised her he would be back to see her.

Tom and Charles arrived at the airport just in time. It helps when you have the police with you. They dropped them off and had the airport security take care of their tickets and take them to the plane.

As their plane was taxiing off, Tom finally said something. Charles knew he would. Tom had been quiet for too long. Tom looked him straight into his eyes. "All right, Charles, I have been quiet long enough. Why did you lie to the police? You are not leveling with me. Now start speaking."

Charles looked at Tom and said, "All right, here is what I know. I will not be sure until we get back to Coal City."

Tom said in desperation, "Well, keep talking."

"You see, about seven years ago, Jake came to visit me. He had a friend with him. I did not know they were even there at all until I came back from golfing. It was a surprise to me. You might remember that day. Jake and his friend were at the tavern when we arrived for our nineteenth hole. Jake already had our beer sitting on the bar. He'd seen us driving in the parking lot. Jake then introduced us to his friend Joseph. You and I were partners in pool and gave them a good lesson."

Tom was thinking and then, out of the blue, said, "Was that the time I ran the table on them?"

"Yes, you ran the table twice that day. After we played pool, I gave you a ride to your house. Jake and Joseph went to my house. When I walked in the house, I knew something was up. Jake always called at least a week in advance when he would come home. I just did not know what was wrong. I did not want to create a scene at the tavern, so I just went along on whatever Jake wanted to do.

"To make this short, while we were playing golf, Jake and Joseph set up a computer system in my den. I never saw anything like it before. I read about them. I just have never seen one. This system, at the minimum, cost eight to ten thousand, which at that time was a lot of equipment. Jake and Joseph told me they were not quite done with it, but by tomorrow, it would be running. I had a thousand questions to ask them. I narrowed it down to one. I asked them where in the hell they got that kind of money. Jake's only explanation was there were eleven of them. They all split the cost, and they picked my house for the central unit. Jake just said, 'Trust me, Dad, on this one.' I told them, 'As long you are not breaking any laws, OK.' Joseph looked at me like, well, they had already broken the law. Jake just said, 'Well, Dad, we are going to be as fair and honest as possible. Just have to trust me.'

"So anyway, you know I like computers. Part of me could not wait to get my fingers on that keyboard. Joseph could not believe how I picked the system up. Jake told Joseph that I was in computers before he was born. I told Joseph I am mostly a hacker.

"The next day, they called the phone company to set up the modem. After the phone company left, Joseph went in Jake's room and came out with a box, just like the one in Jake's car trunk. Joseph hooked it up to my phone line that went to the computer. Then Joseph punched in some letters. The next thing I knew, the disk drive in the den was working. Jake and Joseph were very happy. Jake told me they were done now. Then Joseph told me, 'We are in now.'

"Joseph went back to his job in Kansas City. Jake spent the week with me. We all went golfing that day. In fact, we all shot in the eighties. You remember that?"

Tom looked at Charles. "Yeah, I remember that now. The whole day, all you and Jake talked about was computers."

"Yeah, that is right. Come to think about it, that was probably a boring day to you."

Tom said, "Well, I had better than I had worse, not very many though."

"The rest of the week, Jake gave me a problem with the new system. He wanted me to make a program that could be coded and decoded. So no matter who typed it on, that system could put it in code so nobody could tell it was typed. Jake wanted it basic too. He just said, 'Only two new computers, the rest just basic.'

"Jake went back to New York. This was where Jake was at this time. Well, you know me, when it comes to making programs, I love to do that with computers. I worked on Jake's idea for several months. In fact, it screwed up my golf swing. When I finally got it done, I called Jake. He was so happy you thought I gave him a million dollars. He said we would be there Saturday to check it out. I could hardly believe this because I called him on a Thursday.

"Jake and his friend Nate was there early Saturday morning. I was surprised Joseph was not with him. Jake just said, 'Oh yeah, Dad, this is Nate. I forgot to introduce you. Nate is our best computer expert. Joseph's job is to hook them up, but he is not really our best computer expert.'

"Just after very few words, they went in the den. I remember it was six o'clock in the morning. Nate started to check out my program. In the meantime, Jake put the doorbell to my back door and put a switch to the den door and a special electric lock to the den. Jake explained if the code was not entered right, then the doorbell light would be red. I told Jake, well, that is good, but they can still get in by pressing the wrong code. Jake said they knew that, but you would know if someone was in the computer room without being noticed.

"Nate was astounded about how I made the code for them. I gave them this one disk that you use first. You type just like you always do. Then after you are done, punch in these few keys. Bingo, the material that you wrote changes to a coded one. I told Jake and Nate the only drawback was it would really destroy what you wrote. So nobody could get your material by going in another way to see what you wrote. You have to save it on another disk.

"Nate was real glad except he asked, 'How do you decode it?' I gave them this other disk. I loaded the coded material first. Then I put in this other disk and typed in some key letters, and all of a sudden, the material was decoded. Then you burn the coded disk that had the material on it so nobody could use it.

"Jake asked if I made copies. I gave him eleven disks that would code the material. Jake told me to keep the only one that would decode the material and to always make a copy disk to put in the safety-deposit box at the bank. Jake told me, 'This is very important. You make sure there is always a blank disk every morning and night. Make two copies and two safety-deposit boxes.' I just said, 'Why two?' In case anything happens to either one of us, the survivor can get the disk with no legal bullshit. I will have the keys to both, but he will only have a key to one.

"I walked to the car with Nate and Jake. Jake told me they will check out all this thoroughly. If they find a bug in it, they will be in touched. I told them there is no bugs. From that day on, I have been putting disks in the safety boxes. I say they have over 150 of them.

"In fact, one night, around three o'clock, I heard the phone ringing. I was half asleep when I answered the phone. It was Jake. All he said was 'Dad, you have to change the disk right now.' I started to talk to him. Jake cut me off and said, 'I am sorry, Dad, to bother you, but there is no time to bullshit. Change that disk now.' I went in the den. Sure enough, the disk was full. I put in a blank disk. Even before I turned the light off, I heard the disk chattering. I went to the phone and asked Jake if that was him on the computer. Jake told me it was one of his friends. His friend called and said he could not get on the disk because it was full.

"Jake jumped all over me for not changing the damn disk. I told Jake it was half full yesterday, so I left it till tomorrow. Jake told me, 'Well it worked out. Just hope the phone scrabbled worked.' I told Jake, 'If your friend did it right, the disk worked.' Jake then said, 'Next time, change the damn disk no matter how full it is twice a day.' So from that day on, I changed the disk every morning and night. There is one thing you will not believe, Tom."

Tom looked at him. "Charles, there is more than one thing I am having a hard time in believing."

"Well, I have never looked at what was on those disks. I figured Jake would tell me in time. I promised Jake I would never decode them unless he told me to. Well, you bet your ass, as soon we get home and bury my only child, I am going to get to the bottom of this. Until then, I will not trust anyone except you and Kate. This is why I lied to the police. I do not know what is happening. I will know a lot more when we look at those disks."

Tom said, "We?"

Charles looked at him and then said, "Well, if you want to help me, I would appreciate it."

Tom did not say anything. Then he gave Charles that look. He told him, "You really did not even have to ask, you idiot." Charles thanked Tom.

They made a list of how Charles wanted to handle the funeral. Neither one them knew about detective work. Charles told Tom that some of Jake's eleven friends might be there. "I would think one of them has to get in touch with me for the disks."

Tom agreed and said, "Maybe the murderer will be there also."

"I never thought of that. They might be in Coal City now if they think I have anything to do with it."

Tom and Charles talked some more and came up with a weird plan. They decided not to tell Kate; she would be against all the way.

When they arrived in Coal City, Tom and Charles talked to Kate. She told them, "The visitation will be at the funeral home tomorrow morning right before the funeral. We then go to the cemetery and have dinner at the American Legion for the family and friends." Charles told Kate she did a good job and hugged her.

Tom and Charles went to the funeral home to give clothes for Jake. Dwight thanked Charles and explained what he was going to do. Tom and Charles picked out the casket and took care of the rest of the business. Charles told Dwight, "I have a favor to ask of you."

Dwight just said, "Sure, what is it?"

"I want a video camera set up somewhere in the building where we can make sure we have a picture of everyone that is here."

Dwight gave them a weird look. Then he asked if Charles wanted the guests to see the camera. Tom just said, "Hell no, we do not."

Charles told Dwight, "Tom is right. I want you to hide the camera where just you, Tom, and I know. Do not even tell Kate. We will do that."

Dwight said, "Since we are friends, I will do it." Tom handed the camera to him.

Charles told Dwight, "Just send me the bill after the funeral."

"Do not worry about that now. I know you will take it." Charles then thanked Dwight, and then they left.

Tom and Charles went to the cemetery next. Charles said, "I am glad Coal City is a small town. In the big city, it would be harder to do." They walked up to Ruth's apartment. It was only two hundred yards away from Jake's cemetery lot.

Ruth was surprised to see them. She first told Charles she was sorry about Jake's death. Then Ruth asked, "What do you need from me? In a small town, everybody knows everyone." He asked Ruth if he could have someone to videotape Jake's service from her apartment. Her first question was, for what? He explained to her that he just wanted Tom's son, Bill, to take pictures of the burial.

Ruth had this "who would want that?" expression. Then she said, "If that is what you want, just help yourself and do whatever you need." Charles thanked her, and then they left.

Tom knew his son was at home. He knew he was off today and going to the funeral tomorrow. Sure enough, Bill was at his house. He told Charles how sorry he was. Charles thanked him for that and asked him if he could do him a big favor tomorrow during the burial of Jake. He did not hesitate and just asked, "What do you need done?" Charles told him to videotape the burial at Ruth's apartment.

Bill just said, "Dad, does Mom know about this?"

Tom told his son, "Hell no."

Bill started to laugh, and then he said, "No disrespect to you, Charles, but how the hell are you going to do this without Mom knowing it?"

Charles said, "I do not know, but I will tell your mom soon."

"It better be sooner than later before someone tells her." Tom agreed with that; so did Charles. They all knew Kate would be against this crazy idea.

Tom and Charles left Bill's house. Charles told Tom, "We have to go to the neighbor's house now." They drove Charles's car back to his house. They walked to Ben's house, which covered his back door and all his north side. Charles knew the family was going to the funeral. When he asked them not to go, they were in shock. He explained that he wanted them to videotape anyone who entered his house after he left for the funeral home tomorrow morning. He handed Ben his camera. Ben said, "Keep your camera. I can use mine. It is better."

Ben's wife said she had a better idea. Charles looked at her, and Ben said, "Well, what is it?"

"Susan can do it better than Ben."

Ben told Charles, "Paula is right. Susan is home and would rather do that than go to the funeral."

Charles told them, "That would be perfect." He knew they thought he was crazy, but through friendship, they did not ask what was going on.

Tom and Charles walked to his other neighbor Marvin. His house would cover his front door and all his east side. "I am just glad I live on a corner. Marvin cannot get around very well." Charles knew he was not going to the funeral. He told Marvin to videotape his house after he left tomorrow morning at eight o'clock. Marvin just said, "Sure, no problem." He took the camera, and Charles showed him how to use it. "Hey, I can run one of these. I just do not own one. I have one question."

"What is it?"

"Why not take me to your house and I will watch it for you?"

"Thanks, but I just want to see who comes in."

Marvin said, "OK."

Charles had one window that was not covered. This was on his south side. They went to Mrs. Shull's house. Charles asked her if he could have someone use her garage window tomorrow so they could take pictures of his house. Mrs. Shull was in her eighties; she just said, "Help yourself. I am sorry about Jake." Charles thanked her, and they left.

They went back to Charles's house. He told Tom, "Well, I believe we have all the cameras in place. Do not forget to ask Bill to have one of his friends at Mrs. Shull's garage."

"I am already ahead of you. Bill's friend George will be there at seven o'clock in the morning, an hour before you leave."

Tom and Charles went to the den. Charles knew nobody had been in the den yet; the light was green. Then he checked out the disk. He could not believe what he had seen. The disk was almost full. Tom asked, "What is unusual about that?"

"Jake has always updated this computer. In the past, we started out with floppy disk and then the three-and-a-half-inch disk. Now we have the CD, which holds several more information. I only replace it about every three days. I just see how much memory is left. If it is over half full,

I change it. When we went to Newark, the disk has hardly been used. Now it is almost full."

Tom told Charles, "You are not going to start on the disk now, are you?"

"Yes, I am. You might be right about the bad guys coming here. If they do not only will we have them on tape, they will get this disk. We have to make sure nothing is on it that will tell them what we know."

Charles loaded the first disk in the computer and then the original disk. This would unscramble the disk so they would see what was on it. To his amazement, the first part of the disk did not mean too much to him. It had some dates that resembled trials in a way. One was *Johnson v. Tran Oil.* Another was *Baker v. Middle Oil.* Then it went on and on with other trials.

There were corporation names with people's names after each. To Charles, it seemed like board of directors or the head of the companies. To both of them, this did not mean anything.

The rest of the disk blew Charles's mind. He did not realize that Jake might have given him a message on it. "Dad, I believe they might be on to me. I have to make a quick decision." Then there was some other data about corporations and names. The only thing they were familiar with was Secretary of State John Douglas Jr. He had been on the news lately about foreign oil shipped to the United States. Tom told Charles he remembered hearing him make a speech about the labor force in the country.

There was one more statement Jake wrote. "Check out his grandpa's name, which is John Douglas. This guy was around forty-five in 1963." Then Jake wrote, "Dad, if I do not make it through this, it is because we made a deal with the devil fifteen years ago. You are right, Dad."

Charles made two copies of the disk, plus two copies of the decoded disk. He erased the last two sentences and left this one in the computer. Tom asked him if he was crazy. He told Tom, "Well, we've got to let them think this is real. I do not believe this will hurt the rest of Jake's friends. I have to do what is right."

Tom thought about it for a few seconds. He said, "Well, they trusted you in doing just that, so do it."

Charles reached for another disk to put in the computer. He handed the other disk to Tom and said, "Hold this till I need it."

Tom asked in dismay, "What the hell are you doing now?"

"Do you remember that computer class I took at night a few years ago? I met this computer wizard, and we became friends. Well, years later, he made a computer virus. Well, the disk that I just put in my computer has that virus. I am going to load the disk in your hand and put the virus on it." Tom was getting impatient with him. "It is like this, Tom. I put the virus on this disk. If someone steals this disk and uses it, it will spread the virus on their computers."

Tom just said in dismay, "That is a dirty trick. I have one question."

"What is the question?"

"Wonder if they use your computer and you will have the virus."

"My friend made another disk that will detect the virus and will cure my computer for me."

Tom told him, "You have weird friends."

Charles laughed and told Tom, "He mailed me this virus just days before he killed himself."

Tom then said, "Oh, I remember now. You went to Wisconsin for his funeral. When you came back, you made the comment you have one of the best computer weapons of today."

"I tried it on my old computer, and both disks work."

Tom's eyes were seeing the point. "You hope someone steals the disk and spread the virus on their computers. Big deal."

"If the virus hurts some big business computers, eventually, we will hear about it one way or another. This will, I hope, lead us toward who murdered Jake and Amanda." All this took longer than Charles thought. They were in the den for just less than an hour.

Tom and Charles went to the bank to put all the disks in the safety-deposit box. Tom told Charles that Kate wanted him to eat supper with them. He replied, "That will be great."

After they left the bank, they went to Tom's house. Right before they entered, Charles asked Tom, "Do not tell Kate what we were doing."

Tom turned around. "How the hell are you going to keep that a secret from Kate?"

"Well, I will tell her tomorrow."

Tom said, "Good luck. Get in the house before Kate sends an army after us. Kate is getting worried. She has not seen or heard from us most of the day."

After they ate, Tom and Charles went in the living room, and Kate brought them some beers. She then went to her room to read. Charles thought she did that so Tom and he could just try to relax and watch the ball game. The second Kate went in the bedroom, Tom said, "I cannot wait any longer. How did this all get started? Jake's last statement was 'deal with the devil.'"

"The only thing I can remember is how we paid for Jake's college education. At the time, this was a new thing that was going on. Some of my friends told me about it at work, so I asked some questions. If a student qualifies in grades and signs a five-year contract with the company, the company will pay for the student's college education. We did not have that kind of money at the time. I told Jake about it. Jake and I went to the company and checked it all out. The next thing I knew, Jake made the passing grade, which was a C+ or better. If he did not do that well, I had to pay the company back. If he did do well, the deal is Jake had to work for the company for five years. Jake worked for Eattran for eight years. He then went to Tran Oil and was still there until he was murdered." He was thinking out loud, mumbling what Jake once told him.

Tom asked him, "What are you mumbling about?"

"Jake told me that Tran Oil and Eattran used him back and forth. Remember, a few years ago, Jake flew to Los Angeles once to testify in court? Some person was suing Jackson Insurance Company. Tran Oil let them have Jake for that trial.

"Well, during all this time, Jake made several friends. Most of them got their education and jobs the same way Jake did. He told me that he noticed something very unusual there through the years, and he had seen eleven people just saving data and information that they thought was either very strange or illegal. Then in a few years, they would put all this data together and see what they found out. That was how I got involved in this mess. You can bet your ass, after tomorrow, I am going to decode all those disks and see what the hell they were up to."

Tom talked Charles in staying the night at his house. They had a few more beers, and then Charles slept on the couch. The next morning, he heard Tom and Kate arguing. He overheard Kate saying, "How could you let Charles do such a thing?" He knew right then that, some way or another, Tom told Kate what they were doing. Kate came out of the bedroom. She was really surprised to see Charles there.

Tom yelled out the door, "Charles is here, Kate!"

"Oh shit." Then she just went in the kitchen and started to cry.

Tom came out of the bedroom. He apologized for telling Kate. "She just asked too many damn questions about yesterday."

Charles told Tom, "I understand. Let me go talk to Kate."

Tom just said, "I will get ready for the funeral while you talk to her."

Charles went in the kitchen. Kate said, "You know, you are crazy for doing this. Here it is, your son's funeral, and you and Tom are playing detective."

"Kate, you are right. I am going to find out who killed Jake. Unfortunately, there are a lot of complications."

Kate said, "There should be no complication on the day of Jake's funeral."

Tom came in the kitchen. His first statement was "Kate, be quiet." Boy, that was a mistake. She gave them both hell. Charles was just glad it was early enough to try to settle Kate down; he needed her companionship badly.

He asked Tom, "Let me talk to Kate alone, please."

Tom said "sure" and went back to the bedroom. On the way, he said, "Good luck."

I looked at Kate and said, "Do not say a word. I am going to tell you what I am doing. Do not get mad at Tom. I made him promise not to tell you. I thought it would be best for you. I was wrong. Kate, I believe whoever killed Jake is coming to the funeral. I do not believe they got whatever they wanted from Jake. They think, by now, I have it. I am hoping that some of Jake's friends are going to be here to give me a message. So I came up with all the cameras so I can tell who I can trust."

While Kate was crying, she said, "Here it is, your son's funeral, and you are not showing any remorse."

"Kate, I got your message, but all my love with Jake will always be with me. All the hate I have for whoever killed Jake is in me. I am not going to rest in peace until I find out who and why they killed Jake."

Kate said, "I understand that, but during Jake's funeral?"

"You are right, but this is the only place I can see Jake's friends or enemies without being too suspicious." Kate was calming down a little bit, so Charles promised her that, from now on, he would not hide anything from her. Kate told him she loved Jake too and would be glad to help. Charles then told her, "Let's go to the funeral and respect Jake as I would want Jake to respect my death."

Tom came out of the bedroom. Charles asked him to come with him to his house. "Kate is going to pick us up to go to the funeral home."

Kate told Tom, "Go ahead. Charles needs you now. I will be there in about an hour."

As they walked in Charles's house, he thought the bad guys might have broken in last night. The computer light was still green, and nothing had been touched. He gave Tom a drink while he was waiting for him to get ready. Charles told Tom, "Make two notes telling people that, after the service, we will be down at the Legion. Then also put on it 'Thanks for bringing food, cards, or flowers—Charles.'"

Charles was ready when Kate pulled up. He taped one of the notes on the front door and the other on the back door. He made sure the computer door was shut but not locked and that the green light was on. Then they went to the funeral home, which was only a block from his house. They were an hour early. Charles wanted to see Jake by himself.

After a short while, people started to come to the funeral home. Most of the early ones were older friends of Charles and of the families. They gave their sympathy one way or another.

Charles noticed this young man was crying while he was walking toward him. He could not tell who he was until he was closer. It was Nate, who worked on the computer with Jake. Nate looked at him and said, "Mr. Appel, I am sorry for Jake's murder."

Nate whispered with a broken voice while looking at Jake's casket, "This could have been avoided. We should have not done what we did."

Charles told Nate, "You know something, don't you?"

Nate just said, "We have to talk."

"After the service, we are going to the Legion for lunch. I wish you can come."

Nate told him, "Well, I'll be glad to. I hope I am not imposing, but I need a place to stay the night."

"Good, you can stay with me at my house. We can do all the talking we need to do at the Legion."

Charles introduced Nate to Tom and Kate. He asked the couple to fill Nate in on what they had been doing since they found out about Jake's murder. Nate said in dismay, "What have you been doing?"

Kate told Nate, "You will not believe what these idiots are doing."

Charles told Nate, "Just keep your eyes open, and listen to Kate and Tom."

In the next few minutes, some more friends from Coal City came up to Charles. He was busy talking and did not notice this six-foot man standing in line behind them. He introduced himself as John Martin. "On behalf of Eattran Corporation, we express our sorrow for you."

"Thanks for coming all this way."

"The company felt that Jake was a big help to the company in the last eight years and will be missed." He then handed Charles an envelope. Mr. Martin told him, "I thought it'd be better to give this to you personally." Charles did not open it. He gave it to Kate to keep it for him.

Charles asked Mr. Martin if he wanted to stay and come down to the Legion to have lunch after the service. Mr. Martin told him he would be happy to. He then left Charles and walked to a corner of the room. Charles noticed he was talking toward three other men.

The preacher gave a short but nice service. He gave good word toward Jake. Charles finally broke down and cried. Kate handed him a Kleenex. He noticed Kate and Tom were crying too. He looked up at the preacher after he gave the Lord's Prayer and noticed out of his left eye that two of the men who were with Mr. Martin were gone.

As they were heading for the cemetery, Kate showed Charles the one hundred thousand dollars of life insurance check that Mr. Martin gave to him in the envelope. When they arrived in the cemetery, he told the preacher to make it short and sweet, for he knew Jake never did like any long speeches or sermons. As Charles was sitting down beside Kate, he noticed Mr. Martin had one friend with him, but the other two men were not there.

They all went down to the Legion to eat lunch. The preacher gave thanks for the food, and they started a line to eat lunch. A few minutes went by, and then everyone was talking. Nate sat with Tom, Kate, and Charles. He could not believe what Tom told him about what happened in Newark, and neither could Kate. Nate did not know that Amanda was murdered. "I could not believe this," Nate told them. Nobody heard anything from their friend in Kansas City. Then with Jake's murder, they decided that someone had to get in touch with Charles. Since Nate already knew him, he was the one they felt could come to the funeral and be the least suspected.

Out of the blue, a voice came out. "Well, Nate, it is nice you came out here for your friend's funeral." They all looked up to see who it was. Mr. Martin was looking right at Nate. Nate started to introduce them. Charles explained to Nate that they already met. Charles could tell that Nate was very nervous. Mr. Martin told Charles he had to leave to make it to his plane on time. He thanked him for coming and for the insurance check from the company. Mr. Martin said, "That was the least we could do."

Charles walked Mr. Martin to the door. His car was waiting for him. Charles noticed the two men who were with him at the funeral home. There were also two women in the back seat. Charles was wondering if, by chance, he had them on tape somewhere.

Charles's and Jake's friends had left the Legion by now. There were Tom, Kate, Nate, and Charles. Then the auxiliary was cleaning up the kitchen. Charles knew where the key to the bar was. So he opened the Legion bar, put a fifty-dollar bill in the cash register, and poured Tom a pitcher of beer and himself a Jim Beam and water in the largest glass he could find. On the way out, he picked up some plastic beer glasses. He carried all this in the big room, where they were all sitting around the table.

While Charles was looking at Nate, he told him, "We are going to talk about you and Jake for a while. I want you to tell me everything you know about what Jake did and was doing from the time you met to the time Jake died. We will be butting in with some questions from time to time. After we all get drunk as we want, you and I will go to my house. You will stay with me as long as is necessary or as long as you want. Tomorrow we will have Tom and Kate bring the cassette tapes and check them out. We will start going through all those disks that Jake and all of you made to see if we can get any sense out of all this. We can have Kate to organize all information in an orderly and timely manner, if at all possible."

While Nate poured himself a glass of beer, he said, "Mr. Appel, there is a lot to be told. I will try to explain our actions and how this all came about."

"But before you start, call me Charles because we are in this together no matter where it ends."

Nate just said, "Whatever you say, Charles." He continued. "The first time I met Jake was at a trial. I was a special witness for a computer company. I worked for Tran Oil. They told me to go and testify for Attact Computer Company. They gave me all this material to read and study about the company and the lawsuit. See, this Mr. Kevin Richards was claiming that Attact took a computer chip that he made that would change the computer industry as your mind cannot imagine. Well, anyway, Jake was the lawyer for Attact. The day I flew into Los Angeles, Jake was at the airport to meet me. He introduced himself while we were shaking hands.

"I will never forget what Jake said as we were riding in the car. Jake had my entire life in a manila folder. He even asked how I liked Professor Greenwall. I was amazed that he asked that. Then Jake was laughing. He explained that he was from the University of Illinois also, just three years before me. Jake said he took one computer course with the professor. He went on to say he did not get an A in his class. In fact, he told me he had a hard time in getting a C.

"Jake asked me a funny question. How in the hell did I afford going to UOI? Jake said, 'Let me guess first.' I told him to go ahead. He said, 'I bet your dad worked for a corporation for at least eighteen years or so. The company had this college plan. If you qualify, they would pay all your college expenses only if you work for them for at least ten years after you graduate.'

"I was surprised. I asked how he knew that. Not very many knew about it. Jake just said, 'Looking at your grades and all the colleges and degrees you have in computers that took money, your family, at the most, brought in $33,000 a year. You had no scholarships. Besides all that, this is how I got my college paid for.'

"Jake and I talked about college days the rest of the way to the hotel room. When we entered the room, he told me that I have to answer these questions for him. Jake told me he knew computers but not enough for this trial. So I was brought there for two reasons. One is to convince the jury that Attact had the chip first because Mr. Richards could not have made that chip. I asked Jake what the second was. He said, 'Well, you have to teach me about this chip so I know what the hell is going on.'

"The first day of the trial was boring. It was Jake and the lawyer just getting their footwork down and their case presentation to the jury and judge. That night I will never forget for the rest of my life. We were in the hotel room going over my testimony when the phone rang. It was the lawyer for Mr. Richards. He gave Jake an offer to settle out of court. He told him he would be willing. So they set a meeting time later that night.

"Jake made some phone calls. Attact agreed if they got all the rights to the chip with the statement that it was their chip. In return, Attact would give Mr. Richards fifty thousand dollars. Jake told him Attact would do that in a heartbeat. So Mr. Richards's lawyer agreed. To Jake's dismay, Mr. Richards agreed with the advice of his lawyer and took the fifty thousand. Jake could not believe what happened. He personally believed that Mr. Richards was telling the truth, that Attact, in fact, had stolen it from him. I asked Jake, 'Well, why not do something?' Jake just said, 'I am one of these days but not now.'

"Jake showed me something. Mr. Richards's lawyer was named Steve Lee. He too was given a free ride at university. Steve works for this big law firm that takes lawsuits. Jake told me he thought it was fixed. Mr. Richards would only have twenty thousand after the legal fees. He would not have that if the case went to court very long. This guy, Kevin Richards, worked twenty years on that chip and lost it for fifty thousand. I sure would not give up that easily.

"Jake thanked me for coming, even though I never testified or explained the chip. I told him I only came because my company told me to. Jake surprised me again. He looked at me right in the eye. He asked me if I would help them if he could prove to me that the companies we worked for were stealing, lying, and making millions of dollars through manipulation of people. I told Jake I do not believe in hurting innocent people. Jake told me, 'Think about it. I have four people who are willing to lose their jobs just by keeping track of wearied decision or anything that makes their companies millions of dollars that did not seemed proper. We have all this data in each of our houses. What we need is some computer expert that can put all this on one computer that is in one location that cannot be traced.' Jake told me he does not want an answer now. He told me he had the feeling he could trust me."

Charles told Nate, "If Jake thought he could trust you, then without hardly knowing you, well, I can too."

Nate thanked Charles, and then he went back to his story. "Jake told me he was just putting this on the table to see if I was interested. I told Jake if this could be proved, I might be interested. Jake told me he would get a hold of me later to discuss this. Nothing was said the rest of the night. Jake took me to the airport the next morning. We said our goodbyes, not mentioning what we talked about last night. Just as I was walking toward the gate, Jake said, 'Keep an eye on your corporation, and you will see.'

"I did not hear from Jake till a year or so. At this time, my corporation did three very unusual or unpatriotic decisions. The first decision was selling their computer equipment to China. This was not that bad as such. What bothered me was the same equipment could be used to take information from our own government and satellites. This equipment was all intangible with ours. Our government approved the sale, with the Pentagon stamp on it.

"The second bad thing to me was that our computer company sold two-thirds of our stock to a corporation that was very untrustworthy. This company was well known to buy big blocks of stock to rattle the cage of the corporation. In fact, if made, the company will lose money. Then they will be forced to sell to or merge with another company. This company will end up making twice their investment. This is what happened in less than seven months.

"The icebreaker came with the new computer company that was called Telall. Telall made a contract with our government. We were to make a computer system that could tap in on any business or bank or anyone who had a modem. Unfortunately, I was in this project. I was noted, at this time, as being the best known computer whiz in the country.

"I could not believe what happened in the next two days. On Thursday, someone called me, just fifteen hours after I was told to go ahead with the new project. As I answered the phone, the person on the other end just said, 'If you remember what we talked about a year ago and want to help stop this madness, go to Cook and Adams in twenty minutes, get out of the car, and listen.' This voice sounded like Jake's. I was not sure. After all, it had been over a year.

"So like a dumb idiot, I went to that intersection. As I got out of the car, I heard this phone ringing at the corner phone booth. I let it ring at least ten times. I remembered what he said: keep listening. I ran to the phone. The person told me, 'I thought you are the interesting type.' I asked, 'Is this you, Jake? Damn it, tell me.' Jake started to laugh and said it was him. Without hesitation, I asked, 'What the hell is all the mystery about?' Jake told me it was the new project I was working on as of yesterday. I asked Jake how the hell he knew about that. Jake told me it was a long story. He just wanted to know if I was in with them or not. I must have been quiet for a few seconds. I told Jake, 'Yes, I am with you. We have to be honest with each other and fair to all.' Jake agreed.

"Jake even told me, 'We have a serious problem. I need your help fast. Where can we see each other without being noticed?' I knew this all-night café that would be safe. Jake agreed to meet me there tomorrow night. That next day, we gathered every note or any information I had on the new project. I could not get to the personal files as they were in the safe. I did not have the combination. The company just kept it locked up. I made some notes for myself in case Jake had some questions for me.

"I arrived at the restaurant at around seven fifteen. The meeting was to take place at seven thirty. There were only six people in the restaurant. This was not unusual for this restaurant. It was noted for late hours, not the early hours. I waited forever, it seemed. I looked at the clock, and it was seven fifty. I started to think something went wrong. I did not know why I felt scared, afraid, and very uneasy. I looked at the clock again. It was eight fifteen. I did not know how many cups of coffee I had, but it was several. I had to go to the damn bathroom. I was afraid to leave in case Jake showed up.

"Finally, this couple came in, walking up. It was Jake with this girl. As they walked toward me, I got up and told Jake I would be right back. Jake looked disappointed and asked me where I was going. I told Jake, 'If your ass had been on time, I would not have been drinking all this coffee that is going through me. I have to take a piss.' Jake's girlfriend started laughing. Jake told me, 'Get going. I do not want you to piss on the floor.' As I walked back to the table, I could hear the girl still laughing at me.

"Jake stood up and introduced me to Amanda. Jake sat down and told me he was sorry for being late. Amanda and he had not seen each other for a few days, and they enjoyed each other's company too long. I told Jake I understood. Jake asked me if I was sure I wanted to help them. I told Jake I was sure and then showed him all my notes that I had taken. Jake looked at them. He said, 'This is very good, but we are not doing it this way.' He took a match and burned my notes.

"I was getting aggravated when Jake did that. I asked Jake, 'What the hell are you doing?' Jake told me, 'We do not keep any records in our possession too long, especially no names, times, or places. We do not call or write one another except maybe three times a year.' Jake was telling me he did most of the calling and communication toward all of us.

"Jake explained to me they all had their own home computers. Each one put their information on a disk and then either mailed it or sent it through the modem to his computer. I told Jake that sounded all right. Jake just said it worked but not good enough. They needed a better and safer way. This was where they needed my help bad.

"I told Jake, 'Well, what the hell do you want from me?' Jake told me to settle down and listen. They knew my company was making a computer for the government. I asked Jake what they were called. Jake could not have knocked me down any harder if he used a hammer. He just said the Walton computer. My mouth must have flown open. The government had me and our company make them through this dummy corporation so nobody knew that Attact had anything to do with the computer.

"I could not believe Jake even knew about the Walton. He told me that one of his guys worked in my corporation. In fact, he was one of the vice presidents of our corporation. I was amazed at all this information that Jake had on me and our company. I asked him again, 'What do you want from me?'

"He said, 'We need you to do two things. I told you how we passed our information. We need you to improve our system to be the best. We would like to have our main computer in one location. We need you to help us make sure our main computer cannot be traced. Your company is making the Walton computer that can do this. We need you to make sure that computer cannot trace none of ours. The second item is harder yet. The other person in your company is helping us. We do not need your information. We already have it, plus more. We need you to make us eleven computers that, some way or another, cannot be traced to our main computer.'

"I told Jake he was crazy. Jake gave me this stare and said, 'Nate, there is a very fine line between being crazy and being a genius. To prove what I believe is happening to our country, we have to be very crazy, and we better have a genius with us. In the computers, you are the genius.'

"I tried to tell Jake that we have not started making them for the government yet. I told him I might be able to change some components or make it portable to work in phone booths. Jake just said, 'I have faith in you. Whatever you come up with will work.' I told Jake the problem was money. Jake laughed out loud and said they had the money. I told him they cost around twelve thousand apiece to do what they need. Jake just said they had the money.

"Jake then asked me, 'Are you in or not?' I told him I must be crazy too, and I would help him. Jake thanked me. I told Jake I had a question for him. The government cannot keep this a secret too long. They will probably be on the Carloet in a few years. That will do what we need. Why not buy them then? Jake told me that they have so much information now. Plus in a few years, they will have a lot more that will either prove their theory or not. I asked Jake what he was trying to prove.

"Jake told me, 'It is simple. We are saying that the very rich and big corporations are paying for the education of a certain few. They are getting these people in many fields as they see fit. In return, they make as much money as they can. These same people that they control make laws, change laws, and even break laws to ensure their prosperity forever. They control judges, senators, representatives of the states and nation. We know they have three Supreme Court justices now. We know they have several on county boards, townships, city mayors, aldermen. They have some on the board of trade and several throughout all types of governments. To prove this, all our information is coming in so fast. We need those new computers now, not in two years. We have to find someone to take all this information so that we can get justice done.'

"Well, after listening to Jake, he had me convinced he was right about what my own corporation is getting away with. After all, that was how Jake and I got in this mess, they paying for our education. Why not the rest of them? So my job was simple, according to Jake—just get eleven computers, and make them trace proof.

"Jake surprised me again. He handed me a check for $150,000. Jake just said, 'Spend it wisely.' I could not believe whose signature was on the check. It was signed by Mr. Kevin Richards, the same person that Jake beat in court over the computer chip. Jake must have noticed my amazement over the check. I asked Jake how he got this money. He laughed and explained that, after that lawsuit that nearly broke Mr. Richards, Jake gave him this idea about a board game. Well, eventually, he not only made a few million on the board game but Mr. Richards made other games and toys as well. I could not hold it no longer. I asked Jake what the hell game he had in mind. Jake told me in a calm way it was the Billionaire game. I about passed out. That game became more popular than any other in our nation.

"This Mr. Richards made it to all the top financial magazines for making the best comeback for a businessperson. Jake just told me that Mr. Richards told him if there is anything he could do, just call him. They had been friends ever since. Jake called him up and said he needed some money for twelve computers, one main computer and eleven smaller ones. Mr. Richards gave Jake this check and told Jake, 'Here is an order for those computers. When your friend gets done with them, send them to my business.' He will run them through his business and then give the computers back to us. This way, all his employees will think that he ordered them, and so will the government.

"We left the restaurant under the condition I would have the computers done in three months. Jake and Amanda went their way, and I went to my car and went home. I never found out who the other person was in my company that Jake knew, nor did I ever hear from Jake till three months later.

"The phone rang one night just three months after our meeting. Jake, with no hesitation, just asked, 'Well, are they ready?' I told him they are. Jake asked me if I can meet him at the same restaurant as last time. We agreed to meet at about at eleven o'clock that night. I did not even know if Jake was in town or where he was at. After this, I knew he was in town for something else besides seeing me.

"When I arrived at the restaurant, Jake was already waiting for me. We did some small talk, and I told Jake I wanted him to take a ride with me. Jake was ready to ask me some questions, but I interrupted him. I said, 'Just sit back, enjoy the ride, and pay attention.' Jake told me, 'All right, you are in charge now.'

"I found an empty phone booth that was close to the road. I told Jake this would work fine. I told him to get out of the car and help me open the trunk. When I opened it, Jake could not believe what he had seen. There was a computer system. I told Jake this was it. I pulled out this long cord. We went to the phone booth, dialed a number, and put the phone in this box. We went back to my trunk and hit a few keys, and the computer started to work. This all took less than two minutes.

"I hung up the phone, put the cord and the box back in the trunk, and told Jake to go to my garage. Jake was so happy like a kid getting his first bicycle. On the way to my garage, Jake started asking me all types of questions. I told Jake, 'Just wait until we are done. We will go back to the restaurant and go through all the process then.'

"When I opened the garage door, there was the home computer on the workbench. I told Jake the disk that was in the computer in the car was now in this computer. This would work whether it was a mile or a million miles. I pressed the home computer. It just said, 'This is a test.' I took the disk out of the trunk and put it in the computer, and it said the same thing. Jake was really got over all this. I told Jake, 'Now let's go back to the restaurant, and we will discuss the flaws and anything you want to talk about.'

"I could tell Jake was thinking about all that he had seen. I gave him a piece of paper and told him to start writing down all his questions. Jake did not say a word, but he was doing a lot of writing. We arrived back at the restaurant at twelve thirty. We sat at the same table we were at just a while ago. Jake liked this table. Nobody could get behind us, and we could see everyone who was in the restaurant.

"I took Jake's list of questions and was looking at them while he ordered our coffee. After the waitress left, I started to explain the system. I told

Jake the power was off the cigarette lighter. There was a special detector in the system that if it is getting traced any time during the connection, a red light comes on, and the system shuts down. I told Jake it'd be nice if he could get a way to decode and code the disk, but I did not know how to do that. Jake said it was not a problem. He knew someone who can. I told Jake the only drawback was if you make a disk at home or somewhere and then put the disk in the computer, it will be faster than typing the message while you are hooked up to the phone booth. The drawback is someone could get your disk before you get to the phone. Jake again said we can get around that too.

"I looked at Jake's questions one at a time. I answered them, and he was satisfied. I told him that after we run these, we can get the bugs out of them. Jake asked me if we had any money left. I told Jake we had two thousand left. Jake told me to keep it and have a good year. I told him I can have them all sent to Mr. Richards in a week or so. I had just a couple to finish, and then they would be done. Jake told me that would be great. He had a hookup person that would do that for us.

"I must have showed I was surprised. I could not help it. Jake just said, 'Hey, we need you to make the computers. I do not want you to know who the others are for your safety and theirs.' Jake looked at me real serious and said we were getting close to finding out and proving it. If one gets caught, that will not hurt us as long no one knows the others. I told Jake that makes sense, but I would like to make sure they work. He said, 'Well, if they do not work, I will bring them to you, or we will arrange some way to work it out.'

"The last time I had seen Jake for the computers was here at your house. Jake had some problems with the main computer. He could not get the person that usually hooks the computers up for him. From that time till now, I had only seen Jake a few times. We never talked about the computers or any information. I never did find out who the other person was that work for my corporation.

"I found out later on the day after Jake's murder. I got this phone call. I have one of those answering machines. I was in the same old habit as most people do who own one. Whether I am home or not, I always let the machine answer my calls. If I am not busy, I go answer the phone. I was very occupied with this girl at the time. She was just starting to wash my back while we were in the shower. I did hear the phone ring, but between the phone and the way Carillon was going about washing my back, the answering machine just paid for itself.

"My mind and hands were so interested in Carillon's body I had no idea what the person said on the phone. It was not fifteen or twenty minutes before I was dressed. While Carillon was getting dressed, I turned the answering machine on to play back the message. I will never forget it as long as I live.

"This voice just said, 'You have to go to Jake Appel's funeral to represent his friends. I decided you should go before me.' I know that voice, but he did not leave his name and just said we will get in touch later. I had Amanda's phone number hidden in my desk drawer. Jake gave it to me just in case an emergency came up. This was the only way I could get a hold of Jake. I never had a computer or his phone number. Jake always called me. Amanda did not answer the phone. It was the police. They asked for my name. I panicked and hung up. I found out later she was murdered. I then called your town newspaper, and they confirmed that Jake was murdered but did not give me any details. This is how I got here, and that is all I know right now except I did bring that phone tape. I do know that voice."

Charles told Nate, "I had several things to ask you, but this is not the time or the place. We all will discuss what you said in the next few days. Tom, after you and Kate leave, could you gather up all the videotapes?"

Tom told him, "No problem. I will bring them by tomorrow morning at around nine o'clock."

"That was fine."

Tom, out of the blue, said, "Will you call me if someone took the disk?"

Nate asked Charles, "What disk?"

"I will fill you in when we get to my house. Tom, Nate and I will check out the disk, and I will call you if someone took it. You make sure you bring the tapes. Then after we look at the videotapes, we will go to the bank and get the disk." He asked Nate if he wanted to stay with Charles tonight just to make sure that he wanted to.

Nate looked a little startled and then said, "Sure."

Charles told Tom, "I will tell Nate tonight what we found out. We will meet tomorrow then."

Kate asked Charles, "Are you all right?"

He told her he was fine. "Nate will be with me." So they all left the Legion.

CHAPTER 2

The Videos

Tom and Kate took Nate and Charles to Nate's car at the funeral home. Charles told the couple, "See you tomorrow. Do not forget the videotapes." Tom assured him he wouldn't. Nate and Charles went to Charles's house. Charles told Nate about the computer disk and how they videotaped the funeral and his house. He could tell Nate thought the same way as Kate did but did not say anything.

As they entered the house, the kitchen table had some flowers and food on it. There was a note that said, "We put some ham in the refrigerator for you—Florence."

Charles looked at the light at the same time Nate noticed it. He told Nate, "Someone went in the computer room. Just maybe someone took the bait." They went right to the computer and looked to see if the disk was gone from the disk drive. It was still there.

Charles was very disappointed and told Nate, "They did not take the damn disk." He did not look no more. He just turned around and went to the kitchen to get a couple of beers. They did not say much and just drank their beer.

Charles finally told Nate, "I am going to take a nap and rest. Help yourself to anything you need."

"Do not worry about me. I will be make do."

Charles must have been tired as he still had on his clothes from the day before. The sun was just rising out of his east window. He walked in the living room, where Nate was asleep on the couch. He quietly walked to the bathroom and took a long shower, which felt good. He shaved and brushed his teeth.

Charles could tell he was not feeling any better toward Jake's death but still felt a little better after the shower. He was thinking again. *Rose always laughed at me for years. She just told me I never let my mind be quiet, thinking.* I then remembered that just maybe they made a copy of the disk. Instead of taking the disk, they might have thought if they made a copy, Charles would never know.

He ran to the computer and turned it on. He took out the disk. If anyone made a copy and used his computer, that bug would be in his computer. *All I have to do is run a disk, give it a few commands, and then check to see if that bug is here. If the bug is here, then someone either looked at the disk on my computer and did not take it or made a copy.*

The only matter was that this system was old. The people who were here could not know what kind of system he had. So just maybe they took one of his disks. So all Charles had to do was see if any blank disk was missing. He looked through his box of disks. He had them numbered; there were supposed to be twenty-five, and it was exactly that. He was disappointed again.

By this time, Charles must have woken up Nate; he was walking in the room. He told Nate what he thought. Nate was yawning when he muttered out, "Maybe they put it on one of your old disks." Charles could have kissed Nate. Sure, they might have thought he might not miss an old disk.

Charles reached over to his old disk box. It had dust on it. He told Nate, "I hardly use it anymore. We could tell that someone touched the box. The dust was swept off the edge. There are fifty disks in this box."

Nate said, "How the hell do you know that?"

"I use a couple of these disks sometimes, so I numbered them. I just know there are fifty in that box." He counted them; there were only forty-nine in the box. "Nate, you are a genius. One is missing." Charles looked through them. He laughed and told Nate which one they took.

Nate asked, "How in the hell can you tell, out of all those disks, which one they took?"

He laughed and told Nate, "The dumb asses just pulled one out of the air. Unfortunately, they took my old blackjack game that I made. I always kept that one. I still use it every now and then. The game is not very good. It does not show the pictures. It just says the card number and the suit.

The game is the first program I made on a computer several years ago. This damn blackjack game is gone. I usually play it every six months just for practice."

Charles walked in the kitchen and searched under several plates where he hid the disk that took the virus out of his system. Nate watched him hit a few keys. Then presto, the screen turned a different color. Then it asked to type in coded letters. Nate asked Charles if he knew what he was doing. He told Nate, "Yes, this is the disk my friend made to take the virus out of the computer. All you do is type 'debug' backward, and the disk comes on and runs for a few minutes. When it quits running, I just type 'run.' Then the computer goes through a series of programs. When all this is done, the system is cleaned. Do not ask me how it works. I do not know. My friend just told me it works, so it works. I do not know how it works myself."

Charles cannot wait to see whoever made that copy. "I just hope they do not notice the virus within the next twenty minutes after they put it in their computer. Their system will be so screwed up it will cost them thousands of dollars."

Nate was still yawning. He looked at Charles and asked, "What are we going to do next?"

"I've been thinking on that. Do you like your job?"

Nate, still not fully awake, said, "What the hell do you mean?"

"I thought we might want to be partners in my wild chase in finding out who killed Jake. I just wonder if you would like to live here with me and help me. I am not rich. After all, I just received one hundred thousand from Jake's company. Just think about this for the weekend."

Tom and Kate knocked on the door at nine o'clock, just as they decided on. Kate was always on time. Charles should have been ready for them. He handed Tom a beer and Kate a Diet Coke. Nate and Charles already had a beer. Tom said, "The first tape is Marvin's." Charles put the tape in, and they all watched it.

Kate, right away, noticed the note on the front door. Charles told her, "I forgot to tell all of you. I put a note on the door to use the back door if one have anything to bring to the house. I thought this would make it easier for us." Kate thought that was a good idea. The tape ran for a few minutes; nothing showed up, so Charles fast-forwarded it to see if anyone used the door or read the note. Nobody even walked on the front sidewalk.

From this angle, they could see that a car stopped, and a person walked to the back door. They could not tell who it was at this position. A few minutes later, another person parked the car and walked toward the back door. This black car was driving by going east on the north side. They could not tell for sure what this car was doing.

Tom then put in the tape from the south side from Mrs. Shull's garage. This tape showed nothing either, so Charles ran it fast-forward. They could see the back door a little. They saw two people walk in the house. Then in a few minutes, another person walked in. After a couple of minutes, two persons walked out of the house. They played the tape some more, and then two more people walked in. After a short while, two people left the house. Afterward, one person walked inside, and two left. The tape was blank; this was all they had seen. Nobody tried to get in the window, which what Charles was looking for. He hoped the other video would show more.

Tom put in the north side, which Susan taped. There were two women walking to the house from the west corner to the east. They must have come either from the funeral home or somewhere from the west. This car pulled up and stopped. A woman walked to the back door carrying some kind of plate or something that looked like food. In a few minutes, two people walked out together carrying nothing.

After a while, this other car pulled up and parked. This person was carrying flowers. Just as she was across the street toward the sidewalk, this black car stopped going east and halted by the magnolia tree, which was closer to the west side than the east. This person got out of the car carrying flowers also. It seemed she was trying to catch up to the other person. They both walked in the house together. In a few minutes, two people walked out of the house. They both went back to their own cars.

The tape did not show anything for a minute or two, so Charles fast-forwarded it. In a few seconds, this black car pulled up. This person got out. This time, it looked like she was carrying food. Something looked different, but Charles could not put his finger on it. Everyone in the room did not say anything either. He stopped the tape and played it back. They all said at the same time, "Is that the same car?"

Then Kate said out loud, "She has on another type of jacket or coat." So they all watched carefully to see what was happening. The woman walked in the house, and then in a minute or so, two women walked out of the house.

They all looked at one another. "What is going on here?"

Charles told them, "Let's just play it again, and we will check all this out."

Kate thought out loud, "Maybe we should take inventory to see what flowers and food you received, and then as we play the tape, we can figure out who did what."

Charles told all of them, "Nate and I just never paid any attention to the flowers or food. I wanted to check out the computer disk. I just moved all that other stuff around the kitchen so we could get our beer. I did notice Florence's ham in the refrigerator. I moved it to get to the beer. I thought we might eat it today."

While he was talking, Kate put the cake and flowers together in the middle of the room. She took charge this time. Kate told Tom, "Now play the tape from the beginning. We will put each item where it belongs."

The first two women came in; they both had flowers. Kate laid two flower arrangements in front of the television. The next person brought food; this was Florence. The next person came from one car with flowers. Kate told Tom to stop the tape. She said, "Now look, this is Mrs. Theabal, the florist." So they took the arrangement and looked at all of them. There was a card that had the florist's name on it—Theabal Florist.

Kate then said, "Well, this must be the other flower that the other woman brought. Then here is this cake. This is what the last woman brought. The cake had no name on it, just said, 'Friends from the First Bank.'"

Then two women walked out. Kate said, "Where did this second person come from?"

Tom just said, "I know. Play it back again." They did this several times.

Kate, out of the blue, said, "I got it figured out."

Charles just told Kate, "Oh, let all of us on this."

Kate explained they had to make a few phone calls first. She got on the phone and called Florence. She asked Florence and her husband to come down to Charles's house as soon as possible. Florence told Kate, "In about fifteen minutes."

Kate hung up the phone and called First Bank this time. She asked for Jacky. Kate asked her if First Bank sent a cake to Charles's house during the funeral. Jacky said, "No, we sent some food down to the Legion. But to my knowledge, nobody sent a cake in the name of the bank to the house."

Kate hung up and said in a very clear and forceful voice, "All right, the bank did not send the cake. Let's look at the other flowers. One just said, 'Friends from Eattran,' where you worked at, Charles. The other one says, 'Friends of Jake from Newark.' There were no names on the flower's card, just Eattran. There was no florist name on them either.

"We could eat some food, or you guys have another beer. I will explain all this to you when Florence gets here."

Nate said, "Wait a minute, how well do you know Florence?"

Charles laughed out loud. "In a small town, people knows everyone. Florence is a real close friend of mine. Her husband, Bob, and I are real close friends since early high school days. For about ten years before I got married to Rose, Florence fed me hundreds of suppers. Sometimes Bob and I were not in the best shape in the world, but Florence put up with me because I was a friend of Bob's."

Nate looked at all of us and then said, "I never lived in a small town. I just cannot believe how you are all good friends."

They all were sitting down in front of the television when Florence and Bob walked in. Florence, right away, asked Kate, "What is all the fuss about the ham?"

Kate laughed. "It is not about your ham. It is about the person who walked out with you."

Florence stared at all of them. "That is a good damn question. I brought the ham in the house, and here was that woman putting some flowers on the table. I told her I was Florence and put the ham in the refrigerator. The woman looked a little puzzled and then told me she was Sam from Madison and brought flowers from friends from Eattran, where Charles worked at. I told her that was nice and then wondered why they did not send it through a florist. I even told Bob that seemed strange to me, but we were getting ready for Jake's funeral. We did not talk about it until know."

Kate then asked, "Was there another person in the house with her?"

Florence said, "No or not in the kitchen anyway."

Kate asked, "What was this Sam wearing?"

"She was wearing dark blue or black slacks and a white blouse with a red jacket or vest."

Kate told Charles to run the tape back and let Florence and Bob see it too. They played it back, and there was Florence coming in the house, and here was that Sam with a red jacket on. Kate said, "Now run the tape with Mrs. Theabal coming in the house." This woman was wearing just a white blouse and black or blue slacks.

Florence said, "This is the same one that I've seen."

Tom said, "Boy, that is a nice Madison. Must be a rented car though."

They all looked at Tom. "What do you mean a rented car?"

"The sign on it by the license plate frame." Sure enough, it was a rented car. They never noticed that before.

Charles told Bob, "Thanks for coming. You and Florence are a big help."

Then Kate said, "Tom, the tape to the last. Here is a woman getting out of that black car, which is the same car as the other, unless there are two rented Madisons in town. See, there is the name of it on the plate." They can read this one—Superior Rent-a-Car, Springfield Airport. "She is wearing a blue jacket now and is walking in with the cake. Now look, two people are walking out, one with a red jacket, and the other is wearing a black dress—the same black dress and red jacket as the very first two who walked in the house."

Florence said, "I bet that Sam is wearing a reversible jacket. I remember seeing a blue lining in her jacket. I thought that seemed a little out of place. I would never have blue lining with a red jacket unless it was reversible."

Kate said, "Now run the tape at the beginning, and you will see two women walking in, one wearing a black dress and the other with a red jacket and dark blue or black slacks." Sure enough, there they were. "The one in the dress was in your house all that time, probably in your computer room."

Charles told Kate, "You got it. Now let's run all the tapes again. Maybe Florence and Bob can see something we missed."

They played back the video of the east side. Right away, Bob yelled, "Out there is that black Madison that just went by going south!"

Charles stopped the tape and ran it back and then forward to the car. He asked, "How do you know this is the same car, Bob?"

"Look at the rear right window sticker. The black car on the other tape has the same sticker on it. What are the odds there are two Madisons with the same sticker on the rear driver's side window?" They all looked at that window and saw the sticker. Bob told them, "You should get your other television and VCR and run them both at the same time."

Tom thought out loud, "Why did we not think of that?"

Bob went to the table and started to make a sandwich and almost at the same time opened a beer out of the refrigerator. Florence told Bob, "Just make yourself at home."

"Why not? Charles does it all the time at our house."

Charles even laughed on that one. He could tell Nate could not get over how friendly they all were. He told him, "Just stay around for a while, and you will understand us better."

Nate looked at Bob and Tom and then said, "I just might do that."

By this time, the other television and VCR were ready. They started playing the east- and north-side tapes at the same time. On the north side, the two women were walking toward the house. The east side was nothing, and then a black car cruised by, going north. They could not tell how far north, but it was the Madison.

After a few more minutes, the Madison showed up at the stop sign, heading east, and then took a left. It turned one block to the west. Florence pulled up to the north side of the house. After a few more minutes, Florence and the other woman, Sam, were walking out. After Florence pulled away, the girl got in the Madison. The Madison made various turns around the block, some going right and then some straight, but no matter what, it always was near Charles's house.

Mrs. Theabal pulled up with her flowers; this was when the Madison stopped, and the woman got out in a hurry to catch Mrs. Theabal to the house. In a few minutes, they both walked out. In about five minutes, the Madison stopped near the house on the west side of the magnolia tree, and then this woman got out and walked to the house with a cake. It was not two minutes later when both women walked out of the house to the Madison. Kate explained, "See what happened now?"

Charles looked at Kate. "Good job. I am glad. You and Bob are the most observant ones here."

Bob then said, "Too bad you do not have one of the cemetery. I bet the Madison will be there with at least three or four people in it." Tom started to laugh. Bob could tell. "You did not, did you?"

Tom just said, "We sure did. Here it is." He put the video in.

All the funeral cars were in front. The camera could not pick up all the rest of the cars. To Charles's dismay, there was Mr. Martin standing near the funeral service with another man and two women. One was wearing a black dress and the other a red jacket with dark slacks. Charles was shocked and surprised at the same time. He then said, "It worked. They took the disk."

Bob, in shock, said, "What disk?"

Charles told Bob what they did and why they called Florence, to ask her what she had seen. In a split second, Charles did not know what hit him; but whatever it was, it was hard. As Tom was helping him up, Charles asked what happened. Bob told him in a very angry voice, "You're lucky I did not hit you harder."

Bob was ready to hit him again when Florence yelled at him and said, "That is enough!"

Charles looked at Bob and told him he was sorry. He had known Bob long enough; he knew what he did. Bob told him, "Next time you put my wife's live in jeopardy, you let us know. We will make the decision. You might get someone killed by playing detective."

"You are right. I did not use my head. From now on, I will let all of you know what I am going to do before I do it. That is a promise. I also promise I am still going to find out what happened to Jake."

Bob just stared at him and said, "I do not blame you for finding out. I just want no secrets from you or surprises." Charles agreed with Bob, who handed out his hand. Charles reached for it, and they were shaking hands. "I will help you in any way. From now on, just make sure Florence and I know what we are to do."

Charles laughed and told Bob, "I will be glad to ask, but I really do not think I need you, but if I do, I will ask you in a heartbeat and tell you first what I am doing."

"That will be nice." Then they all sat down and started to figure out the tapes some more.

CHAPTER 3

Coming up with a Plan

They all were looking at one another very quietly after what Bob had said. Charles told them, "Hey, we know Mr. Martin and his friends know something. They also know that I have some kind of disk that they or someone wants. The worst thing is they know either I know something now or I will know soon." What bothered Charles was no one knew who was helping Jake. "We need to find out who they are before Mr. Martin does. This is what they want badly. I do not think they will bother us until they get that information."

Bob then just stood up and stared at Charles. With his eyes, Charles could tell he was worried. Bob said, "Yes, you might be right. If that Mr. Martin thinks we know who they are, then they will come after us to find out what we know."

Kate then spoke up. "Bob is right on that. Look what they did to Jake to try to find out who the rest of them are."

Florence even said, "Sorry, Charles. They are right. Eventually, they are going to be after us." They were all very silent, and then all you could hear was Bob's heavy breathing; he did that when he was mad or upset. Charles had him feeling both; that was hard to do in less than an hour, and Charles did that.

Charles looked at Nate; he was not saying anything. Then Charles looked at Tom. He was very quiet also. Charles then stared at Bob again. "You know what, I think what we should do is this. I am going to make a phone call in the other room. You all can talk about whatever you want, and then when I get back, I will tell you all what I think."

Charles went to the other phone in the computer room. He dialed a number. He could not hear the others talk at all. Finally, someone answered the phone. "This is the Parkers. Jack is speaking."

"Jack, this is Charles Appel from Coal City. Is Joe there?"

Jack said, "Yes, hang on. He is at the food counter. I will get him."

Joe finally answered the phone. Charles told Joe, "You are always eating."

Joe laughed and then told Charles how sorry he was about Jake. Charles thanked him, and then Joe was telling him he remembered when Jake first was playing golf with his father. Joe laughed. "That was a very awful experience sometimes."

Charles told Joe, "Yes, it was."

Joe laughed again. "Hey, Jake finally beat your ass." Charles laughed too. He did not know why, but talking to Joe made him feel better.

Charles explained to Joe he needed a favor for tomorrow. Joe just said, "You need a tee time to just relax."

"I sure do."

Joe was looking at the tee times. "Since you are a good customer, here's what I can do. We have an outing at nine thirty. I will tell the starter to put you out right before the outing." Charles thanked Joe. "In fact, I will do better. Doug is the starter. Just walk to Doug, and tell him I let you on. Hey, Doug is on the course today. I will tell him to just let you play."

"We will be there by nine o'clock and pay you then."

Joe said, "Be here by nine in case we get off to a good start, but, Charles, I do not want your money. This is on me." Charles thanked him and then hung up.

Charles made one more phone call, and Karla answered. He asked her if Richard was there. She said, "No, Charles, but I will tell him you need a golfer tomorrow. What time?"

"Tell Richard I will pick him up at eight fifteen tomorrow."

"And if he cannot go, I will tell you soon so you can find another."

Charles laughed and told Karla, "You know us too well."

Karla just said, "Well, you guys are too predictable." Then she hung up.

As Charles went back to the kitchen, Bob and Florence were gone. "They had to pick up Susan to take her to a volleyball game," Kate said and, out of the blue, added, "You made a tee time for tomorrow."

Tom looked at Charles. "You did?"

"Yes. I called Joe, and he worked us in." He could tell Kate was mad. Before she could speak, Charles told her, "Well, Jake would rather me do that than sit at home and do nothing."

Kate said, "Well, I suppose so, but it just is not the thing to do."

"This is exactly the thing to do. We can all sit back, relax, and think on what Bob said. Monday, we will meet at the bank at ten to check out the safety-deposit boxes, and then we will all decide our next step. Nate can decide to stay with me or go back to his town. You and Tom can decide to help me or not. Either way, I am going to check out all that I can to find out who and why they killed Jake."

Kate shook her head. "Well, that does make sense. But still, you have to go golfing."

Charles just told her, "Yes, Tom and I have to see how good Nate is anyway."

Tom asked Nate, "Are you any good, Nate?"

Nate just said, "Well, if over a hundred is good, then I am damn good. I do not have my clubs with me."

Tom started to laugh. "Come with me. We will pick you out a set of clubs." Nate got up off the chair in a surprised motion.

Charles told Tom, "You know where they are. Just pick one out."

While Tom and Nate went to the basement, Kate started to talk. "Charles, I do not mean to be mean. I just think like a woman since I am one."

Charles told her, "I understand. Just that I had to do what I thought will get to the truth. If you think this will be too dangerous or you do not want to help, just think it over and tell me Monday."

Kate started to cry. "I do not mean to be on the other side or against you. I just want you to think of what might happen or at least respect Jake."

"Do not worry, I need you to keep Tom and me on the right track. I need you just because you are you."

Kate took a few seconds. "I will be glad to help you not because I agree with you but just because Tom and I love you."

Charles told her, "Thanks, and do me one favor."

Kate said, "What is the favor?"

"Just do not change and be you."

Kate just stared at Charles and said, "You do not have to worry about that," and out of the blue added, "I wonder what Tom and Nate are doing down the basement."

Charles told her, "Let them be. I want Tom to get to know Nate, and then when Tom and I play golf tomorrow, we will compare notes."

Kate told him without him asking, "Do not worry, I will keep that between us."

"Well, you and Tom, I know, will compare notes. Just do not let Nate know nothing."

By this time, Tom and Nate came up from the basement. Charles could tell Nate was amazed down there. Nate just said, "I've never seen so many golf clubs in my life."

Tom told Charles, "He tried them all out—the Titleist, King Cobra, the Pings, and your homemade Golfsmiths. He wanted the Kings, but I told Nate they were Jake's, and he should not take them."

Charles looked at Nate and just said, "I hope you understand."

"Hey, the way I play any of those sets, I am not good enough to use."

Tom told Nate, "Hang around us long enough. You will learn."

Nate just said, "I know where I will be tonight. I cannot believe the practice net and carpet Charles has down the basement. You have a regular indoor golf course down there."

Tom laughed. "I could not get him out of there. If Nate practices as much as you do, he will beat us both in no time."

The phone rang just then. Charles went to the phone; it was Richard. He just told Charles he would be glad to play. Charles asked how he shot today. Richard just said, "Well, not real good, but I scrambled a ninety-two at Ironwood."

"That was great. We will pick you up tomorrow."

"I know, at eight fifteen."

"See you then." Charles told Tom, "Richard is in for tomorrow."

Tom said, "Good. Nate, you ride with Richard."

Charles told Nate, "Good luck."

Nate asked in a worried way, "What is wrong with Richard?"

They both said at the same, "Nothing, just wait till you ride the cart."

Kate told Tom, "We have to go. Our family is coming for supper."

Tom had that dismayed look. Charles told Tom, "You forgot again."

Kate just said, "Hell, you both forget everything except your damn tee times." They laughed on that one while Tom and Kate walked out the door.

Charles told Nate, "Come on with me, and bring the clubs with you." Nate grabbed the clubs, and out the door they went. Charles told Nate that he went outside of town and practice. "Sometimes I just hit the golf balls just to relax."

As they pulled up, Nate could not believe it. He told Charles to turn the car around and go back. Charles told Nate, "Do not worry, I always come out here and practice. Then afterward, I go visit the people's graves."

Nate said in dismay, "This is a cemetery."

"Well, yes but not in this area. It is a big place where I can practice golf without driving twenty miles. If you want to get good, we have to see where your ball goes so I can tell you how to practice in the basement."

Nate said, "I cannot believe this. Jake's grave is only down there, about 300 yards to the left."

"Well, really, it is 285 to me. It is a driver. Hey, I've been doing this for at least thirty years. I know more people in the cemetery than I do that are alive. When we leave, I'll give you a tour. In fact, that one on the left, I call him my second dad."

Charles threw several balls on the ground and gave Nate a six-iron. Charles told him, "Take nice, easy swings to get loosened up. Then when you are ready, just hit one."

Nate hit the ball way right. Charles started to laugh. Nate looked at him and just said, "They go all that way." Nate was right; he hit several balls, and they all went that way.

Charles told Nate, "That is enough. Let's go."

"I am not done yet. I just got started."

"Sure, you got started by hitting them all right. We will go back to the house, and I will fix it for you without losing any of my golf balls."

They went back to the car. Charles drove very slowly. He told Nate, "Here's another friend of mine. He rode to work with me for fifteen years." He took a right and then went around this little curb and stopped.

Nate asked, "Why are you stopping?"

"You hit the damn balls. Go out there and pick the ones you can find."

Nate got out of the car and started to look for his golf balls. Charles could see Jake's grave from there. He thought it looked good. After a few minutes, Nate got back in the car; he had twelve golf balls. Charles looked at him and said, "You better have better eyes to find them golf balls, or you will need three hundred tomorrow."

Nate said in a disgusted voice. "That is not funny."

As Charles put the car in drive in the middle of the road, he made a big U-turn. Nate could see they were going right by Jake's grave. Charles stopped, and they got out. Charles told Nate, "Here is my wife's side of the family and mine." They walked by the aunt, grandma, grandpa, mom, and dad of Charles's wife.

Nate could hardly believe it; there were Charles's wife, Rose, and his daughter-in-law, Charlet. Charles told Nate, "She had no other place to be buried, so Jake wanted her here. So naturally, we had to buy another row of plots. Rose's grandpa bought the first row. Then there were Jeramy and then Jake." Charles started to cry. Nate just put his arm around him. They stayed there for fifteen minutes.

As they went back to the car, Charles asked Nate to drive. As he went around the little building, Charles told Nate to go about eighty yards and stop. Charles got out of the car, and Nate got out too. Charles told Nate, "This is where my mom and dad are buried with my grandpa and grandma on my mom's side. Grandma and Grandpa on my dad's side are across the tennis court." Charles started to leave.

Nate just said, "You stop here all the time?"

"Well, not all the time, just the times I practice golf here, which is about once or twice a week. Let's go back to the house. I need a beer."

Nate got back in the car and went down the path that ran to the main road. He looked at Charles. "Oh, take a right." Charles had to tell him how to get back to the house. "Monday, I will give you a tour of this small town."

Charles and Nate went down the basement and got two beers out of the refrigerator. Charles opened one of them, not the other. He told Nate, "Now hit some golf balls in that net." Nate hit ten of them, and then Charles told him to stop. "Now see the yellow line on the mat?" Nate said yes. "Well, on the back swing, follow that line. Then on the forward swing, follow the white line that leaves the tee. This is your right swing. Just keep doing that over and over, and you will have a draw or a straight shot. Do that fifty times, and then you can have your beer."

By the time Nate did that, Charles already drank both beers. Nate went to the fridge and got him one. Charles told Nate, "If you get one, by george, get me one too." Then Nate hit some more while Charles was practicing his putting. They were down there for at least two hours. Charles could tell Nate had enough practice and beer.

Charles did not realize how late it was. He called the pizza place and ordered a large sausage and cheese for him. Then he asked Nate what kind he liked. Nate said, "Well, if I have my choice, I like it all."

Charles shook his head and said, "I should have known."

Charles ordered one large supreme and two salads. "Just bring one package of all your salads." He told Nate, "I'll know what you like next time."

Nate and Charles did not say too much that night. They ate their pizza and drank a few more beers. Charles could not help himself and said, "Nate, if you go back to work at Tran Oil, they will probably be after you. They might think you know something. Maybe you should just quit your job and stay here." Nate did not know what to say. "Just think about it, and next day or two, you can decide. Right now, just keep it in mind." Nate thanked him and went to bed. Charles stayed up for the rest of the night watching TV and crying.

The next morning, Charles woke up in the chair; the TV was still on. He took his shower, went down the basement, hit fifty golf balls, and practiced putting for fifteen minutes. He went upstairs and woke Nate up. Charles told him, "We have a tee time. We have to get your ass going."

Nate, in a sleepy voice, said, "What time is it?"

"Seven o'clock. You remind me of Jake all the time. Did you guys sleep through college or what?"

Nate said, "No, but we both made sure our first class did not start before ten."

Charles laughed. "That is why it took you two extra years to graduate."

Nate said, "Well, that was part of it. The rest was just, say, growing up slowly."

Charles asked Nate if he liked bacon and eggs. He said, "Well, that is all right."

"Take it or leave it. That is all I know how to fix."

"That'd be all right."

Nate was getting ready to take his shower. Charles told him, "After we eat, you have about twenty minutes to warm up your golf swing."

Nate, in a surprised voice, said, "Do what?"

"Well, if you want to be better in golf, it does take some work. Just go down there and loosen up at least. It really helps me."

Nate finally was ready to go. He could tell Charles was a little upset. Nate just looked at him. "All right, what did I do wrong?"

"Well, Nate, some things you can be late on, and golf is not one of them, especially when Joe worked us in." Nate just shook his head. It reminded Charles of Jake. Jake did not really respect golf; he just hit the ball and expect he could do it.

Charles told Nate, "Well, by the day, you are going to learn a lot, especially playing with Richard."

Nate, in a sarcastic voice, said, "Who in the hell is Richard?"

"You will meet him in about fifteen minutes."

When they loaded up the car, Charles got in to start the engine. He remembered the beer. Charles told Nate, "Do not get out of the car. I will be right back." He had the beer down the basement and opened the refrigerator door. He could not believe it; he only had ten cans left. He knew they drank too much last night. He filled the cooler up, threw in some ice, and was back to the car in less than three minutes.

As Charles got in the car, Nate was laughing and told Charles, "You forgot the cooler."

Charles said yes as he was backing out. "When we golf at Parkers, we have to bring our own. I just hope that Richard does not have one." Nate did not say a word on that. Then Charles told him, "Just put your seat belt on."

When they arrived at Richard's house, just at the same time, Nate figured out the safety belt. For once, Richard was ready. Charles told Nate to open the trunk. Nate opened the glove box and found the button. Richard put in his clubs and cooler in the trunk. As Richard got in, he said, "You brought a cooler too."

Charles said yes, and Nate was laughing. "We have plenty of beer now."

On the way to Tom's house, Charles introduced Nate to Richard. They were at Tom's house in two minutes. Tom was always ready, and they were on the highway in no time.

Richard started to ask Nate what he was doing. Nate explained that he worked for DATABASE Corporation in Alexandria, Virginia.

Richard asked Nate, "What the hell is that?"

Nate laughed. "Well, we collect data for corporations from all over the world. When the company wants that information, we send it to them. Some of the information is about governments, other corporations, people, investments, just about anything that corporation wants us to find."

Richard said, "Well, that sounds like your company is a paid spy."

"We usually just use information that comes from the Internet or other former employees of corporations."

Tom turned around and, out of the blue, asked Nate, "How did you know Mr. Martin?"

Nate told them that Tran Oil owned DATABASE. "Mr. Martin used our business for Tran Oil." Nate was personally in charge of the business, and Mr. Martin was the person he reported the information to.

Charles turned and asked Nate, "Did Mr. Martin know you and Jake knew each other until the visitation?"

Nate, in a nervous voice, said, "You know, I really do not know. I thought Jake might have told him."

Charles told Nate, "You know, at the funeral home, he might not have seen you."

"Yes, that might be true because I did not see him until we were at the Legion."

Tom looked at Charles, and then he said, "You know, I bet when Nate goes back to work, Mr. Martin will be there waiting for him."

Nate looked scared. "You know, I better find out something good or bad before I go back to work."

Richard looked at Charles. "You know, I do not know what you crazy people are talking about, but I came to play golf, so let's change the subject, or take me home."

Charles told Richard, "Yes, you are right, no more talk except golf, beer, and pool."

Richard, in a happy voice, said, "Good."

By this time, they were at the golf course. They all walked toward the club house. Joe was outside talking to some golfers. As they walked by Joe, he left the golfers and walked right to Charles. He told Charles how sorry he was about Jake and handed him two cart keys. "Here, take these keys, get loaded up, and see Doug. We have an opening fairly soon." Charles thanked him, and then Joe walked back to the golfers.

Tom and Richard had this funny look. Charles just told them, "I know, this is the first time we never had to check in. Joe told me to not worry about it. He is taking care of it." Richard jumped in the cart and told Nate to get in. Tom told Charles to drive. They all got their clubs loaded up with the beer. In less than five minutes, they were at the starter.

Doug looked at Tom, Richard, and Charles. He said, "Have a good time, and good luck, Nate." They could all see Nate's eyes; he could not believe that a starter would know his name.

Richard told Nate, "Once you are with us, everyone knows you."

Nate looked at Richard. "This would never happen at our golf course unless you are rich."

Richard said with a big smile, "You have not seen nothing yet. Just stick around, and you will learn what friendly people are."

Tom and Charles were on the tee. Tom already hit his drive. Charles was getting ready when Richard and Nate was getting out of their cart. Charles's ball went to the right. Tom asked Richard, "What took you so long?"

Richard looked at Nate and then said, "Well, Nate just cannot figure out how the starter knew his name." They all laughed.

Tom told Nate, "You have not seen nothing yet."

Nate looked at Tom. "That is what Richard said."

Richard hit his ball down the middle. Nate addressed the ball; when he hit it, it went straight down the middle but only two miles high and less than a hundred yards. Richard told Nate, "Get in. I will straighten your game if you listen to me."

"I told you I do not play very often."

"Well, if you stay here with Charles, you will get a lot better, or we will be drinking off you."

They all bogeyed that hole except Nate; he shot a seven, which was not bad for hitting two bad shots. The next hole, Tom hit his left. Charles got up and hit his left too but more than Tom's. Nate went down the middle but only a mile high this time. Richard hit his straight down the middle.

As Charles went to Tom's ball, Tom asked him, "Why did you aim your ball left?"

"You notice that."

Tom said, "Yes, I know when you aim left, and that is what you did."

Charles told Tom, "I want to talk to you about Nate today without him knowing it."

Tom, while he was lining up his shot, looked up and then said, "You got a hell of a way in doing it." He hit his shot in the middle of the fairway.

They had a hard time finding Charles's. While they were looking, Charles told Tom, "I want to know what was said down the basement when you and Nate were looking at the golf clubs."

Tom was not surprised; he just said, "I was wondering when you were going to ask." He then told Charles to hit the ball. "I will tell you everything as we play." Charles had to chip out; he made a seven. Richard parred, and Tom bogeyed, but Nate shot a seven too.

During the next few holes, Tom told Charles, "Nate could not believe how friendly you are letting him in your house. He just kept saying he has never met a friendlier and kinder person. I told Nate, 'Just do not get him mad at you because he does not like to be lied to or threatened.' I also told him you are very stubborn."

Charles thanked him, and Tom just said, "Well, it is the truth. I also told Nate if you are proved wrong, you do admit you're wrong."

"Hell, I want to know what Nate knows, not what you told Nate about me."

Tom laughed and then said, "Really, he did not tell me much about himself at all."

"You know I like Nate a lot from the start. I am going to let him stay here if he wants to. I have one favor to ask you and Kate."

Tom asked, "What is that?"

"If you or Kate sees something or suspects something about Nate, you do not hesitate and tell me."

"Why, you don't trust him?" Tom then said, "Or is it he knew that Mr. Martin?"

"I do not know. Just do what I ask, and if I do not listen to you, make sure I listen to Kate."

Tom gave me his funny look and then said, "You do not have to worry about Kate telling you."

I looked at Tom. "Yes, I know, that is why I want you and Kate to just watch Nate."

Tom looked at Charles in a funny way. "Kate told me you told her about the same thing."

Charles said, "Yes, I did. I just wanted to make sure I told both of you."

Tom and Charles were talking so much that they did not realize they were on the eighteenth hole. Richard was hitting an eighty-five, Tom an eighty-nine, Nate a ninety-five, and Charles a ninety-three. Richard was laughing at Charles and just said, "Hell, if you do not get your ass out of your head, Nate might beat you."

Charles told Tom, "Let's make them a bet."

Tom said, "OK."

Charles told Richard, "Tom's and my score will beat yours and Nate's for a beer at the Leaser."

Richard said, "You're on." He did not even ask Nate.

Richard hit another good drive, and Nate hit this one good; instead of going high, it went long, and Tom looked at Charles and said, "We are in trouble."

Richard walked up to Tom and said, "Well, let's see what you can do."

Tom hit a good one but not as far as Richard and Nate. Charles hit it long but left. On the next shot, Tom was short of the green, and Charles was short to the left. Nate was short. Richard hit a good one within five feet of the pin. Tom and Charles got on and two-putted. Nate got on and made a twenty-foot putt. Richard missed his first putt but made par.

Richard picked up his ball out of the hole and told Nate, "Well, we know who is buying the second beer."

As Nate and Richard was putting their clubs in the car, Nate asked, "Who buys the first beer?"

Richard said, "This tavern we go to buys the first one as long we show the score card." Nate just shook his head and then put the cooler in the car.

Charles told Nate, "Wait a minute, there is one can left. Who wants it?"

Richard said out loud, "Hell, we know you want it, so take it."

Charles drank the beer while Tom and Richard took the carts back. Charles asked Nate if he enjoyed the game. "I had the best golf game of my life, not the score, just having fun, and still shot good for me, even drinking three beers."

Charles pulled the car where Tom and Richard would be. He finished drinking the beer. He told Nate to throw the can in the Dumpster by his window. He threw the can right in it. Charles told him he usually missed and had to get out of the car to pick it up. Nate had a laugh on that.

By this time, Tom and Richard were in the car. They were at the Leaser in six minutes. As they walked in, the bartender had seen them. Charles told her, "Three and one."

She said, "OK."

Before they sat down, the bartender had three Busches and a Miller Lite. Charles thanked her, and she said, "I know, count to two hundred."

Nate said, "What was that about?"

Tom tried to explain. "When we first walked in, Charles came up with this two-hundred count. When she counts to two hundred, she brings another round. This way, Charles figures no matter how busy she is, we get our second round."

Charles and Tom walked to the corner of the bar. There were popcorn and hot dogs for the customers. Charles put five hot dogs on a plate, and Tom filled two containers with popcorn. While they were doing that, Nate told Richard, "This is unreal. I cannot believe you just walk in a place, say very few words, and end up with four beers, popcorn, and hot dogs."

Richard told Nate, "You have not seen nothing yet."

Nate looked at Richard. "You know, this is at least the third time I heard that today." Richard just said, "Well, when you have friendly people and you do not act like a jerk, you get a lot more for your money and have a real good time."

Charles and Tom were back to the table in no time. Charles looked at Nate and could notice he was looking bewildered. Richard told Charles, "Do not worry about it. Nate is learning what small people are all about."

Nate looked at Richard. "I would not call you small people, just very fair and happy people."

Tom looked up, "Well, just do not get Charles mad. You will see a very fair person turn into . . . well, let's just say you do not want to see that."

Charles looked at everybody. "Well, here come our beers that we have to buy, Tom."

Tom told Charles, "Well, you lost it for us, so you pay."

The bartender put the beers on the table and asked, "One more round?"

Richard told her, "Well, hell yes, we need two more before we leave."

She asked, "Another two hundred?"

Charles told her, "No, count about five minutes or so."

She smiled and said, "I will be back."

Nate was looking at her very closely and asked, "What is her name?"

Richard said, "Yeah, Charles, what is her name?"

Charles laughed. "Well, we've been coming in here for the last fifteen years or so. Her first name is Susan, or that is what they call her. I never asked her name. I just talk to her when I come in here. Through the years, she knows what I drink, and I leave her a good tip. She probably knows my name, but she never called me by my name, and I never call her by hers."

Nate looked at all of them but told Charles, "That is weird."

"Yes, it is, but why screw up a good friendship? I tell you something, though, if I needed a favor that I thought she could do for me, I bet she'd do it."

Tom told Nate, "I bet on that too."

Nate still looked puzzled. Tom told him, "Well, one year, we could tell Susan was having a bad day. She had a black eye, in fact. Charles jokingly asked her if she tripped on a doorknob. Susan told him, 'None of your damn business.' Charles told her he was sorry that he made the joke. Susan told us, 'Well, my husband beat on me the other night. I told him to leave.' Charles told her, 'Why not get rid of the bum?' Susan told us, 'Well, I went to a lawyer. He wanted two thousand dollars up front.' Charles asked her if he is good. Susan told us he is one of the best in Decatur.

"Well, Charles went out to his car. He kept his golf fund money in a separate account so Rose would not have to worry about the joint account. Good for Charles, Rose did not know how much was in it. Well, anyway, Charles came back with a check and sat it on the table. He filled the check out for two thousand dollars. When Susan came back with our next round, Charles gave the check to Susan. Charles just told her, 'If you get rid of the bum and do not take him back, here is the best tip you will ever get.'

"Susan could not believe what she'd seen. She started to cry and said, 'I do not even know your name.' Charles told her, 'Well, you'll know it when you see my signature on the check, and I will know yours when I get it back. But I'd rather just keep our friendship the way it is, and if you need help, you just ask. And if I need your help, I will ask you.' Susan still could not believe it. Charles just told her, 'Good luck, and if you need more to get rid of the bum, just ask.'

"Well, from that day on, we asked Charles what her last name was. He told us, 'Well, when the check came back, it is sort of funny. The credit union get the checks. I just keep this carbon copy. On the carbon copy, I never wrote her name except 'Susan, the bartender at the Leaser Lounge.'"

Nate asked, "Is this really true?"

Charles told him, "Yes, it is true. She divorced the bum, remarried, and had two kids. To this day, I do not know her last name of either marriage."

Tom told Nate, "Now you know why she makes sure we get our beers as fast as possible."

Nate then asked, "Well, did you get your money back?"

Tom and Richard looked at Charles. "Hey, did you ever get that money back?"

Charles stared at the three of them. "Well, not really. One day I came in here after she remarried. She handed me eight hundred dollars. Susan told me she will pay the rest back as she gets it. I do not know what got over me. I told her, 'Save the rest toward your fifteenth anniversary, and take a small trip with it.'"

Richard told Charles, "That was stupid."

"Yes, it probably was, but then again, if the money helped Susan get a better life, it was worth it. Let's have one more here before I ask Susan for my money back."

Tom started to laugh. "That would be the day."

They drank their last beer and were walking out when Nate asked in a nervous way, "Well, it's time to get back to your house."

Richard and Tom asked Nate, "What are you talking about?"

"Well, we had four beers each on the golf course and then another four at the Leaser. I just thought we'll be going back to Coal City."

Richard told Nate, "Who is driving?"

"Charles is driving."

"Well, Charles will tell us when we go home."

Tom told Nate, "Unless you have a special place you have to go."

"Hell no, I am with you, guys."

Richard told Nate, "Well, we go home when the driver tells us. When Charles drives, God only knows."

Charles told Richard, "I remember one time you had to find a way home from Dave's."

Richard told Charles in sharp voice, "Do not remind me. Karla reamed my ass on that one."

Tom started to laugh and then said, "I missed that one."

Charles told Tom, "If you were not a workaholic, you probably would have been there."

By this time, they were out of Decatur, heading for Coal City. They went around Johnstown, and Tom asked Charles, "Are you stopping here?"

"No, I figure we go to De Land and just give them some business." Charles pulled into the Luckies about five minutes later.

Nate asked, "What is this place?"

Tom told Nate, "This is a tavern and restaurant."

"I did not see this place on the way."

Charles said as he opened the car door, "We were all talking and probably did not pay any attention to it."

As they walked in, Charles yelled, "Hey, Jasper, are you in here?"

A voice yelled back, "Yes! I am cleaning up! Just help yourself, Charles!"

Richard and Tom sat at the bar. Charles went behind the bar and served Richard his Miller Lite and Tom and Nate their Busches. Nate asked Charles, "What are you doing? You cannot just walk in a place and serve ourselves."

Charles told Nate, "Relax, we do it all the time. Hell, Jasper even knew my voice." He gave Nate his beer. "Nate, just relax and have fun."

Tom put some quarters in the pool table. Charles told Tom and Richard, "You guys play just one game here. We will have one more and then go to Dave's."

Tom told Charles, "Well, we just want to warm up."

"You need to."

Charles could tell Nate was watching Richard and Tom play. He asked Nate, "Hey, do you shoot?"

"Well, I am better at pool than golf."

"Hell, do not tell Tom and Richard that we will challenge them when we get to Dave's."

"Hell, the way I am going, I will be drunk."

Charles took Nate's beer and gave him a cup of coffee. "Here, drink this until we get to Dave's." Nate thanked him, and Charles drank Nate's beer. "Do not want it to go to waste."

Charles served one more beer and gave Nate another cup of coffee. Tom beat Richard in the game of pool by one ball. Charles told them, "Well, drink up. We are leaving."

He laid fifteen dollars on the cash register. Charles yelled, "Hey, Jasper, thanks! I put the money on top of the register! Want me to lock the door?"

A voice came out of the back. "Yes! Sorry I am in the kitchen! My hands are full!"

Charles yelled back, "Understand, and keep the change!"

Charles walked out last, turned the sign to Closed, and locked the door. Nate was shaking his head. Tom asked him, "What is wrong?"

"I cannot believe this. We walked in a tavern, played one game of pool, drank six beers and two coffee, and never saw the owner or whoever was back there. This Jasper knew Charles's voice and just said 'help yourself,' so we did. Had that been in Alexandra, we would be arrested or shot."

Tom told Nate, "Hey this is a small town. Everybody knows Charles."

They were at Dave's Tavern in less than six minutes. The bar was pretty full, so they sat at the table. Richard went to the bar and ordered the beers. Tom went to the pool table and put some quarters in. Tom asked, "Who wants to be partners?"

Charles told Tom, "Well, since Nate is my guest, Nate and I will take you and Richard on."

While Tom was racking the balls, Charles told Nate, "Hey, do not drink coffee, but just drink very slow. We will beat these guys in pool."

You're the boss. I just cannot believe how you guys can do this."

"Just takes practice, like anything else."

Richard came back with the beers and then asked, "Who is playing?"

Tom told Richard, "We are taking Charles and Nate."

Richard told Charles, "For your sake, I hope Nate plays better pool than golf."

Charles broke the balls and did not make anything. Tom made four small balls. Nate shot and ran the table. Charles told Richard, "Well, I guess Nate can play pool better than he can golf." Tom had this dismayed look and just could not believe what he had seen.

Nate just told everyone, "Well, I was a little lucky."

Tom told him, "Sure, just a little lucky." He started to rack the balls.

Charles broke and did not make anything. Richard's shot made three stripes. It gave Nate a very hard leave. Nate missed, and then Tom ran all the stripes off but missed the eight ball. Charles shot, ran the table, and made a one-rail bank on the eight. Tom just said, "I will be damned. If Nate does not do it, Charles will."

Richard just said, "Must not be our day in pool."

Charles told them, "Hey, there are days like that."

The next few games went back and forth. Nate told them, "Hey, I cannot drink anymore, even drinking the beer slowly."

Tom told Nate, "We do not leave until the driver says so." Nate told them they might have to carry him.

Charles told them, "One more game, and I will buy the last round, whoever wants one." Nate told them to leave him out.

After the game, they had all the beer gone, so Charles told Nate, "Well, let's get going."

Charles took Richard home first, even though it was out of the way. Richard thanked them and said, "Let me know when you need another golfer to go."

Charles told him, "Do not worry."

As Charles pulled into Tom's driveway, he got out and said, "Meet you tomorrow at John's Tap."

"What time?"

"Eight thirty."

"Sure."

"Tell Kate, if she wants to help me, to meet us at the bank at ten o'clock."

"Do not worry, Kate will be there."

"Well, if she is not, I will understand."

Charles got back in the car. Nate could not wait. "Did I hear you tell Tom eight thirty at John's Tap?"

Charles said, "That's right."

"Hell, I will not be alive by then the way I feel now."

Charles laughed. "When you eat some food and get some sleep, you will be fine."

Nate and Charles were home in a short time. Charles called Howard's Pizza, ordered one large sausage and cheese, and then asked Nate what he liked. Nate just said he liked everything on his, so Charles ordered one large supreme. Howard told Charles it would be delivered in about fifteen minutes or so. Charles thanked Howard and hung up. Nate was sitting on the couch and, in a slurring voice, said, "You did not give your name or address."

"Oh, in this town, they know you by your voice if you give them enough business. I do this a lot." Nate could hardly keep his eyes open.

The pizza came. Charles gave the delivery boy twenty-five dollars and told him to keep the change. Nate must have been hungry because he had both boxes open and was eating his before Charles was back at the table.

After they ate, Nate told Charles, "I am going to bed."

"OK."

Nate asked in a strange voice, "Where do you sleep?"

"I usually just fall asleep in the chair. When I wake up, I take my shower, and then I am ready to go. My bedroom is at the right of the living room."

Nate just said, "You know, I did not even notice that."

Charles laughed. "Well, when you sober up, you will remember better." He changed the channel to watch some news and was just thinking what their game plan would be after tomorrow or if Tom and Kate would show up at all.

The next morning, Charles woke up at about six, took his shower, and cleaned up the house a little. He cooked some bacon and eggs. Then he yelled up at Nate, "It is time to get up!"

Nate said in a very slow and somewhat angry voice, "What time is it?"

"It is seven thirty. We are going to meet Tom in an hour uptown, remember?"

Nate came slowly down the steps. Charles said, "Here, eat this."

Nate asked, "What is it?"

"Bacon and eggs. This is the only thing I know how to cook on the stove, so you take it or leave it."

"I will take it." Nate could not believe it. Charles drank so much beer yesterday and played golf and pool, and here he was at seven thirty, wide awake and ready for the day.

With Charles's help, Nate was ready by eight o'clock. They went to the car. As Charles started it, he said, "Shit, I forgot the safety-deposit keys." He ran in the house to get them.

While Charles was doing that, Nate fell asleep. Charles came back to the car and saw Nate sleeping. Charles turned the radio on full blast. Nate jumped up, hitting his head on the roof. Charles started to laugh. Nate just said, "What the hell is going on?"

Charles, while he was still laughing, just said, "I thought I'd wake you up."

They pulled up to John's Tap in no time; it was only four blocks away. Charles got out and was on the sidewalk even before Nate was out of the door. Nate noticed the tavern was not open yet. He started to tell Charles at the same time Charles picked the papers and was opening the door. Nate asked in surprise, "What the hell are you doing?"

"I am opening the tavern up for Charlet. Either Skip or I does this if we can get up here in time." By that time, the door was open. Charles turned on the window lights and told Nate, "Well, come on in." Charles walked to the end of the tavern, turned on the rest of the lights, and plugged in the coffeepot. He told Nate he was going get a bag of ice.

While Charles passed the cooler, he asked Nate, "You want some kind of pop?"

Nate just said, "Coffee will be fine."

Charles went out and came back with a bag of ice. When he walked back by the cooler, he reached in for a Coke. Nate told Charles, "Coke at this time?"

"I do not like coffee, too early for a beer."

Tom drove up and walked in. By the time he sat down, Charles handed him a cup and then said, "The coffee is not done yet. It will be in about five minutes."

Tom started reading the paper and just mumbled, "I am in no hurry. Nate, how was the bacon and eggs?"

"They were very good. How did you know that?"

Tom started to laugh and then said, "That is the only thing Charles knows how to fix on top of the stove."

Charles grabbed the coffeepot. "The coffee is ready." He poured Nate and Tom some. Charles then put in a dollar and seventy-five cents in the cash register. He asked Tom if Kate was going to make it.

Tom could tell Charles was nervous, so he told him, "Hell no. She said it is your own problem." He could tell Charles was very disappointed, but he could not keep a straight face. Charles then could tell something was up. Tom started to laugh. "I got you. Kate will be at the bank at ten o'clock, just as you said."

Charles was smiling and then said, "Are you trying to give me heart failure?"

"No, but I was told we were out too late yesterday."

Nate said out of the blue, "Tell me about it."

A few minutes went by, and a tall person came in. Tom got up and then walked toward the back table. He picked up a deck of cards and started to shuffle them. Charles asked the newcomer, Darrell, if he wanted coffee. Darrell said, "Yes, that will be fine. Who is this person?"

Charles said, "This is a friend of Jake's. His name is Nate."

Darrell asked, "Hey, Nate, can you play cards?"

Nate told him, "Not very good."

Darrell then told Charles, "Well, he is your partner."

Charles just said, "OK."

Tom told Nate, "Get over here. While Darrell drinks his coffee, I will teach you this card game."

Charles told Nate, "Pay attention. I need the money."

Charles went to the phone to call the bank. He asked for Andy. In a few seconds Charles was talking to him and explained to him they would be there at ten o'clock to check out the safety-deposit boxes. "We might be there for quite a long time."

Andy told Charles, "Do not worry. If we can, I will give you my office."

"Thanks and see you at ten." Then they hung up.

Charles walked to the table. Tom already dealt the six cards. Charles asked Nate, "Well, you understand how to play?"

Nate replied in a very nervous way, "I think so. Jake showed us this years ago, if I remember right."

Tom looked at Nate. "Well, are you better at this game than golf?"

Nate told Tom, "Worse."

Tom told Charles, "Well, that is good for us because if Nate was better at this game than pool, I should probably pay now."

Tom and Darrell won the first games. Tom could tell Charles was not paying much attention to the game. He looked at the clock; it was nine fifteen. Tom told Charles, "You know, I think it is time for a real drink. Charles, get us three beers and a Bloody Mary for Darrell."

Charles told Tom, "All right, just one before we go to the bank."

Nate told Charles, "Leave me out."

Darrell told him, "If one of us drinks, we all do."

Charles handed them their drinks while Darrell shuffled the cards for him. Charles sat down, started to deal, and then told Darrell, "This is our last game and drink until we get back from the bank." Darrell told them he had to leave too.

At this time, Charlet walked in. She said hi to everybody and asked, "Where is Skip?"

Charles told Charlet he did not know. "Maybe he went camping."

"Oh, that is right. They went to Clinton Lake. Thanks for opening up."

"No problem. Thank you for letting us play cards."

Charlet then lay down her sacks and at the same time asked Nate, "Well, who won at the golf course, Nate?"

Nate said, "Well, it was not me."

Charles told her, "Richard and Tom won golf. Nate and I won pool."

Charlet asked Tom, "Well, you found someone who can beat you?"

Nate told her, "Well, I was lucky."

Charles, with a laugh, said, "Luck? Hell, we beat them."

After a few hands, the score was twelve to eight. Tom just said, "Well, hell, let's get this game over with." And he bid four.

Nate asked, "What happens now?"

Charles told him, "Well, you dealt. It is up to you. You can either bid four and take it away or let Tom have it. If you let Tom have it and he makes the bid, then they win."

Nate said, "Pass."

Darrell told Nate, "Well, that might be a bad move."

"I do not think so." Tom made it in clubs. Nate gave all of them this dumb look and then said, "I'll be damned. I had three deuces, and none of them was a club."

Tom led with the ace. Darrell threw the jack. Tom told Darrell, "All we need is low and game we win." Charles did not look very happy. Tom came back with the two of clubs, and Darrell threw the king.

Charles said, "Shit." And he threw the ten of clubs. Nate threw a nine of clubs and just said, "Well, we should not have sold out."

"Hey, do not put. We put you."

Tom was laughing, went to the blackboard, wrote Nate's name, and then said, "Hey, what is your last name? I do not know it."

Nate told him, "Andrews. What is this?"

Charles told him, "Whoever sold out gets his name on the board until someone else sells out. Hey, we owe four dollars total and three drinks."

Nate, in dismay, said, "What?"

Charles told him, "We play a dollar a game and twenty-five cents a set. We lost three games, and we had four sets."

Tom then told Nate, "And a drink a game. Charles already bought the first one, so you and Charles owe two more."

Charles told Charlet, "Give us another round." Charlet served the drinks.

Then Darrell said, "Forget my other one. I have to go."

Charles said, "Oh, hell, we can be late fifteen minutes, can you?"

"No, I have to go." They quit playing cards.

Time went faster than they realized. They finished the last beer by ten o'clock. Tom was glad. He told them, "I do not think Kate would be happy waiting on us when she found out we were here."

Charles told Tom, "I was thinking the same thing." He turned to Darrell. "We will finish that other drink some other time." Darrell thanked them and walked out just behind them.

Charlet told all of them, "See you later."

Charles said, "We will be back soon."

The bank was just half a block away. Charles told Tom, "We might as well walk." Tom started to walk. As he looked up, he could see Kate getting out of her car.

Kate waited for them and then said in a funny voice, "Just had to play cards."

Charles explained, "Well, your husband won anyway."

Kate told all of them, "Well, I will not see the money." Then she looked at Nate. "What are you shaking your head for?"

Tom started to laugh. "Well, Nate, Kate is beginning to know you."

Nate told Kate, "I just cannot get over this town. We went in a tavern that was locked. Charles had a key, and we helped ourselves to some drinks."

Kate said, "Oh, you boys had a few drinks. How many? Ten?"

Nate laughed. "No, just two."

Kate shook her head and then said in a soft voice, "How did I ever get in a position I never know?"

Tom told Kate, "Honey, I heard that. You just love me."

Kate looked at Tom. "I do not know about love. For so many years, I just put up with you."

Charles started to laugh. "You both know you love each other. I am just glad you are both my best friends."

Kate told them, "Let's get inside before it gets too deep out here." So Charles walked in first.

Diane was at the counter; she walked around and told them to follow her. Andy must have told her they were coming. Charles signed the register, and they went in the safety-deposit area. She unlocked the bank's lock, and Charles unlocked his. Diane said, "If you need help, just come out and get one of us." Charles thanked her. Diane turned around. "No problem."

"The first box," Charles told everyone, "is old stuff. It still has Jake's first baseball cards in it." Nate could not believe this. "Well, I just keep them now. There are some stocks' papers I forgot I had. Jake and I bought them when he was in school. He wanted to buy some kind of stock. So I took him to Madison to a stockbroker I knew."

The next box had more stuff in it. Charles did not remember Jake had so many baseball cards. Kate asked, "Where are the disks?"

"The next two boxes." Charles opened them up. Kate could not believe how many they were. "Jake and his friends were doing this for a few years."

Kate just said, "Looks like a hundred years."

Charles told Kate and Tom, "You go through this box. Nate and I will go through the other one."

In a very short time, Kate and Tom found another deposit key. So did Charles and Nate. Charles said in a surprised voice, "I wonder what is going on here."

He opened the other two boxes. The first box was a list of the stocks with the broker's name at the bottom of the page—Tom Bensly. Charles explained to them, "This is John Bensly's son, who took over his father's business." There were all sorts of stocks and papers under this paper. The next box was a letter in a sealed envelope. On the envelope, it said, "To Dad only."

Kate told Tom and Nate, "Maybe we better leave the room until Charles reads this." Tom thought this was a good idea. Nate was just staring at the letter; he did not realize how long he was staring until Kate spoke. "Well, let's leave Charles alone." Nate looked up and started to walk out. Tom gave Charles this funny look. Charles thanked them.

After they went out of the room, Charles opened the letter. There was a list of corporations; at the bottom, there was this message:

> Dad,
>
> If you are reading this, I must be dead. This list of companies, the first eleven, is where the team works at. I did not put their names down, but if you use your memory, I know you can figure it out. Just think whom you met or I talked to you about. You know them all one way or another. (Do not trust no one except your close friends.)
>
> The rest are the ones who, we believe, is trying to take over or change our government. They have a lot of power. I believe their goal is to control Congress and the president. They already have the Supreme Court. In the following papers are names and places and a few bank account numbers. I hope the disk backs up what I am saying here. Oh, Dad, if you do not proceed with this, that is fine because I doubt that if I died of natural causes, you are reading this.
>
> P.S. Oh, Dad, go talk to Tom. You will be very surprised what he has to say.
>
> Love,
> Jake

Charles stood there for a few seconds; to him, it seemed like an hour. He just sat down and cried. After a few minutes, he realized he had to get his thoughts back. Charles took a piece of paper that was on the table and copied down the companies on Jake's list. He thought, *Find Jake's friends first.* Charles put the letter back in the box.

As Charles was just about to go tell them to come in, he put the paper in his pocket. Then he took a blank piece of paper and folded it in half. Charles then told them to come in the room. He made sure they all had seen that he put in his front shirt pocket the paper that was folded in half. He told them he had the letter there.

Charles started to put all the boxes back with the keys in them just like how they found them. Kate and Tom helped. Nate asked, "What are we going to do next?"

Charles asked Kate, "You are the most sensible one. What do you think?"

Kate was surprised Charles asked her. She thought for just a few seconds. "Well, if I were you, I would go to Madison to see what this Tom has to say."

Charles told her, "OK, that sounds good."

Even before Charles could ask "what's next," Kate said, "Then we should organize the disks after Tom and I come back from Chicago."

Tom told Kate, "Charles needs one of us here." Charles laughed.

Kate said in a strong voice, "Like hell you are. You are going with me. We are leaving tomorrow to see my brother. We will be back Friday." Kate looked at Tom. "Do not argue with me on this one."

Charles told Tom, "You two go to Chicago. Nate and I will go to Madison, and then we will meet Saturday."

Kate said, "No, we will meet Friday night at the Company so I do not have to cook when we get back. Then you guys can golf either Saturday or Sunday, or hell, you'll probably golf both days."

Tom thought out loud, "Will you make the tee times?"

Charles said, "Where at?"

Tom told them, "I do not care. You make it, and maybe Richard will play again."

Nate told them, "He might have to go back Saturday."

Charles told them, "Just plan on Friday. I will make a tee time. We will just have to play it by ear."

As they were leaving the bank, Charles had seen Andy. He went up to him and thanked him for the cooperation. Andy just said, "Anytime." Charles made sure the safety box's key was in his pocket. He really wanted to make sure the paper was in there. Charles deliberately made sure everyone had seen the other paper in his front pocket.

As they were outside, Kate went toward her car and told Tom, "You be back by one o'clock to help me pack, and be sober."

Charles thanked Kate and told them, "Well, let's see if Darrell is back and finish our game and drink."

Tom was delighted with that and then said, "Remember, I have to be back by one."

Charles told Tom, "We heard Kate. Do not worry, I will not keep you late this time."

When they walked in John's Tap, Charles asked Charlet for another round. "Can I use your phone?"

"Sure."

By this time, Charles already had the phone book in his hand. He looked up Tom Bensly's phone number. Charles then made the call. A nice, friendly voice answered, "Tom Bensly Investment."

"This is Charles Appel from Coal City. Could I speak to Tom?"

"It'll just be a few minutes. Please hold."

"Sure."

A voice answered in a few seconds. "This is Tom. Charles, I am sorry about Jake. Dad and I did not know for sure what to do. Dad decided you call us when you are ready. Could you be here tomorrow at eight thirty in the morning?"

Charles told him, "Sure, but you do not open till nine."

"Well, Dad wants to be here with me. He thought it'd be better for you if we did not have any interruption."

Charles told Tom, "All right, eight thirty tomorrow. Thanks."

"No problem."

Charles hung up the phone and told Charlet, "I am sorry. I forgot to use my credit card. Here is five dollars for using your phone."

"Forget it."

"No, here, keep it."

Charlet told Charles, "Are you sure?"

"Yes, I am. Thanks."

Tom started to walk toward the table. Well, let's start playing. Darrell just pulled up."

As Darrell walked in, Charlet already had his drink in front of him. He thanked Charles even before Charlet could tell him who bought it. Darrell asked Nate, "Think you learned how to play this game now?"

Nate told him, "I think so."

Charles told Nate, "Hell, you better. You are getting expensive."

Tom already had the cards dealt and told them, "Get your ass over here. I am running out of time."

Darrell was walking toward the table and told Tom, "What is your hurry? Does Kate has plans for you?"

Charles told Darrell, "She sure does. They are going to Chicago."

Nate was already sitting down. Darrell took one look at his cards. "Well, hell, you are so much in a hurry I bid four in clubs."

Tom told Darrell, "Hey, wait a minute, I am your partner."

"Hey, you are the one in a hurry." Charles started to laugh. By that time, they were all at the table. Nate asked for five cards, Tom asked for six, Charles asked for four, and Darrell asked for one.

Darrell told Tom, "What a load for being in a hurry."

"Hell, I did not bid."

Darrell gave his usual Natele. Charles knew right then they were in trouble. Darrell led the ace. Nate asked, "Do you have to follow suit?"

Tom told him, "Hell yes."

Nate threw the jack of clubs. Charles told him, "What the hell are you doing?"

"Hey, it's the only one I had."

Tom threw a six of clubs. Darrell told Tom, "Hey, Nate was better than you."

"Hell, I drew one, but it was a six."

Charles threw a seven. Then Darrell led the king of clubs. Charles said, "Oh shit." Nate threw a five of diamonds. Tom threw a ten of hearts. Charles threw a ten of clubs.

Tom asked Darrell if he had the deuce. Darrell said, "Wait until the hand is over." He then threw a nine of clubs. Nate threw a four of spades. Tom threw a king of hearts. Charles threw a three of spades.

Darrell then told them, "Hell, none of you have trumps. I will take the rest." He laid down the ace of spades and the two of clubs. Tom could not believe it.

Charles told Darrell, "You asshole." Nate could not believe what he had seen.

Darrell told Tom, "I thought to have your dollar too."

"Not in your life."

Charles told Nate, "I am sure glad Tom has to leave. This could be a long day."

Tom told Charles, "Well, I did not have nothing."

Darrell told him, "That is no shit. You are a load."

So Charles started the deal and told Nate, "We cannot let that stop us."

Darrell told them, "Hey, you cannot beat luck."

Nate told him, "I do not know you very well, but to me, that was shit." Charles told Charlet to bring a round of drinks.

They played five more games. Charles and Nate only won one game. After they paid their last round of drinks, Tom told them he had to go. Charles told him, "Good. I cannot afford you anymore today. When you have a chance, I like to talk to you before you go to Chicago."

Tom was happy about that; it was killing him Charles did not talk about the letter. "What about after supper, say, around seven?"

"We will be down at seven." Tom then left the tavern.

Darrell was getting ready to leave. Charles asked him if he wanted one more for the road. Darrell told him, "Thanks, but I better get home myself."

Nate and Charles left the table and walked up to the bar. "Give us one more, Charlet, and then we will leave too." Charlet gave Nate and Charles their beer.

Nate looked at Charles. "What are you going to do next?"

Charles knew he was talking about Jake and the letter. "I do not know for sure. After Tom and Kate come back from Chicago, we will make a detailed game plan, I hope. I have to think. Let's go hit some golf balls. You need to practice, and I need to think. I can think better hitting golf balls."

"I think I had too much to drink to practice golf."

"I know we both have."

"Then why are we?"

"Just pretend we are on number twelve or thirteen. We're probably in that shape anyway."

Nate started to laugh. "Well, I guess that is right."

They left the tavern and went behind the cemetery. Charles told Nate to hit one. "Let's see how bad it is." Nate took a seven-iron. The ball sliced its way to the right. Charles started to laugh. "I wish you drank that much the other day."

Nate told Charles to hit one. Charles took his seven-iron. He took a little more time than usual, and then when he hit the ball, the paper fell out of his pocket. Nate bent over and picked it up. He slowly handed it to Charles and asked if that was what he was thinking about. Charles told him yes. Then he told Nate, "Did you see my ball?"

Nate forgot all about the ball. Charles told him it went straight at about 140 yards. "Well, it takes practice to play with no beers or several beers. You have to learn your own strength and weakness so you change with your game. To answer your question, yes, this letter is a list of corporations that Jake told me his team worked at. I would have to figure out who they are. Jake told me I met them some time or another. He told me if I think on it, he knew I will figure it out. This is to make sure if someone else finds this letter, they will have a hard time."

Nate asked, "What are you going to do?" Charles put the letter back in his pocket. He noticed Nate could not tell it was a blank piece of paper.

They practiced for few more minutes. Nate told Charles he had to go to the restroom. Charles told him, "OK, let's go home."

When they got in the house, Nate went right to the restroom. Charles walked in the computer room and opened up a little safe he had. He deliberately waited until Nate came out. Nate asked, "Where are you?"

"Come in here. I am putting the letter in my little safe." As Nate was walking in, Charles put the letter in the safe and shut the door. "It'll be in good hands here. Let's go out to eat, and then when we are done, we will go to Tom and Kate."

Nate was still looking at the safe. Then he said, "That sounds like a good idea."

"I am going to change shirts in case we play pool. I do not want chalk on this shirt." When Charles went in his room, he grabbed an ink pen and put it in his pants pocket. He switched shirts and came right out.

Nate was not around. Charles walked in the computer room. Nate was not there. Nate came down the steps from the bedroom and told Charles, "I'm just getting ready too."

They arrived at the Company to eat some burgers and fries. Nate put some quarters in the pool table and told Charles, "Go ahead and break."

Charles broke the balls; two fell in. He was laughing. "Now they fall." They played till seven o'clock. Charles told Nate, "Well, hell, we played ten games, and we broke even. Nate asked to play the tie off. "Hell, let's just quit here and continue some other time. We have to go to Tom and Kate anyway."

Tom's house was only a block and a half from the tavern. Kate answered the door and told them to come on in. Tom came out of the restroom, went to the refrigerator, and handed them a beer. Nate told Tom to forget him; he had enough for the day. Charles took his and told Tom, "No more after this one."

Kate told Tom, "Hey, you had enough. We are leaving early tomorrow." He told her he was going to drink a Coke.

When they were all at the table, Charles told Kate and Tom about the letter. "We have to be real careful on how we handle this. Jake does not want to take a chance on his friends getting killed or my friends."

Tom told Charles with a laugh, "That was very nice of him."

Kate said, "That is not funny."

Charles told Tom and Kate, "After tomorrow, Nate and I will know a lot more. The way Tom talked, they had something to tell me. Plus, we have to figure out where and how to translate all those disks. Maybe Chick and I can solve that before you get back from Chicago. Kate, you and Tom have a good time. We will see you at the Company for supper Friday night unless something changes. Nate, let's go home so Tom and Kate can go to sleep."

Just as they were to the door, Charles told Nate he had to go to the restroom. As he walked away, he could hear Kate talking to Tom and Nate. While Charles was in the restroom, he pulled out of his front pocket the copy of the list of companies he made at the bank. On the other side, he wrote, "Tom and Kate, make a copy of this. Give me one back without Nate knowing, and hide the other copy anywhere you want. Just make sure you two are the only ones who know. I put the original one back in the safety box. Do not ask questions until I tell you to." Charles put this in Kate's medicine cabinet by her makeup, which he knew she would find. He then flushed the toilet and came out.

While they were walking out, Charles told them both to have fun. Tom said, "I know Kate will."

Kate yelled back, "I know Tom will because he will be with me!" Charles laughed while he was getting in the car.

Charles and Nate were back at Charles's house. Charles turned on the television, and then he sat down. Nate was already on the couch. Charles told Nate, "You know, you have to decide if you want to stay here with me or go back to work and take your chances. I have enough money if you want to stay here. I just do not know how much money I need to catch Jake's killers. Whatever it takes, I will find a way."

Nate told Charles he had a few thousand to get by with. "Maybe I could find a job around here and help you find Jake's killers."

"Hell, after tomorrow, maybe Jake already has our war chest. I cannot believe Jake would not tell me about his investments."

"Well, he probably thought you would worry less."

"I wish I never did what I did for him now. I tell you something, though, I am going to follow through where Jake left off until the end."

"We might want to know where that is."

"I am going to eat some hot dogs. There is luncheon meat in the refrigerator if you want some. Then I am going to bed to rest and think."

Nate told Charles, "I am going to stay up for a while, if that is all right.

"Hell, to me, this is your house, so just do what you want." Charles went in his bedroom, turned on the television set, and then shut the door.

Nate went in the living room and started to watch a movie Charles had on tape. After the movie, Nate walked to Charles's bedroom door to see if he was asleep. The television was off; there was no sound. Nate figured Charles was real tired through all his misfortune in the last several days. Nate went back to the television, sat down, and watched a television movie.

After forty-five minutes, Nate went back to Charles's bedroom door. He could not hear anything. Nate was fairly sure Charles was asleep. Nate walked in the computer room. He went right to the safe. He wrote down the model number of the safe. He even measured the height, sides, and top. Nate started to turn the knob to try to open it. Then he stopped. Nate noticed the knob was set in one particular place. He was afraid if he moved it, Charles might notice. Nate then went in the living room to finish the movie.

Charles came out of his bedroom; he noticed Nate was still up. He looked at the television and noticed his favorite movie was on. Charles asked Nate, "Is that a great car scene or what?"

"Yes, it was unbelievable."

"Hey, you know, I never could figure out what kind of car was the black one. Did you notice?"

Nate told him, "No, I could not tell."

Charles told him he always thought it was a Charger. He then asked, "What about the Mustang? Did you know what kind that was?"

Nate did remember seeing the car. He said, "Yeah, that was a good-looking one."

Charles told him he had one of them and that it was that year. "But mine was burgundy."

"I bet that ran good."

"It sure did." Then Charles asked, "Did you notice how that black car hit that truck?"

"Yes, really tore it up."

"It sure did."

Charles went in the restroom. After he took his piss, he looked in the mirror. He asked himself, *I wonder what Nate was up to.* He knew, in this movie, the black car went in a gas station or something like that. Then he wondered if he went in the computer room.

Charles came out of the restroom to tell Nate he was going back to bed. He noticed before he spoke that the television was off and that Nate was already in his bedroom.

The next morning, Charles was up at five thirty. He had his shower and started to cook his bacon and eggs. Just as he was done cooking, Nate came down the steps. He told Charles, "You know, I am getting used to smelling your bacon and eggs. That smells good."

Charles laughed. "That's what I thought when I was a kid. My grandpa fixed eggs real early in the morning. I went downstairs, and he always gave me his while he cooked some more. Here, you eat these before they get cold." The toast just popped up. "There, get that toast, and put in two more for me." Nate went to the toaster and did just what Charles asked.

Even before Nate was eating, Charles's eggs were done too. Nate could not believe how fast they cooked. Charles told him, "Eggs do not take long, just the bacon." He poured some orange for Nate and himself.

Charles told Nate, "We will leave at eight o'clock to Madison."

Nate asked, "Sure you want me to go?"

"Sure, so maybe both of us together can figure what they say." Nate told Charles he was not very good with investments. Charles said he was not either. "Years ago, I was, but I lost interest after Jake moved away."

When Nate took his shower and was ready, it was time to leave. Madison was about a fifteen-minute drive. They were in front of Bensly Investments in twenty minutes. Charles and Nate were just a few minutes early.

As they walked to the door, a voice spoke up. "Mr. Appel, wait, I will unlock the door." There stood Tom Bensly. He sat his briefcase down and shook Charles's hand. Charles introduced Tom to Nate, and when Tom unlocked the door, they walked in.

Tom told them, "My dad will be here shortly. Please just sit down. I will get some coffee on."

John walked in. Charles got up, went to John, and started to shake his hand. Charles told John, "Thanks for coming." Then he introduced Nate to him.

Tom came over. "We have all the information for you in our main conference room." He picked up the pot of coffee and two Coke cans. He handed Charles a Coke and asked Nate what he wanted.

Nate told Tom, "Coffee will be fine."

Charles told Tom, "Hell, you remember that I do not drink coffee."

"Well, really, Dad did." Charles thanked them both. Tom asked, "Charles, are you ready for this?"

"Yes."

John told Charles, "If you want to quit or take a break or ask any questions, just let us know. We have a lot of information that will surprise you. The first order is that we might not handle this very well. When we heard about Jake, we were gone on business. We did not know about Jake until after the funeral. We left a message on your answering machine. You did not call us back. We figured you were not ready yet."

Charles started to laugh. "Hell, I do not listen to that damn box very often. So I am the one to apologize."

John told Charles, "I am going to have Tom explain this. Tom is more familiar with Jake's finances than me. I am here mainly for you."

Charles thanked John for that and told Tom, "I am not trying to be smart about this. Could you go through this slowly? I am a slow listener."

"That is what Dad told me to do to all our customers. Charles, I am going back as far as we can so you can understand the whole picture." Charles told them that was good. Tom explained, "Remember, back in 1990, you brought Jake in when he was ten? You invested a thousand in the Ashland Company."

Charles told him, "Yes, that is still in the safety-deposit box. Jake had a note to talk to you if he died. That is how we got here."

Tom said, "Good, now do you know what that is worth today?"

"No, I never cared. We did try to teach Jake about the stock Carloet."

Tom told Charles, "You have to be praised. You taught Jake very well. This stock sold out to another company, and then that company sold to another. The stock in your safety box is worth nothing. Through the years, Jake kept track of it. With our help, he kept on buying more of the stock no matter what company. Today this stock has a value of thirty thousand dollars."

Charles could not believe what he was being told. Then he asked, "Well, that was very nice. Just keep doing whatever you are doing with it." Then he started to get up.

Tom said, "Hey, Mr. Appel, I am not done yet. You see, Jake had been doing other things. Do you remember about every six months, he came home? He handed you papers to sign."

Charles told them, "Yes, but I never read them. I just signed them."

"Yes, we know. Jake always laughed about it. For years, he always told us, 'Dad does not know nothing yet. He just trusted me enough to sign the papers.'"

Charles asked, "What are you telling me?"

"Well, your son was making $250,000 a year for the last twelve years. Did you know that?"

Charles said in shock, "Hell no. I told Jake, 'Whatever you make, I did not care' or 'It was not my business.'"

"That was what you told him. Well, in the last twelve years, Jake put in one hundred thousand dollars a year to invest for him. Well, I am proud to say the CDs, stocks, trust funds, mutual funds—we have his money scattered all over. He always told us that you told him, 'Never keep all your investments in one place. Scatter them out.' Well, that was what Jake told us to do.

"To this day, all this stock and money is in Jake's and your names. This is what you've been signing all these times. You were co-owner of all this. The total cash value of Jake's financial worth in our investment company is $2.5 million. Jake, in the last twelve years, gave us $1.2 million. We made $1.3 million after all expenses."

Charles was shaking and trembling. "You are telling me I am a millionaire right now?"

John told Charles, "Yes, because of your son."

Charles did not know what to say; he just froze. It seemed he was like that for an hour, but it was just really a few seconds. Charles turned toward Nate. "Hell, we have a large war chest now."

Tom asked, "What do you mean?"

"Well, I am going to find out what really happened to Jake. This will take more money than I have. Now in one short day, I can afford anything to catch those murderers."

John went to the phone. Charles could not hear everything. John asked to the person on the other end, "Could you come over here now?"

"Did you tell him?" John said yes.

In a few minutes, this tall man came walking in. John introduced him to Charles. "This is Carlo Anderson."

Carlo told Charles, "It is nice meeting you." Charles then introduced him to Nate.

John told Charles, "This is Jake's taxman. Carlo is a good friend of mine. Jake told me to find a good taxman."

Charles told them he had seen his commercials. Carlo told Charles, "Who does your taxes now?"

"Really, nobody. The little bit I have, I just file short form."

"Well, that stops right now."

Charles and Nate still could not believe what they were hearing. Tom told Charles that Jake and he started to be friends during this time. "Jake made me promise, no matter what happens to him, to not let you know how rich he was. Dad will know what to do when the time comes." Tom started to say something and then stopped. "You know, Jake told me the same thing."

Charles asked, "What was that?"

"The money was their war chest. Jake told me to never mind about that. He never brought it up again."

Charles asked, "Well, if he needed a large sum of money, could he get the money?"

"Sure." Then Tom asked Carlo, "Is that true?"

Carlo told them, "Yes, but you have to pay more taxes on the money you withdraw."

Charles told them, "All I am going to find out is who killed Jake. I want to know, is there any way a powerful company or government agency can freeze this money from me?"

Tom told Charles, "You know, Jake was worried about that too."

Charles asked, "What do you mean?"

"Well, just about two months ago, Jake told me to move half his fortune to another account. This account pays only 3 percent. I told Jake this was not one of his best ideas. Jake told me, 'Well, do it anyway. You see, I think they are on to us. We will need that money soon.'"

Charles asked, "Where is this money?"

"He has it in our business account. I told Jake I can keep it in this account for six months before I have to move the money to another account. When the money is in this arrangement, we pay 3 percent. We put this money in a bank account that pays us 5 percent. I told Jake, through this arrangement, we make 2 percent for doing this."

John told them in a very strong voice, "Wait a minute, I did not know this."

Tom told his dad, "Well, this might not be proper or maybe illegal. I did it for Jake."

Carlo jumped in. "I knew about it, John. There was not nothing illegal about it directly."

John told them, "This is not good business."

Charles broke up their talk. "Wait a minute, could I transfer, say, two hundred thousand dollars to the AJ Trust and the same amount to the Chicago Bank in Coal City right now?"

Tom told Charles, "Sure."

Charles then asked, "What about put two hundred thousand in four other banks in a passbook account? Could I do this?"

Tom and Carlo said, "That'll be great."

Charles then told John, "I know it will take away some of your business. Would you rather do that than the government find out about this other deal?"

John told them, "Do it. Jake had plans with this money. I feel like you are carrying out Jake's plan. Good luck. You make the arrangement with the banks. The money will be there when you want it."

Tom made out a list of banks he would recommend, and then he told Charles, "Use my name, and tell them to call me if there are any questions."

Charles stood up and told Tom and Carlo, "Thanks. We will be in touch." He turned to Carlo. "Whatever you do you, make sure all this is legal, and make sure all the taxes are paid in full."

"Do not worry, Jake told me the same thing when we set all this up a few years ago."

Charles told Nate, "We have things to do by three o'clock." He thanked all of them; as he was to the door, Charles turned around. "Oh, Tom, you just do whatever you've been doing with the rest."

"Yes, sure."

Charles started to walk away. "One more thing, what do you usually make off your clients?"

Tom told Charles, "Between 5 and 10 percent."

"From now on, anything you charge my account, take 20 percent. I am sure Jake would want that. If you need that in writing, mail me the papers. I will sign them and mail them back to you."

John told Charles, "You do not have to do that."

"John, your son helped my son. The least I can do is help your son for Jake. I know that is what Jake would want."

Charles and Nate went to the first bank on Tom's list. The Chicago Bank was just two blocks from Tom's office. As Charles and Nate walked in, Charles told Nate, "They remodeled this place a lot."

They were walking toward a teller window when a voice asked, "How are you doing, Charles?"

Charles turned to his left, and there was this nice-looking woman sitting down at a desk. She could tell Charles did not remember her. Right away, she told Charles, "I am Chila Winters."

Charles told her, "What a surprise. I have not seen you for years. How did you recognize me?"

"Well, between your walk and bald head, it could only be you."

"You are really looking real good from the last time I've seen you."

Chila just smiled. "Since Richard and I divorced, I lost weight and changed my hair, having the best time of my life."

Charles introduced Chila to Nate, and then she asked, "What can I help you with?"

Charles told her, "I need to start a savings account. Tom Bensly thought this bank would be glad to help me."

"Here, you two sit right here. I can do this for you." Chila stood up from her chair, walked to another person's desk, grabbed some forms, and came right back. She told Charles, "There are just a few questions we have to fill out, and then we will give your account number, and you will be set."

Charles asked her if he could see the paper. Chila handed the form to him. Charles showed it to Nate. Then he handed it back. Charles told her, "OK."

The first few questions were name, address, and social security number. The next question was if Charles wanted any other name on the account. He told her, "No, not right now but maybe later. Is this hard to do?"

Chila told Charles, "No, we just need the same information as you gave, plus your written signature if you agreed."

Charles then asked, "Can I have one of the forms so I can keep it with me?"

"Well, we usually have them. Come in the bank."

"Well, I do not know if I want to do that."

Chila asked, "Well, how much do you want to put in savings?"

Charles looked at her without changing his expression. "Two hundred thousand dollars."

Her mouth fell so far open that you could drive a semi in it. Chila asked, "Did you say two hundred thousand dollars?" Charles told her yes, and then she handed him extra forms. "You can do what you want on that matter."

Charles told her, "The money won't be here until a couple of days. Tom will be sending it to you. Just tell Tom how you want to handle it, and then I will get in touch with you."

"Yes, that would be fine." Then with a big smile, she said, "Thanks for doing business with us."

The next bank on Tom's list was Logan Bank, just three blocks from the First Capital. On the way, Nate told Charles, "Hell, even they know you in this town."

"I knew her husband years ago. I thought Richard died. I did not know they were divorced. He was a drinking buddy of mine years ago when I worked here in Madison."

When they walked in Logan Bank, Charles told Nate, "I've never been in this bank."

"Well, this is nicer inside than the Chicago Bank." Charles told him he noticed that too.

By that time, a person walked up to them. This six-foot-six man asked, "What can Logan Bank do for you?" Charles told him he wanted to start a savings account. The man told them go to Mrs. Jones's desk, the second one on the right. Charles and Nate walked over there.

Mrs. Jones asked, "Are you opening an account with us?" Charles told her yes. She asked the same questions as the Chicago Bank. She had the same look as Chila did when Charles told her how much. Mrs. Jones told them she would call Tom, set up the change, and be glad to do whatever it took to make him a happy customer.

Charles and Nate went to the Madison Credit Union next. Charles told Nate, "Years ago, there was a girl I knew that worked here. She retired two years ago."

They were not in the bank yet when Charles told Nate, "Hell, I do not believe it. There was Mary walking out." Charles said hi to Mary.

Mary said, "Hi, and how are you, Nate?" Nate was dumbfounded.

Charles started to laugh. "Mary was one of the people in the auxiliary that helped in Jake's funeral."

Nate apologized for not remembering. Mary told Nate, "Hell, in a small town, everyone knows the stranger."

She could not wait to ask, "What are you doing here, Charles?"

"I am going to start a savings account here."

"Go over to the first desk, and talk to Joan. Tell her I sent you. Joan will do a good job." Charles thanked Mary, and then they went in.

Charles had seen her name plate on the desk that just said "Joan," no last name or an official heading. Joan noticed Charles was looking at her name plate. Charles just said, "You have a friendly atmosphere, just first names." Charles told her he liked that. "I am Charles, and this is Nate. I want to start a savings account." Joan went over, grabbed another chair for Nate, and asked them to sit down. She handed Charles a form.

"Look this over, and fill out all the first four lines, or I can do it for you." Charles filled them out in no time. Joan told Charles, "Well, you must have done that a lot." Nate started to laugh. Joan gave an expression that if she knew the inside joke, she would laugh too.

Then she asked, "Well, Charles, how much do you want to start with?"

"Two hundred thousand dollars."

Joan looked up and told him, "Is this some kind of joke?"

Charles told her no. "If you do not believe me, call up Tom Bensly."

Joan reached for the phone and punched one button. Charles and Nate did not know whom she was talking to. "This is Joan. I want to talk to Tom now." To Charles's dismay, Joan asked Tom, "Who in the hell is this Charles Appel? He says you know about this two hundred thousand dollars." Tom asked Joan to put them on speakerphone.

Tom told Charles, "Well, it does not take you long. You've been to the Chicago and Logan. Now you are at the Credit Union." Tom said he just hung up on Logan Bank and told Joan it was true.

Tom then told Charles, "Let me introduce you to my sister Joan. Joan's married name is Alexandra."

Charles asked, "You do not mean Mr. Alexandra that everyone knows in Madison?"

Tom started to laugh. "I sure do. She married his son." He told Joan, "Remember about a year or so ago I had Jake look at our computer? Jake called his friend, and over the phone, they fixed it."

Joan told Tom, "I forgot all about that."

"This is Jake's father."

Out of the blue, she asked, "This is not the Jake who died, is it?" Tom, in a quiet voice, said yes. Joan could not believe what she just asked her brother. She looked across the table. "Mr. Appel, would you forgive me?"

Charles told her, "Forget it. I would like the phone number of that person that Jake called to fix your computer though." Joan did not know.

Tom told Charles, "You know, I might have that. Just a minute."

Joan told Charles, "If you do not want to do business here, I will understand. Me and my big mouth."

"Jake trusted your family. Then I trust you with my money."

Tom came back on the phone. "Sorry, I thought I had his name written down, but I could not find it."

Nate then spoke up. "Was this about a year and half ago?" Joan and Tom both answered yes. "That was me. I forgot all about that. You just bought the computer. If I remember, it was the Super One Thousand."

Joan did not know what to say. "That is right."

Nate told them, "You hooked the cables wrong that, for some reason, when you tried the computer, it screwed it up."

Tom said, "Yes, that was it. Then you told me to go in the computer somewhere and type in something, and then it corrected the program."

Charles then thanked Tom and Joan. "I guess you are happy with everything now?" Joan asked.

"You did a good job. When Tom gives you the money, just put it in the new account."

Joan asked Tom, "Did you tell Charles to go to the Savings and Loan?"

"Yes."

"I know Mr. Fox real well. I will call him right know."

Tom told Joan, "That is what I should have done."

Joan hung the phone up. "Well, Mr. Appel—"

Charles interrupted her, "Call me Charles."

"Well, Charles, ask for Mr. Fox when you go over there. He will know all about it." Charles thanked her.

The Savings and Loan was on the other side of town. Charles told Nate, "This will work out just right. I will take you to a neighborhood tavern I know real well."

When they arrived at the Savings and Loan, this man walked right up to them. "I am Mr. Fox. Are you Mr. Appel?" Charles told him yes. "You must be Nate." Nate told him yes while they were shaking hands.

Mr. Fox had all the information from Joan. "Just sign on this line." Charles signed the paper. Mr. Fox told him, "I never had such a large account in less time in my life."

Charles told him, "Well, Tom must trust you, so I do too."

Mr. Fox told them, "Should I call you when the money is here?"

"No, I will talk to Tom when all this is completed."

Charles, on the way out, commented, "Now this is how I like to do business. No bullshit, just get it done. We will be at John's Tap in less than three minutes."

The second Charles walked in the tavern, four people told him they were sorry about Jake. Charles thanked them and introduced them to Nate. They were there for an hour when Charles told Nate, "We have to go to one more bank back in Coal City." He thanked all of them, and then they walked out the door.

Nate said, "I cannot believe it. We did not buy one drink in the place."

"I told you it was a friendly tavern."

They were back in Coal City. Charles pulled up to the drive-up window. He told Nate, "Actually, the bank is closed except the drive-up window." Charles rolled his window down. "Hi, Ronda. I would like to speak to Will, if that's all right."

"Just a second, Charles. I will check." When Ronda came back, she said, "Sure, go around to the front. Will has unlocked the door."

By the time they parked the car, Will was already at the door waiting for them. Charles introduced Will to Nate and then told him, "I do not want to waste your time. Here is the deal. Jake somehow made two million dollars. I have all of it now."

"What? I could not believe it."

"I am in shock still too." Charles told him to put two hundred dollars in four banks in Madison. He wanted a savings account here and two safety-deposit boxes. "Could this be arranged soon?"

Will told him, "Here, just sign this on the bottom line. I will fill out the rest."

"Is that it?"

"Well, where is the money?"

Charles told Will, "I forgot to tell you. Tom Bensly is going to send it to you. Then when you get it, I will come back, and we will finish our business."

"That'll be fine."

"Tom told me it will be done in a few days."

"That will work." Will told Nate, "Nice meeting you again."

"You too."

Charles was laughing by the time they were at the car. "You met Will at the Legion."

Nate said, "I'm sorry for not remembering."

"Well, Will is my cousin. That is why this worked out so fast. We will not bother the AJ Trust. I would like to see their faces when they see the money."

Nate started to laugh. "Hell, I would like to see any of the money when any bank receives it."

"You know, I am not going to believe it either until we have some real money in our hands. I want to go home now."

Nate still did not know Charles very well. But he did know something was bothering him. "What is bothering you, Charles?" Nate asked.

"You know when Tom told us he left a message on the answering machine?"

"What is unusual about that?"

Charles explained, "Nothing in a way. I do not use that answering machine very often. In fact, I keep it in the computer room under the desk. The damn phone is not even on the machine. Jake kept leaving me messages. When he would come home, Jake would give me hell for not taking the calls."

Nate said in a worried voice, "Well, what does that have to do with anything?"

"Hell, Jake could have left me a message the night he was murdered. I never checked the machine weeks before he was murdered. I am afraid Jake called me that night."

Nate hastily told Charles, "You have to listen to it sooner or later."

While Charles was looking at Nate, he was wondering if Nate should listen to it. Then again, why not?

When they walked in the house, Charles went right to the machine. He then went to the desk and grabbed a spare tape. Nate watched Charles as he took one tape out and put in the blank one. Nate asked, "Are you not going to listen to it?"

"Do not worry, I am just making a copy of the tape."

Charles rewound the tape. The first few calls were about tee times. He told Nate, "See what I mean? This is two weeks before Jake was murdered." The next message was from the dentist's office reminding him of his appointment. "Hell, I missed that one."

The next voice was Jake's. Charles started to cry as he was yelling, "I knew he called, and I was not at home!"

Jake's voice was saying, "Dad, you were right. Look at the computer. You have to check this out. I think they might be on to us. See you soon." Then the tape went off.

Charles was just speechless. He never heard the next ten messages from people calling to ask if they could help. Charles did not know how much time went by. Then there was Tom Bensly's voice telling him to make an appointment with him. "The number is 672-5325."

When Charles was getting his senses back, Nate handed him a beer. "I think we need this." Charles thanked him while he was taking the tapes out.

Nate asked, "What did Jake mean by that?"

Charles told him, "On his last disk, he said the same thing. I think I know now. I always told Jake that the oil companies killed President Kennedy. The disk we have must have something. Really, I could not tell, just a lot of names. You know, I have to make some decisions right now."

Nate started to speak. Charles told him, "No, you listen to me first." Nate stopped talking. "Nate, how serious are you with this girl, Carillon?"

Nate said in a real surprised voice, "How in the hell do you remember her name? I only talked about her right when I arrived in Coal City."

Charles asked again, "Well, how serious is it?"

Nate told him, "If it is any of your business, I am not very serious at all. Can I ask why the hell did you ask that?"

"Well, hell, I thought you just might want to live with me since I am rich now. You do not have to worry about your job." Nate did not know what to say. "Just listen and hear me out. First thing is there is something on the disk. We know that. We just cannot figure it out yet. Second, there are eleven others out there who need to be brought to safety before they are murdered. Third, I cannot do this myself. I need help. I am asking you to stay here and help. I will even let you have a joint bank account at Will's bank, plus whatever we put in the two safety boxes. Do you like this kind of arrangement or not?"

Nate was amazed; he just stood there with his mouth open. Nate told Charles, "Well, at least I know I can trust you better than anyone at work. What the hell, I will stay."

Charles was delighted; he told Nate, "Hell, if you want to leave anytime, just let me know. You can take the money that is in Will's bank."

"That will not be necessary."

"Hell, I'd rather you have it than anyone else."

Nate asked Charles, "Well, what is our game plan now?"

"Tom and Kate will be back Friday afternoon. I am going to make a tee time for Sunday."

Charles was on the phone for several minutes. Finally, the Ripply Golf Course came through. Charles hung up the telephone and told Nate, "You will like this course."

Nate asked, "How hard is it?"

Charles laughed in his usual way. "Well, it is longer than Pharis and has more sand traps and more water. The bright side is the sand is soft and easy to get out of. The greens run through and fast."

"That is the good part of it."

Charles called Richard. Karla answered the phone. He asked if Richard was playing on Sunday. "Yes, he is with Bill and Dick. If you need a fourth, call Dwight." Charles thanked her.

Charles then called Dwight. Penny answered the phone. "Can Dwight play Sunday?"

Penny asked, "This is Charles, right?"

"Yes."

"Well, what time did you make it?"

"Ten forty-eight. I will drive."

"I will tell Dwight you will pick him up. What time?"

"Ten o'clock. We are playing at the Ripply."

"OK, but I have one thing to say."

Charles said in a laughing voice, "I know. Be home a lot earlier than the last time."

"You better if you do not want me to flatten your tires sometime."

Charles hung up the phone. Nate could not wait to ask, "How late were you guys out last time?"

"Well, the last time, we had Dwight home by two thirty in the morning. He had his birthday two days before, so we celebrated two days late." Then Charles told Nate, "We cannot do nothing more today. Let's go uptown to see if we can play cards. This will give us time to think on our next move. The banks will be open tomorrow morning. We will make our decision tonight on what to do."

As they walked in John's Tap, Darrell was still there. He walked toward the card table. "Mike and I will take you and Nate for three games."

Charles told him, "Cut for deal."

After twelve beers and nine games, Charles told them he had enough. Nate said in a desperate voice, "I sure the hell hope so. We only won one game."

Darrell told Nate, "Well, that makes up the last time."

Mike told Nate, "Well, this is the first time I met you. I am glad to take your money."

Charles told Mike, "Hey, there will be another day."

Darrell spoke up. "What about tomorrow?"

"No, I and Nate have business to do."

Mike asked if they had a foursome for Sunday. Charles told him he just called Dwight. "He is playing."

Mike said in a disappointed way, "Well, I am caught up at the farm."

Charles told him, "Why not call Richard? I think they have a threesome the way Karla talked." Mike thanked him and left with Darrell.

The time went by fast; it was five thirty. Charles asked Nate if pizza was OK. Nate told him it did not matter. Charles asked Charlet if he could use the phone. She asked, "Are you going to order pizza?"

"Yes."

"Well, tell me what you want. I will order, and then you can go home." Charles told Charlet what they wanted, and then he ordered another beer for Nate and himself. Charlet made the order. "The pizza will be at your house in fifteen minutes."

"Hell, we can have one more beer for the road." Charlet served the beer. "Hey, Charlet, Nate and I will not open up tomorrow. I have to go to the bank right when they open."

"No problem. Skip is in town this week."

When Charles and Nate was to the car, Nate asked, "Who is Skip?"

"Well, he opens up the bar too in the morning."

Nate could not believe it. "How many people have keys to her tavern?"

Charles smiled. "I really do not know. I say three or four."

"You mean to tell me Charlet has three or four people who can open her tavern anytime they want?"

"That is right. That's the good thing about a small town."

Just as Charles parked the car at his house, the pizza boy just pulled up. Charles yelled, "Mat, we will take the pizza now!"

Mat walked up to Charles. "It will be twenty-two dollars." Charles gave him twenty-five told Mat to keep the change. Mat thanked him and then went back to his car.

Nate asked in disbelief, "Is there not one person you do not know in this town?"

"Sure, you just have not met one yet."

Charles opened the back door. They walked to the kitchen. Charles put the pizza on the table and went to the refrigerator. He told Nate, "I am having a Coke. What do you want?"

"I had too much beer. I will just have water."

While they were eating, Charles told Nate, "You know, I have been thinking. We will go to AJ Trust first and then to the bank. I will deposit the hundred-thousand check that Mr. Martin gave to me. Do you think the check will be good?"

"Hell yes."

"Well, if it is, we will put that money in the safety-deposit box at the First Bank."

"You do whatever you want. I am going to stay whether you have your money or not."

"I meant what I said. You will have the money at the First Bank. I do not want to talk about it anymore."

Nate rose from the table. "You know, I either drank too much or am just tired. I am going to bed."

Charles told Nate, "Well, the bank opens at eight. I will wake you up at seven fifteen."

"That will be fine." Then Nate asked, "You think the money came in from Tom Bensly?"

"Hell, we will know the first time we walk in the bank."

Charles went to his favorite channel and turned on a Western. Like usual, he fell asleep in the chair. Charles woke up at five thirty in the morning. He took his shower and was dressed by six thirty. The television was still on; he changed the station to the weather channel. The forecast for Sunday was still good.

Nate came down the steps and told Charles, "What about that? I woke up on my own."

Charles was just starting his bacon and eggs. "They will be ready when you are ready."

Not a word was said; they just ate and went to the bank. Charles walked in first. Nate was right behind him. They did not even walked five feet when Andy walked up to him. Andy had never done that all the years Charles banked there. Right then, Charles knew the money arrived. Andy asked Charles to come to the back room. Charles told Nate, "Hell, you might as well come too."

Charles could tell Andy could not believe the deposit. "I called Tom up twice just to verify the cashier's check." Charles told Andy what Jake had done through the years. Andy asked, "Is there anything I can do?"

"There sure is—in fact, three things."

Andy looked at Charles. "Just tell me. I will do it."

"Well, first, I want to put one hundred thousand in savings. Second, I want fifty thousand in checking."

Andy then asked, "What is the third thing?"

"I notice you have that little empty corner on the other side."

"You mean by the safety-deposit room?"

"Yes, that corner."

Andy asked, "Well, what about it?"

"I want you to let me have a computer there, and I want to have Kate to run that computer for me. I would like you to hire her, but I will pay you back. You can take it right out of my savings or checking."

Andy had a very puzzled look. "Well, I guess I can. What is she going to do?"

Charles told him, "I am not trying to be a smart-ass, but this is not any of your business. Can she or not?"

"Yes, I will let you do that." Charles got up, shook his hand, and thanked him.

Andy still could not believe all this was happening. He even stuttered when he told Diane to give Charles fifty thousand cash and how to put the money in the proper accounts. Nate did not say a word the whole time. He was just was as amazed as Andy and could not believe Charles turned into a millionaire overnight.

Diane could not believe she was counting the fifty thousand. She asked in a shaking voice, "Do you have something to put it in?"

Charles told her, "I forgot to do that. Just put it in a sack for now." She counted the money and found a sack.

Charles and Nate walked out of the bank. Nate told him, "Are you crazy, walking around with that much money?"

"Hell, everyone knows me. By the time we make it to Chicago Bank, the whole town will know. No one will do nothing except tell me good luck."

When they walked in the Chicago Bank, Will was standing right by his office. Charles whispered to Nate, "See, I bet you Andy told Will."

Nate whispered back, "Yeah, but he already knew."

"Yes, but Will did not tell Andy."

Charles and Nate walked right in Will's office. Will told Charles, "The money is here."

"I want Nate's name on the accounts too."

Will, who was very surprised, asked, "Are you sure?"

"Nate is staying with me." Charles told Will he can make this a joint account in savings and checking with Nate's name on the two safety-deposit boxes.

Will told Charles, "OK, how do you want it?"

"One hundred thousand in savings, one hundred thousand in checking. Then I want you to cash this check that Jake's company gave me. I want half of this to go to one safety box and the other half in the other."

Will talked to Marla and explained what she was supposed to do. She filled out the safety-deposit forms and made the account changes. All this took two hours. Charles was getting hungry. He asked Will, "Well, is that it?"

"Well, the checks, how do you want them?"

Charles gave him his information and then told Nate, "Well, tell Will how you want your checks."

Nate told Will, "Just my name will be fine."

Charles was walking out the door when he remembered something. "Oh, I forgot. Can you give us more hundred and bigger bills on the fifty thousand?" He pulled it out of the sack.

Will told him, "You cannot walk around with that much money."

Charles told him he was not going to. "I am going to give Nate ten thousand right now. Tonight I am going to give Tom and Kate thirty thousand, and I will keep ten thousand."

Will walked back to Marla. She could not believe she could see that much cash at once. While she was counting the money, Charles asked Marla, "How is your boy doing? What is his name? Anthony—is that right?"

"Thanks for asking. He has to go to a specialist at mails next month."

Charles went in his billfold, pulled out a Farmers check, filled it out, and handed it to Marla. "Maybe this will help."

Marla looked at the check. "I cannot take this."

"Hey, I know Jake would give it to you if he knew, so keep it." Marla kissed Charles and started cry.

When they left the bank, Nate could not wait to ask, "All right, how much did you give her?"

"Do not worry, it was from the Farmers account."

Nate grabbed Charles. "If you think I care about that, you are dead wrong."

Charles told him, "Hell, I know you do not care. I wrote her a fifteen-thousand check. Anthony has been sick for over a year. I know they need the money."

Charles could tell Nate could not believe he did that. "Look at me right now." Nate turned around as Charles stared right in his eye. He told Nate, "I will give anyone this money, but I will make sure you will be all right, and I will for damn sure keep enough to find Jake's killer or die trying."

Nate did not know what to say. Finally, he told Charles, "I do not care about the money. I just want to make sure you do not waste your money."

"We will let the money take care of itself for now. We have to be real organized before Kate and Tom come home."

Nate asked, "Where are we going now?"

"We are going home for a few minutes and then go uptown to play cards."

Nate said in a very sensitive voice, "How is that going to help?"

Charles, with a funny smile, replied, "Hell, I think better while doing something rather than just thinking about it all the time."

Charles called Steve Cambell on the phone. He told Nate, "Hell, I got the damn answering machine."

After the beep, Charles said, "I need a computer for the Internet with a good firewall. I will pay extra if you have it ready by Tuesday. I want to make sure my computer will be by itself, but they should both use the same printer. The most important thing is the computer must be similar to the one you made Kate last year. I will be at John's Tap playing cards, or call me as soon as possible later tonight."

Nate told Charles, "That is a very interesting message."

"Hell, Steve will help me. He knows what I meant, sort of."

"You know, I do not know you very well yet, but I think you have your game plan already in your mind."

Charles told Nate, "Yes, I do. I will run it through you after I talk to Steve Cambell. Well, let's get going. I feel lucky today."

Nate walked in John's Tap first. A stranger asked, "Is this the new kid who is learning how to play pitch?"

Charlet looked at the guy and just said, "Give Nate a break, Charlie."

Charles then walked in. Right away, he had seen Charlie and told him, "Hey, you have not met Nate yet. Nate, this is Charlie. He thinks he is the best pitch player around."

At the same time, Darrell was coming out of the restroom. He told Charlie, "Hey, Nate and I will take you and Charles on for five games."

Charlie could not get the words out fast enough. "You are on."

Charles told Charlie, "Well, cut for deal."

Darrell drew a ten. Charlie drew an eight. Darrell told him, "Hell, we will set you the first hand, won't we, Nate?"

Nate looked at Charlie. "You bet your ass we will."

Sure enough, Darrell and Nate won the first two games. Charlie could not believe it. He looked at Charles. "How well did you teach him?"

Charles said in a joking voice, "Too damn well."

The phone rang several times. It always took Charlet at least five rings before she answered the phone. "John's Tap."

"Is Charles Appel there? This is Steve Cambell."

Charlet told him, "Sure is. Just wait." Charlet yelled at Charles. "It is for you, Charles! It is Steve Cambell!" Charles went right to the phone; as he reached for it, he told Charlet to buy everyone a drink.

Charles told Steve Cambell he needed a computer as fast as possible like the one he built for Tom and Kate last year. Cambell told Charles he had one almost done and that he was a few days early. Charles told him, "I will give you a thousand extra for it. I will give that other person five hundred to let me have it first."

"You want this real bad."

"Well, I am short of time. Tom and Kate will be back tonight. I want the computer ready to go as soon as possible."

Cambell told Charles, "At that price, I am sure it is yours."

"One more thing, the one at my house."

"You still use that one?"

Charles told him, "Hell yes, but I need you to move it to the AJ Trust. This is where the new one is going too."

Cambell asked, "At the bank?"

"Yes, at the bank. One more thing, I need a printer that will go from both computers. I want you to make sure nobody can hack or get in either one. I also do not want my old computer to be connected to the Internet, just the new one."

Cambell asked, "Is there anything else?"

"Well, could you install a program I made into my old one so it could help Kate's?"

"I can probably do anything you need if you have the money."

"No money problems."

"Well, I will have everything by Tuesday, best I could do."

"That will be fine. We will meet you Tuesday in AJ Trust at seven in the morning."

Cambell said, "Hey, the bank will not be open."

"Andy will be there with me."

"OK, see you then."

Charles hung up the phone and told Nate, "The computer will be there Tuesday."

Then he asked Charlie, "What is the score?"

"Ten to eight, not in our favor."

Darrell told Charlie, "Maybe you should take a card lesson from Nate."

Charles told Darrell, "The way the cards are falling, anyone can beat us today."

Charles and Charlie managed to win one game out of five. Charlie drank his last beer and told them he had to go home. As he was walking out the door, he turned around and told Nate, "You are a lot better than I thought." Turning his head in disbelief, he walked out the door.

Darrell was laughing at Charles. "Did I hear you right about a new computer?"

"Yes, I bought one from Steve Cambell."

"I still have the one he made me three years ago, still had no problem with it."

"That is why I called him. I do not know if it is luck or what, but he does a good job."

Charles looked at the clock; he noticed it was four thirty. He told Nate, "We better be leaving too."

Darrell told him, "I bet you five dollars you are not leaving."

"How the hell do you know that?"

Just then, the door opened. Charles turned his head, and it was Tom. Charles told Darrell, "Sure am glad I did not bet you."

Tom noticed Darrell was laughing. He asked, "What did I miss?"

Charles told him, "Nothing. Darrell must have seen you pull up just as I told them we were leaving. Well, how was the trip?"

Tom just said, "Give me a beer. I am ready for one. Kate's brother is OK and the rest of the family. I am glad to be home."

After Tom drank his beer, he told Charles and Nate, "We are still eating at the Company?"

"We sure are. Nate and I have a lot to tell you and Kate."

Nate was grinning, so Tom asked, "Well, what is it?"

Charles told Tom, "Let's have a couple more. We will tell you at the Company."

Tom gave Charles a disappointed look and then asked, "Well, hell, did you make a tee time for us, or is that a secret too?"

"We have a tee time for Sunday—you, me, Nate, and Dwight."

"If you did not have a tee time, I was going to leave right now." Even before he could get a breath in, he asked, "Where are we playing?"

Charles told Nate, "You tell him."

Tom said in disgusted voice, "Someone tell me soon."

Nate told Tom, "The Ripply, wherever that is."

"That is good. That is a hell of a golf course."

Charles and Nate had two more beers. Charles said to Tom, "Try not to get drunk yet. Wait till later so we can all get drunk tonight."

Tom told him, "Well, I have to be home in a few minutes. Kate already gave me the third degree."

"Well, I have some important stuff I want to tell you. I also have a big favor from Kate."

"Well, what is it? I will tell her to just do it."

Charles told Tom, "No, not now, later."

As Charles and Nate were on the way home, Nate asked, "What do you think will happen when you give them the money?"

Charles said with a smile, "Tom will take it. Kate will think I stole it. This evening is going to be very interesting."

Charles and Nate were ready by five thirty. Charles told Nate, "Well, hell, let's get going. I want a certain table where we can talk."

They were at the Company in five minutes. Terry was attending the bar. Charles went right to her and ordered their drinks. He asked if they could use the back room tonight. Terry answered, "Sure, is something wrong?"

Charles explained, "No, nothing is wrong. I just want a little more privacy tonight."

Terry told him, "As you go back there, just tell Sally, and she will let you have any table you want."

Charles thanked her. As he turned right, he yelled, "Oh, Terry, Tom and Kate are coming! Let them know where we are!"

"No problem!" Terry yelled back.

Sally asked Charles if he had a bad day. Charles told her, "Why?"

"Well, you never eat back here. I just thought something was wrong."

Charles told her, "No problems, but on the way back, give Nate and me another beer."

Sally was at the bar when Charles heard her voice say, "Kate, Charles is back here."

Charles and Nate could hear Kate ask, "What the hell are they back there for?"

Sally told her she did not know. "Just that there are no problems."

When Kate and Tom were at the table, Sally already had Tom's drink and the two beers. She asked Kate, "You want a Diet Coke?"

"Yes." Sally came back with the Diet Coke and asked if they needed a menu.

Charles told her, "Yes, we better. Nate is not familiar with your food yet."

Kate told Charles, "All right, what is this important stuff you want to talk about?" Nate had this grin on his face. "What is so funny, Nate?"

He did not know what to say. Before he came up with something, Charles gave Kate the envelope. "Merry Christmas."

Tom said in a surprised voice, "Hell, Christmas is not another six months or so." Kate's eyes were getting really big; she could not come up with any words. Tom asked her, "Well, what is it?" Kate showed Tom the envelope. He did not have any problem until he had seen the money. "What the hell? Did you rob a bank?"

Charles told him, "No, we did not rob a bank."

Sally came with the menus; she could tell something was up. Kate was real quiet. Sally asked again, "Are you people all right?"

Nate told her, "We are fine."

Charles said, "Give us ten minutes before we order." Sally turned around. "Oh, bring . . ." Charles could not get it out.

Sally said, "I know, another round when I come back."

Charles told Tom and Kate, "I will explain how I got the money and why I need your help in my game plan right now. First of all, the money. Jake, through the years, played the Carloet. He put my name on all his investments. Just happens Jake, through the years, made two million dollars."

Kate said in surprise, "Two million?"

Tom told her, "Not so loud. Charles, it was a good idea to use the back room. Two million dollars?"

"I gave you both thirty thousand in cash. I just thought you might need some extra money. Do not worry, I will give you all you need through the years to come."

Sally brought back the drinks. Nobody but Nate looked at the menu. Kate just told her, "Give me my usual." Tom told her the same thing.

Charles told her, "Hell, just give the same also." Nate ordered a fried chicken dinner with ranch dressing and twice-baked potato with sour cream.

Sally asked, "Is that it?"

Charles told her, "Yes, and I am paying tonight."

Kate could still not get over the money. In a very nervous voice, she asked, "What important stuff do you have to talk about?"

Tom told her, "Hell, what more is there besides the two million?"

"Think about it. Charles has an idea or a plan that involves us. Is that right?"

Charles told Kate, "You are right."

"Well, what is this important stuff?"

"Since you and Tom have been gone, a lot of things have changed. First, I have the money to find Jake's killers. Second, I have talked to Andy, and Steve Cambell is going to install a new computer close to the one he built for you. I am going to put my computer along with this one at Andy's bank.

"This is where you come in, Kate. I would like you to go through all those tapes and put them in some kind of order, maybe by dates or names or whatever you think will be the best way of doing this. You can use the new computer to look up anything that is on the tapes, like businesses, companies, names, whatever you need to know.

"Tonight or early tomorrow morning, I need you to find plane reservations for Nate to Kansas City to find Joseph. I need tickets to New Hampshire to see Amanda's parents. Then from there, I am going to Newark to talk to Lieutenant Steel and pay a visit to Mr. Martin.

"After you find the times of the planes, I am going to call Amanda's parents and set up a meeting. I am going to call Lieutenant Steel for two reasons. One is to find out about Toad."

Kate told Tom, "You were right. He does like that lieutenant."

Charles told her, "Just wait one minute. Maybe I'll take her out to eat but just for business."

"Maybe some funny business."

"Well, anyway, this is what I want from you and Tom."

Tom told Charles, "Hey, wait a minute." Then he paused when Sally came with the food and drinks. The second she left, Tom went on. "Hey, what the hell am I doing for you? Nothing."

"No, when Kate comes up with questions about companies or names, you go to that town and check them out. I do not mean follow anyone. Just go to the town and ask questions about them. Then you come back to town, and we will see what happens. I want to be back in town by next Monday to play golf. I will miss Sunday, but you better have a tee time for Monday."

Tom told Charles, "Just because you cannot play does not mean I cannot play."

"It is true, you dirty dog."

Nate told Tom, "I might be back by then. I can play with you."

"We will just plan on that. Maybe Richard and Dwight can play."

They were done with their supper. Sally cleaned the table. Charles gave her seventy-five dollars and told her to keep the change. Sally could not believe the tip and asked, "Kate, is he sick?" Kate laughed.

Charles told Sally, "Just say I am in a real good mood." Sally thanked Charles and then walked away.

Charles told Kate, "Before you answer me, I do not expect you to work every day. Just do a few tapes a week. I set it up that Andy is going to pay you so it looks like you work for the bank. I am going to pay Andy back."

"I will do it for noting."

Charles, in a stern voice, told Tom and Kate, "While I have all this money, who would I rather have it than you two? So just tell me you will help me. That is all I want to know."

Kate said, "I will under two conditions."

Charles asked in a soft voice, "What is it, Kate?"

"Well, one thing, if we get close, you will not get Tom or me killed, not counting you and Nate. The second one is easier. On one of these trips, I get to go to Hawaii.'

"You book the flight. You can both go after I get back from Newark."

Kate told Charles, "We will be glad to help."

Tom said, "Hey, if Kate gets a trip to Hawaii, I want to go to Vegas."

Charles told him, "Hell, I will go with you on that one."

Kate told them, "Not without me. I would not trust you two alone."

CHAPTER 4

The Team

As they were walking toward the bar, Charles asked Tom, "Let's have one more for the road."

Tom turned his head and looked at Kate. She told them, "OK, just one more, and then that is it."

Charles told Terry, "When you have the time, we all like one more drink."

"No problem. It'll just be a minute or so."

While they were waiting, Charles handed Kate all his credit cards. "What are these for?"

He told her, "Well, I do not know if they are good or not. If you can find one, use it for the tickets."

"I would have the other ones updated or whatever it takes."

"That would be great. Tomorrow maybe you and Tom could go down to my house so I can show you my computer at, say, around one o'clock."

Kate said in a disgusted voice, "Sure, you guys will play cards, and then you want me to come down your house and put up with three drunks."

"I promise we will behave. We will just play cards and be on our best behavior."

Kate said in a demanding voice, "If I think any of you guys have too much to drink, the deal is off."

Charles told her, "I need you bad. I will be in good shape."

Tom stepped in. "I will make sure Charles is all right to show you the computer."

Kate started to laugh. "This is like the blind leading the blind. Nate, you better make sure they are sober, or you are worse than they are."

Nate told her, "We will be there. We will be sober."

Charles told Kate, "Do not worry, just be at my house at one. Anyway, I am going to call Amanda's parents and Lieutenant Steel. I do not want to mess that up now, do I?"

Kate said in a soft voice, "Well, I suppose so. I will be there, and I will be the judge if I stay or leave."

"That will be fair, all I can ask for."

Terry brought the drinks. Charles gave her a twenty and told her to keep the change. She gave Kate this smile. Kate told her, "No, he is not drunk, maybe a little off his rocker."

Charles told Terry, "This is a special occasion. Do not get used to it." They all laughed. When they finished their drinks, they all walked out the door at the same time.

As Tom was opening his door, he yelled at Charles, "I will see you at about eight!"

"That is right, and remember, three drinks only!"

Kate yelled back, "That will be the day!" Then they pulled away.

Charles and Nate were headed for his house; as they drove by John's Tap, Charles pulled in. Nate asked, "What are you doing?"

"Well, hell, one more drink."

"I think I had enough."

"Well, hell, you can have coffee. Charlie is in there. Maybe we can have a rematch tomorrow."

Charles and Nate walked in. Mary and Charlie were in the first booth. Charles ordered two beers. As the beers came, he asked Mary, "Is Charlie coming in town tomorrow?"

"Why? You want to have a rematch?"

"Charlie told you."

Charlie interrupted, "I have already seen Darrell. He will be here at eight, and so will I."

Charles drank his beer fast. Nate still had half of his and told him, "This is not coffee."

Charles apologized. "I forgot, so just drink it, and we will leave." Nate finally got his beer down.

Charles told Charlie, "See you at eight."

"Maybe we ought to practice tonight."

"Hell, the cards speak for themselves anyway. See you later."

Charles and Nate went home. As they walked in the door, Charles told Nate, "You know, since you are staying here, from now on, this is our house." Nate did not know what to say. Charles could tell he was speechless. "Nate, forget it. That is the way it is. This is not right, but for once, I am going to bed. You just do whatever you want."

While Charles was sleeping, Nate could not believe what was happening. Through the past several days, Charles took him in and gave him a joint account worth two hundred thousand dollars. Then now he told him, "Just call this your house."

Nate went to the couch and turned on the television. He was watching a movie that was the only one on at the time. It was about how this person's best friend turned him in for being a spy. Nate turned the television off and went upstairs to his room. He grabbed his phone and started to dial. All of a sudden, he could tell that Charles was up. Nate thought there would be a better opportunity to call, so he disconnected.

The next morning, like usual, Charles had breakfast ready. Nate came down, took a bath, and was ready to go. Charles already had the food on the table and told Nate, "We have to eat. We might as well be on a full stomach than an empty one."

After they ate, Charles told Nate, "You and Darrell will not be that lucky today."

Nate laughed. "Hell, you never know."

Charles and Nate arrived at John's Tap just at eight o'clock. The tavern was closed, so Charles opened it. Between Nate and Charles, the bar was ready in ten minutes.

Tom walked in and asked if the coffee was ready. Nate told him, "It'll be in ten more minutes."

Tom started to laugh. Charles asked, "What is so funny?"

"Hell, about three weeks or so, Nate did not know where the pisser was. Now he knows when the damn coffee is ready."

Darrell walked in just a few seconds after Tom. Before he could reach the cooler, Tom told Nate, "Just take out a Coke too." Darrell thanked Tom.

While they were talking, the phone started to ring. Charles answered the phone. "John's Tap." A woman's voice came on. Charles knew right away it was Mary. Charles asked if Charlie was all right. "Well, he is having breathing problems today. He will not be able to play cards.

"You just make sure he is getting better, and good luck." Charles hung up the phone and told Tom, "Well, Charlie is not coming. I guess Nate and I will take you and Darrell on."

Darrell looked at Tom and told him, "Hell, Charlie and I beat them last time. We will have no problem."

Tom walked toward the table. "Well, let's start playing. Remember—"

Charles interrupted him, "We know. Do not drink too much, or Kate will not help us."

Darrell started to laugh. Charles asked, "What is so funny?"

"I do not know what you guys are up to, but from now on, I know who the hell the boss is."

Tom asked, "Well, who is the boss?"

"It sounds to me Kate is the boss." They all started to laugh.

Charles told Tom, "Well, I believe Darrell is right on that one."

Tom just said, "Deal the damn cards."

After the first three games, Darrell and Tom won all of them. Charles told Nate, "You know, if we do not get any better cards, we might lose the damn farm."

Nate asked, "Do you own a farm?"

Darrell told him, "Hell no. I own a farm. Charles just lives off us farmers."

Nate was shaking his head. Tom told him, "That is just an expression we use around here, like saying you two are losing, and we are winning."

The next few games were no better. Tom and Darrell won the next five. Charles went and opened a beer. Tom looked at him. Charles told Tom, "Hell, one beer or two are OK. Kate just said we all better behave." So they all had a beer.

Charles and Nate won two games in a row. Nate told Charles, "Maybe we play better having a beer."

Darrell told Nate, "Hell, you guys just finally got the cards, that is all."

The time went by fast. The bar was almost full; most of them were watching the card game. Charles did not even notice that Skip was attending the bar until he got up to get them another beer. Skip told him, "Just sit down. I've been helping you for the last fifteen minutes."

"Thanks. I did not even notice. Just buy the whole bar a drink and one for yourself."

Skip, without even thinking, asked, "What the hell did you do, hit the lotto or something?" Tom looked up, just wondering what Charles was going to say.

Charles just said, "Well, hell, I never buy a round very damn often. I just thought this will be the day."

Skip told everyone, "The drink is on Charles." They heard at least ten thanks.

Charles turned around to Skip. "Oh, one more thing, we do not want any more beer over here."

Darrell told Skip, "That does not mean me."

Charles laughed. "That is right. That does not mean Darrell, just Tom, Nate, and me."

Darrell told them, "That is not Charles or Tom speaking. That is Kate speaking."

Tom said, "You got that right."

Charles looked at the clock; it was eleven fifteen. Charles told Tom, "Three more games, and then we leave."

"That would make Kate very happy."

Things did not change. Nate and Charles lost two out of three. Darrell told them he would buy a drink. Tom said, "No, we are leaving."

Charles told him, "That is right, and thanks for the lesson again."

Nate told Darrell, "You must be one of the luckiest persons."

"Hell, you did good too."

Charles told them both, "You guys are full of shit. Nate and I lost sixteen dollars. That Tom drew out of his ass, and Nate did play good, but I made a few mistakes."

Tom told Darrell, "Well, that is right. You did play bad."

When the three arrived at Charles's house, Charles went to the phone and dialed a number. He made an order to go. He asked Tom and Nate what they wanted. Charles relayed the order. He asked Tom what Kate would like. Tom told Charles, "She usually orders."

Just then, Kate walked in. Charles asked her, "What would you like from the Company?"

"A cheeseburger with everything and fries." Charles placed the order and then hung up phone.

Kate was sitting at the table, all ready. She asked, "Who is picking up the food?" Charles told her he was.

Kate went to the phone. Tom asked, "Who are you calling?"

"The Company." To whoever answered the phone, Kate just said, "This is Kate Parkes. The order Charles Appel just ordered, do not make that to go. We will be there in five minutes to eat." She hung the phone up. "You can all have two beers. That is it. Then we will come back here to go over the reservations I made and the computer."

There was not one word said for a few seconds. Charles told Kate, "That is fine with us."

Tom said, "Hell, that makes sense, and then we will not mess up the papers."

Kate told him, "That is exactly right. Charles will not mess up the papers."

Charles started to laugh. "Are you saying I am a messy eater?"

Kate looked at him. "That is what I am saying."

"Well, hell, everyone knows that."

They all went down to the Company and ate. They just had their two drinks, and Kate had Cokes. Charles paid the bill and told Kate, "Thanks for helping."

"Well, thanks for staying sober." They all left the Company and were back at Charles's house by one forty-five.

Kate laid all the reservations on the table. She told Charles, "You know, the three credit cards you gave me, only one of them was good. The other two you have not used for two years. So they dropped you."

"Well, hell, I use that one to buy golf supplies and tee times."

"Well, hell, at least it was good. I called the other two. They will send you forms to fill out." Charles thanked her.

Kate told Charles and Nate, "Your tickets to Saint Louis is the same once you get there. Nate's flight to Kansas City leaves at four thirty. Charles, your flight to Manchester leaves at five. Your plane will go to Concord first and then a flight to Manchester. You should be at Manchester by eight thirty."

Kate then gave Nate a piece of paper. "Here is your hotel reservation confirmation number. You are staying at the Crown Center. Charles, I did not make one for you yet. After you call them, we will do it right after you hang up. I do have your hotel in Newark. It's Newark Plaza. Your flight to leave Manchester is eight o'clock, Wednesday night. Your plane goes to Concord and then Newark. You should be at your hotel by eleven thirty. Whatever you do, get some rest. I have a surprise for you on Thursday morning. Just do not mess it up."

Charles asked, "What is the surprise?"

"I am not telling you or anyone in this room. Just do what I asked you. Promise?"

Charles told her in a childish voice, "I promise."

"You will leave Newark at eleven, Sunday morning. So you can all play golf Monday."

Nate asked, "Will I be back?"

"I forgot. Yes, I have you leaving Kansas City Sunday morning at eight o'clock. You and Charles will be on the same plane coming home from Saint Louis."

Charles told Kate, "You did a hell of a good job. You already earned your trip. Are you ready to learn the computer?"

Kate told him, "No. You have to make two phone calls, one to Amanda's parents and the other to Lieutenant Steel, right?"

"All right, I will do it right now."

Kate told Tom and Nate, "Why not we go in the living room while Charles makes the phone calls?"

Tom looked at Kate like, *Why should we move?* Kate gave him a look that only Tom knew. The look told him, *Get your ass in the other room now.*

Tom got up and told Nate, "Let's leave Charles alone." Charles thanked Kate, and then he went to the phone.

Charles looked up the number that Lieutenant Steel gave him. As he was dialing, Charles could tell he was getting nervous. He just hoped he would not make them upset. After five rings, a woman's voice came on. "This is the Tulmans' residence. How can I help you?" The voice sounded just like Amanda's when Charles called her at Newark. Charles paused, and again, this voice said, "This is the Tulmans'."

He answered, "I am Charles Appel from Coal City. I am Jake's father."

The voice on the other end started to cry. Charles did not know what to say. Then he told her, "Are you Mrs. Tulman? If you are, your voice sounds just like Amanda's."

Mrs. Tulman handed the phone to her husband. He, in a very disturbing voice, asked, "Who the hell is this?"

"I am Charles Appel. I am Jake's father."

Mr. Tulman was surprised too. He told Charles, "You know, your voice sounds a lot like Jake's."

Charles laughed. "That is what I just told your wife, that she sounded just like Amanda's."

Mr. Tulman did not know what to say; they both were just breathing, saying nothing. Charles finally broke the silence. "The reason I am calling is I would like to fly to Manchester to talk to you and Mrs. Tulman personally. I have some information for you, and I hope you can answer some of my questions."

Mr. Tulman did not hesitate. "You most certainly can any time you want."

"I have tickets to Manchester for eight thirty, Tuesday night. I can stay all night at the airport hotel and see you Wednesday."

Mr. Tulman did not even think. "That is ridiculous. You can stay at our house. Janace will be more than glad to talk to you after she gets her composure back."

Charles asked, "Are you sure?"

Mr. Tulman said in a very sincere voice, "You bet I am. We have a lot to talk about. When you arrive at the airport, just go to the bar. The bartender's name is Russell. Just tell him you are waiting for me. I will be waiting for you at the bar."

Charles asked again, "Are you sure you want me to stay at your house?"

"Yes, we have to talk."

"All right, I will be there Tuesday night. Thanks."

"No thank you." Then they hung up.

Charles walked in the living room and told them what happened. Kate did not seem too surprised the Tulmans asked him to stay. Charles told her, "You knew that?"

"Well, Tom and I would have done the same thing. So would you."

"Well, I suppose so."

Tom told Charles, "Hell, you tell anyone to stay."

Kate told Charles, "Now go make your other call before you change your mind."

Charles looked up the Newark police number that Lieutenant Steel gave him. The phone only rang once. "This is the Newark Police Department. Detective Roger is speaking."

Charles, in a very nervous voice, asked, "Is Lieutenant Steel there?"

Detective Roger told him, "No, she is off duty today. Can I help you?"

"No, I will call later." Charles told Kate she was not at work.

Kate said, "Just call her at her number. After all, she gave it to you."

Charles dialed the other number. The phone was ringing several times. The answering machine kicked on. "This is the Steels. Just leave your number. We will call you as soon as possible."

Charles started to leave his message. Just as he told the machine, "This is Charles Appel from Coal City," a voice answered the phone. "This is Ciara. Can I help you?"

Charles, without thinking, asked, "Are you all right? You sound out of breath."

Ciara asked, "Who is this?"

"I am Charles Appel, Jake Appel's father. You gave me your number. I called the police department. They told me you were off duty, so I called this number you gave me."

Ciara was getting her breath back. "I am sorry. I just took my dog for a jog. The phone was ringing as I was just on the steps. I hurried as fast as I could to answer the phone."

"That is fine." Out of the blue, Charles asked, "Are you married?"

Ciara answered in a disturbed voice, "No, I am not married. I told you that."

"Well, on the machine, you said the Steels."

She started to laugh. "Well, I say that so if strangers call, they think there are more than one person at my house."

Charles felt bad and apologized for getting personal. Ciara told him, "No problem."

"Well, I have two things to ask. The first one is I am coming to Newark Thursday afternoon. I am staying till Sunday noon, when my plane leaves for Saint Louis. I want to talk to you about Jake's murder."

"That will be fine. I will be at the station till six at least. I need to ask you some questions too." Ciara then asked, "Well, what is the other thing you want to ask?" Charles hesitated for several seconds. Her voice came back. "Are you still on the line?"

"Yes, I am still on the phone." Charles then told her, "This is not very easy for me. I have not done this for fifteen years, so just bear with me."

"Are you all right?"

"Yes, I am fine. I just want to know if you could have supper with me Thursday night after you get off work. We could talk about Jake and just maybe about each other."

Ciara asked in a nervous voice, "Are you asking me out on a date?"

Charles was really getting nervous now; he could tell it in his voice, so he knew she could too. "Yes, I am asking you to go out with me for supper."

Ciara could not believe it. She thought about it for a few seconds. "Yes, I will be glad to go out with you."

Charles was in shock. "Are you sure?"

Ciara started to laugh. "Yes, I am sure. I will pick you up at the hotel you are staying at."

"That will be great. I am staying at the Newark Plaza."

Ciara asked in a dismayed voice, "At the Plaza?"

"Yes, is that a bad one?"

"No, it is the best one in town. I just did not think you would have that kind of taste."

"Well," Charles told her, "I had a friend make the reservations."

"You know, they have the best restaurant on top. I never ate there, but I doubt we could get reservations."

Charles laughed. "You meet me, say, at seven thirty at the lobby. I will have the reservation."

"You have a date. If by chance you do not get the reservation, I know a place where we can eat."

"Goodbye. See you Thursday."

When Charles hung up, he went right to Kate. She asked, "What is wrong?"

"Ciara is going to have supper with me Thursday night. I have to make reservations at the restaurant on top of the Plaza." Charles gave Kate this stare.

"This will cost you."

Tom told Kate, "Who cares? Charles has the money now."

Kate looked up the number. After a few minutes, she was talking to the restaurant. They told her they were full that night. Kate started to talk back. She told whoever was on the other end, "I want to talk to your boss now." The person told her that it was not possible. "Give me the hotel manager."

After a few minutes, a voice said, "This is the Plaza day shift manager."

"Mr. Charles Appel has a reservation at your hotel from Thursday to Sunday noon."

After a few seconds, the manager confirmed, "Yes, we have it right here."

"If you cannot get a reservation for the restaurant that is on top of your hotel, not only will I cancel the room reservations but I also will make it very hard on you next time Mr. Appel stays in Newark. I know you are not very busy during the week. Mr. Appel is spending a lot of money at your hotel. He could spend it somewhere else."

The manager told her to wait a few seconds. He came back on. "I tell you, if your friend Mr. Appel will give a sizable tip to me and the restaurant manager, we can get you your reservation."

"I will tell you only once. You add one hundred dollars to the hotel room, and you and your friend can split it."

The manager told her, "Just a second. I will give you the restaurant back."

In a matter of seconds, a voice came on. "The Plaza Restaurant."

Kate told him, "Do you have the reservations for Mr. Appel now?"

"Yes, what time did you say?"

"Seven thirty, Thursday, for two."

The man told her, "Everything is taken care of."

"One more thing, it better be a good table." He assured Kate it would be one of the best tables. "Make sure you have a good wine for his table also." The man told her it would be taken care of. Right before she hung up, she said, "One more thing, what is your name so Mr. Appel can look you up in case of bad service? If you lie to me, we will find out."

"I am Mr. Joseph Madigan. I will be here personally to make sure Mr. Appel will get the best service, but it will now cost you another fifty."

"Deal, he will pay you in cash after the meal."

Charles asked Kate, "What did you do?"

"Well, I got you your reservations there. Just one little item."

"What is it?"

"Well, I just spent one hundred and fifty dollars so you can surprise your lieutenant Steel."

Charles told her, "Well, hell, a few days ago, I would have shit my pants spending that kind of money. Today I do not seem to mind."

Tom told him, "Hell, it better be worth it."

"With all that done, teach me your computer." Tom and Kate could tell Charles was already a different person. Kate just hoped the date would be a good one.

Charles went in the computer room. Tom was watching, and then he said, "This is too deep for me. I am going to watch television." Nate stayed in the room. Charles really did not want him in there, but he could not figure a way to get him to leave.

After just an hour, Kate could break right through the disk. She learned how to scramble and descramble it. Charles was amazed at how fast she learned. The trouble was Nate knew how too. The only thing that Charles knew that nobody else did was he still had one more backup hidden. Charles disconnected all the cables and put the computer on the kitchen table. He told Kate, "Tuesday, it will all be ready to move."

Charles called Cambell up. "Everything will be ready Tuesday morning." Charles told him they had a plane flight leaving on Tuesday afternoon. Cambell assured him they would be done in time.

Kate told Charles, "Well, now that I know how to run the computer, what are we going to do now?"

Tom looked at Nate, who looked at Charles like, *Well, come up with something.* Charles told Kate, "I guess we could go."

Even before he could get the words out, Kate told Tom, "No way, you guys are going tomorrow and Monday. I let you play cards today. You are coming home with me right now."

Charles started to laugh. "I was going to say, 'Let's go to the Depot to eat supper.'"

Kate looked at Charles. "Are you serious, or are you just saying that?"

"I am serious."

"Good. You pick Tom and me up in an hour and a half."

"Nate and I will be there." Then Tom and Kate left the house.

Nate asked, "Charles, is that what you were going to say?"

"Hell no. I thought we would go uptown and try to win our money back. I was not going to say that after Kate put her two cents in." Nate was laughing. Charles asked him, "What is so funny?"

"I'm beginning to believe Kate does run the show with you and Tom. It's just that you guys do not know it."

Charles thought a few seconds. "You know, that would be right. Well, anyway, we do play a lot of cards and golf."

Nate then told Charles, "Do not forget the pool games."

"Hell, I forgot about that."

Charles and Nate picked Tom and Kate up for supper. Kate had not been in the Depot for a few years, so she was looking forward to the supper. Right when they were in the car, Kate told all of them, "Let's enjoy tonight, and no talking about golf or computers."

Charles told her, "That is a deal."

When they arrived at the Depot, a guy recognized Tom just as he was sitting down at the table. Tom introduced him to Nate and Kate. "This is Stanley. We used to work at Stayleys together."

Stanley right away asked Tom, "How is your golf game going?"

"Hell, it could be better."

Charles asked Stanley, "How the hell is yours?"

"Hell, Tom and I could beat you and any one of your friends anytime."

Kate was turning red. Charles could tell she was mad. After all, they told her no talking about golf. Charles just told Stanley, "Hell, Nate and I will take you and Tom for twenty-five cents a hole and a dollar for total."

Stanley did not hesitate. "Where are you playing at?"

"At Atlanta at nine o'clock, Monday. We have a nine-twenty-four tee time."

Stanley looked at Tom, who told him that would be OK with him. Stanley told them he had to go back to his table. "I will see you Monday."

Kate said in a sharp voice, "I knew better. You guys cannot go anywhere without talking about golf."

Charles told her, "Wait a minute, that does not count. Stanley came to us."

Tom was laughing. Charles asked him, "What is so funny?"

"Hell, Kate is right. No matter how hard we try, we always end up talking about golf."

Kate did enjoy her meal after that. There was not one word said about golf. They talked about the trip she planned out. Charles told her she did a real good job. Kate just told him, "Do not forget, you have to get some sleep Wednesday night at Newark."

"I will. Just tell me what you did."

"Wait and see."

Charles looked at Tom, who told him, "Hell, I do not know either."

Kate said, "Hell, I do not trust you, Tom, or Nate. You just have to trust me."

When they were done with dinner, Charles took Kate and Tom home. He drove by John's Tap. Nate asked, "We are not stopping?"

"No, I want to go over the arrangement Kate made for us."

Nate said, "That is a good idea. What do you want me to do in Kansas City?"

"Try to find Joseph. I believe he worked for Bensoil Corporation. I am not sure. His last name is Cline. Yes, that is it, Joseph Cline. I remember I met him just two times, if my memory is correct."

Nate gave Charles this funny stare. Charles asked him, "Are you all right?"

"Yes, there is nothing wrong."

Charles then asked, "You have any friends in Kansas City?"

"Well, I had this coworker that moved to Kansas City some years ago. I might look him up."

"You do whatever you want. Just make sure you can locate Joseph."

"I'll do my best."

Charles then told Nate, "Before I go to bed, I am going to practice some golf." Nate asked if he could join him. "I thought you should, if you want to beat us tomorrow."

After they practiced for an hour or so, Charles told Nate he had enough. "I am going upstairs."

"I am going to practice some putting, and then I will be up."

"Help yourself."

When Nate came up from the basement, Charles was in the chair watching television. Nate told him, "I am going to bed."

"OK, I will see you in the morning." He yelled at Nate, "Remind me to call Tom to make sure who is driving!"

"I thought you were driving tomorrow and Tom is driving Monday."

"You know, I believe you are right, so let's make sure we are ready by nine thirty so we can pick up Tom and Dwight." Nate told Charles he would be ready.

When Nate went up to his room, he started to use his cell phone again. Nate dialed the number. As it was ringing, Charles was at the bottom of the steps. He asked Nate if he wanted bacon and eggs or go uptown to eat. Nate, surprised, hung up the phone. Charles asked, "Are you all right? You need something?" Nate was at the top of the steps; he threw the phone under the pillow.

"No, I am all right. Let's eat at the restaurant."

"OK, we will go uptown at around eight." Charles then went to the bathroom. Nate was shaking his head, wondering how in the hell he was going to make that phone call.

The next morning, Charles called Tom and asked if he wanted to eat uptown with them. Tom told him, "Yes, Kate is going to sleep in today."

"We will be there at eight o'clock."

Charles, Nate, and Tom went uptown. As Charles just got in the door, a tall person just came out and just asked, "Charles, is it true you are a millionaire?"

"Larry, just sit down and mind your own business." Charles sat down and started to think about how he treated Larry. He went to him, and then he had seen several others watching. Charles asked if he could have everyone's attention for a few seconds.

Larry told Charles, "You have mine."

Charles apologized to Larry for the way he talked to him. Then Tom could not believe what he said next. "Yes, it is true I am a millionaire now. Thanks to Jake's wise investments. I am going to use the money to find out what happened to Jake and who killed him. In that process, I will give a lot of the money in some way or another to our town. I ask you all, please do not ask for money or make my life miserable. I want to stay in town as if nothing changed. I know it will be hard for all of us. Please make it as easy as possible for all of us in town."

Larry looked at Charles. "Hey, we go a way back. I will help you and not bug you about your new wealth." Charles thanked him and went back to the table.

A couple went up to their table and told Charles good luck and that if he needed their help, they would be glad to. Charles thanked them. He then stood up. "Oh, one more thing, I am not going to waste this fortune I was lacking that Jake had. But then again, all of you are my friends, so I will help you out as I feel fit. Today is a special day for all of us, so today the breakfast is on me."

Tom told Charles, "I hope they did not take that wrong."

"I hope so too, but what else was I supposed to do?"

"Hell, Kate will tell you how to handle your money in Coal City anyway."

"You know, that might not be a bad idea."

"And my big mouth."

They left the restaurant and went to pick up Dwight. He was ready, waiting by his door. After Dwight put his clubs in the trunk, when he opened the back door, he looked at Charles. "Well, hell, I just heard, so I guess you are paying for the golf today."

Charles, with a surprised look, told Dwight, "Are you crazy?" Dwight could not help from laughing. "When did you hear about it?"

"Hell, Penny heard it at the beauty shop yesterday." Dwight then looked at Charles. "You know, no matter what changes, we will always be golfing buddies, right?"

"You bet we will. Thanks."

The tee time was right on time. Charles shot badly that day. Nate still was hitting the ball good. Tom and Dwight played real good. Charles and Nate lost three dollars total. On the way back, Dwight said in a laughing voice, "You know, this has been a good time. Tom and I should have played you guys for a million."

Charles told him, "Very funny."

Charles drove through the country on the way back. They stopped at a bar in Dawson. Tom told Charles, "Went out of the way for this one."

"Hell, I never gave them much business yet this year." They all had two drinks, and then they went back to Coal City.

Nate was walking in the bar first and then Dwight, Tom, and Charles. As Charles entered the bar, the few people who was there clapped their hands. The beer was waiting for Charles on the bar. He thanked all of them for their support. One of the guys went up to him. "I do not know you very well. If I can help you find Jake's killer, you just ask." Charles thanked him.

Tom told Charles, "Well, hell, what you said this morning must have been right."

"I sure am a lucky person to have so many friends."

They had several beers in Dave's Tavern. Everyone bought their share of drinks. In fact, as Charles was walking out, he told Tom, "You know, I spent less today as I ever have."

Dwight told him, "Well, hell, if you want to spend more, just let Tom and me take you and Nate on in golf. That is easy money."

By that time, they were at Dwight's house. Charles told Dwight as he was getting out, "Next time, we will whip your ass." Dwight thanked them for a good time.

Charles then dropped Tom off at his house. Tom told him he would drive tomorrow. "That will be fine."

"I will be at your house at around eight thirty."

When Tom got in the house, Kate was waiting for him. She asked Tom if he was sober enough to listen. Tom told her, "Let me sit down and drink some water." Kate gave him a glass of water and then sat down. She asked Tom if he was still driving tomorrow. He told her yes. Kate said, "Good."

"What is good about that?"

"I need you to keep Charles's golf clubs in your car while he and Nate are gone."

Tom said in a very strange voice, "Why do I want Charles's club while he is gone?"

"That is the surprise. Tuesday, after their plane leaves, you have to get Charles's club on the next plane that leaves. You have thirty minutes to do this."

Tom looked at Kate. "What the hell are you talking about?"

"The surprise I got Charles. I got him a tee time at Newark, Thursday morning at around ten thirty."

"You did what?"

"I got Charles a tee time."

Tom told Kate, "That was a good idea."

"I thought so too."

"I will do my best, but I will not promise I can do it."

"If you want to live here, you will."

"All right, I promise I will get Charles's clubs one way or another."

Charles and Nate went home. Charles grabbed a few beers and told Nate, "Let's grill out some steaks tonight."

"That sounds good."

Charles was getting the grill ready while Nate was drinking his beer. Nate asked Charles if he was nervous about meeting Amanda's parents. He told him, "No, not at all, but I am nervous about seeing Lieutenant Steel."

"Charles, do you think you like her?"

"Hell, I liked her when she was at the airport waiting for Tom and me."

"I hope I get to meet her."

"We just have to see what happens."

The next morning, Tom picked Nate and Charles up. They were in Atlanta plenty of time. Stanley was waiting on the practice green. While they were waiting, Tom asked, "Who are partners?"

Stanley told them, "Hell, I do not care."

Tom said, "Hell, Stanley and I will take on Charles and Nate."

Stanley told them, "That will be fine with me. Tom, just put your clubs in my cart."

Charles told Nate, "Hell, we can beat them the way you are hitting the ball."

"I do have more confidence in my swing than I ever could imagine just a few weeks ago."

Tom told them to shut up and just play. Charles laughed and told Tom, "Hell, we will win."

Stanley told Charles, "Hell, last time we played, you and Richard beat Tom and me."

"Hell, Nate is playing better than Richard now."

Stanley just shook his head and looked at Tom, who said, "Well, not quite that good but close."

After a few holes, Tom and Stanley were up three holes. On the next shot, Tom's ball went left, a straight pull shot. Nate and Stanley were on the right side of the fairway. Charles took his drive and hooked it left real close to Tom's ball. Nate dropped Charles off to his ball. Charles told Nate, "I will take the rest of my clubs and meet you on the green." While he was saying this, Charles was looking right at Tom.

Tom told Stanley, "I will do the same." So Nate and Stanley drove to their balls.

Charles thanked Tom. Tom could tell that he wanted to talk to him alone. Charles said, "We do not have much time. Tell Kate to check out on the Internet anything she can find out about Joseph in Kansas City."

Tom hit his ball left of the green. They then walked to Charles's ball. Charles told Tom, "Hell, that was not bad. I just hope I can do the same." Charles hit his, just four yards from Tom's ball.

While they were walking, Tom asked, "Is that what Nate is to do?"

"Well, yes, I just want to compare the difference."

Tom said with a dismayed look, "You still do not trust Nate, do you?"

"Well, I only know I can trust you and Kate for sure. Anyone else is up for grabs. The people I want to find are rich and powerful and have control over everything." Tom told Charles he would tell Kate.

By then, Tom hit his third shot; the ball went in the hole. Charles's ball was short of the pin, and then he parred. Stanley and Nate both parred the hole. Charles told Nate, "Hell this might not be our day. "At the same time, he opened a can of beer.

At the end of the round, Charles and Nate lost four holes and the total. Stanley asked, "Where do you guys want to go for the nineteenth hole?"

Tom started to laugh. Nate asked, "What is so funny?"

Tom told Charles, "You explain it."

"There is only one tavern in Atlanta that I go to on a weekday." Nate asked the name of the tavern. Charles told him he could not remember.

Tom told Nate, "Hell, Charles never remembers the tavern's name. He just calls it the tavern across the library." Stanley told them he would meet them there. Tom started the car, and Charles and Nate got in.

When they walked in the tavern, the bartender said hi to Tom and Charles. "Who is your friend?"

Charles told her, "His name is Nate."

"He will have a Bud," Tom told her.

Just as they sat down at the table near the pool table, she came with their beers. Nate could not believe it. He asked, "Is there not a tavern that does not know what you guys drink?" Charles told him no. Nate looked at Charles's beer. "What the hell are you drinking?"

"At this tavern, I drink Pabst."

Tom asked Nate, "Do you really want to hear this story?"

Even before he could answer, Charles explained, "A long time ago, I and my working friends came here. They drank Pabst back then. To make it easy for them, I ordered Pabst too. Ever since then, all the bartenders know that is what I drink, so I never change my beer at this tavern."

Nate shook his head. "Now let me get this right. At this tavern, you drink Pabst. Then you drink Miller Lite and Busch at Coal City taverns."

Charles told Nate, "If you could remember more on your golf swing, we might have won today."

Stanley was just walking in when he noticed nobody was playing pool. He asked Nate if he played. Tom told Stanley, "Put the quarters in. We will take Charles and Nate on. Now we will lose." After several games and beers, Charles and Nate not only got their golf money back but they also made five dollars.

Stanley finally told them he had to go. Tom told Charles and Nate, "It is time. We better head for Coal City." Charles agreed, so he walked to the bar and gave the bartender a five-dollar tip and thanked her.

She told Charles, "See you guys next round."

"You can bet on that."

When they arrived in Coal City, Tom pulled into Dave's. Charles told him, "We have a big day tomorrow. Maybe we should just have two more."

"Whatever you say."

Just as they walked in, George was at the pool table. Charles told Nate, "Shit, we will be here for a while now."

Tom told Charles he would challenge first. Charles replied, "Put some quarters up for Nate and me." Charles went to the bar and bought the drinks.

Nate, with a know-nothing look, asked, "What is this about?"

"Well, hell, George beat us last time we played pool. We told George the next time we run into him, we will try to win our money back, so here we are."

"How long does this last?"

Steve, the bartender, overheard the conservation and just told Nate, "Last time, they closed the bar down."

Nate looked at Charles. "Hell, I cannot drink that much."

"Well, they have pop and water."

They all played pool until midnight. Tom was winning the most money. George finally told them he had enough. Nate could not have been happier. He told Tom, "Let's take us home."

Charles started to laugh. Tom asked, "What is so funny?"

"This is the first time Nate called my house home."

"Hell, to me, that is a good idea."

Charles and Tom finished their beer. Charles told Tom, "Well, let's get the hell out of here before we end up closing Dave's down."

Tom opened the door. Steve told them to drive carefully. Charles said, "Tom is driving. He is the best one to drive."

As Tom pulled out of the tavern, he told Charles, "Why not just leave the clubs in my car?"

"That is a good idea. Neither Nate nor I am in the mood to mess with them."

By that time, Tom was driving by the square just two blocks from Charles's house. Charles noticed some kids were standing on the square. He asked Tom to stop the car. Tom asked, "What for?"

"I want to talk to those kids a minute."

Nate asked in a mysterious voice, "Why do you want to talk to those young kids at this time of night?"

Charles told Tom, "Just stop the car and park by them." Tom did what he said.

Charles rolled down his car window. He asked the closest one to the car, "Are you Ken, Horney's kid?"

The boy told him, "Yes, I am. Who the hell are you?"

"Hey, kid, I have a financial arrangement I want to make with you and your friends."

Another boy went up to Ken and told him, "Hey, that is Mr. Appel. My dad told me he is the one whose son was murdered and left him some kind of stock."

Ken asked Charles, "Is that true?" Charles told him yes. "What is this financial arrangement you have in mind?"

"I will give you and your friends fifty dollars a week."

Ken asked, "What do we have to do for this fifty dollars a week?"

"All I want is for you and your friends to watch my house while I am out of town. I do not mean live in it. Just drive by it at least once an hour or so."

Ken walked up a few steps to talk it over with his friends. He came back. "Is that just to drive by your house and watch it?"

Charles told him, "Well, a little more than that. I really want you to keep an eye out for strange cars that come in town, anything that you feel is different or unusual. Write down the license number, and give it to Burt."

Ken laughed. "You mean you want us to drive around town and write down any license plate number that we feel is a strange car in town?"

"Yes and to make sure nobody breaks in my house."

Ken told Charles, "Hell yes, for fifty dollars a week, we can do that. Give us, say, a month in advance, and it is a deal."

Charles handed Ken four hundred dollars. "I trust you, guys."

"Not only will we keep track of strange cars in town but we also will guard your house."

"No, just if you see anything suspicious, just tell Burt." Ken thanked Charles, who told Tom, "You can take us home now."

Tom, while he was backing up, asked Charles, "Are you nuts?"

"Hell, those kids run around town till God knows when. Remember when we were that age? We always knew who was in town before Andy did."

"Well, that is true." Tom was shaking his head.

Charles asked, "Now what?"

Tom turned his head. "You know what those boys will do with that money, don't you? Well, I have an idea. They will probably buy beer with it. Probably when we were that age, there would be no 'probably' about it."

Charles told Tom, "Hey, the deal is to watch the house and for strangers. What they do with the money is their business."

By that time, Tom was making a left turn off the square. Burt was sitting at the gas station. Charles told Tom, "Hey, pull beside Burt. I will tell him what is going on."

"No, we all have been drinking too much to talk to Burt tonight. You can talk to him tomorrow."

Charles thought about it. "Yes, you are definitely right. Take us home."

Tom pulled in by the house. Charles and Nate got out. Tom asked Charles, "Still at the bank by seven?"

"Yes, and do not be late."

"Hell, you and Nate not be late." Then he pulled away.

Charles opened the door to the house. Nate walked right toward the steps to his room. "You better wake me up tomorrow. I am going to pass out."

Charles told him, "Get to bed. I will wake you up at six thirty." While Nate was walking up the stairs, Charles took off his clothes and turned on the television set. In just a few minutes, he fell asleep.

Charles woke up when the five-thirty news was on. He took his shower and loaded the car with his computer very carefully. This only took a few minutes since everything was ready. Charles started to cook some bacon and eggs. By this time, it was six thirty. He yelled up at Nate, who finally woke up and asked, "It is not time yet, is it?"

"You want some bacon and eggs real quick?"

"Hell no, just coffee." Nate came down, took his shower, and was dressed by ten till seven.

Charles handed him some coffee in a cup. "You can drink it on the way up to the bank."

They pulled up to the bank. Steve Cambell was there waiting. Just as Charles was getting out of his car, Tom and Kate pulled up. Andy was already in the bank and just opened the bank door for them.

Nate and Charles carried the computer from Charles's car while Tom and Steve Cambell carried the equipment from Steve's car. As they were walking to the spot where the computer was going, Andy already had the area ready. Charles was amazed at how fast Steve Cambell hooked up all the equipment. Kate was doing a great job in learning both system. Kate told all of them that learning Charles's the other day helped a lot.

While Kate was getting the tapes ready, Andy gave Charles another safety-deposit key. He thought Kate could put the new tapes that she was making in this one so her disk would not be confused with Charles's disk. Charles thought that was a good idea.

As the bank employees were walking in, they were all looking at Kate. Andy told Charles some of them felt that Kate was butting in and might take one of their jobs. Charles told him, "Well, I tell you what, let's change the game plan. Can I rent this spot from you and I will call Kate my personal secretary? I will pay her from my own money."

"I believe this would work out for everyone concerned."

Charles asked Andy, "Could I talk to all your employees when they arrive?"

"Yes, you could." After all the employees were at work, Andy asked all of them to come in the main part of the bank.

Charles stood there for a few seconds. He knew most of the employees one way or another. Charles started out and thanked all of them for their patience and understanding. "As of this minute, Kate is working for me. Kate does not or will ever have any ties to the bank. Just that there is an important disk that I do not want to leave the bank. So I asked Andy if he could rent this space from me until Kate is done going through all the disks."

Diane raised her hand. Charles asked, "What is your question?"

"I do not know how to put it, but does this has to do with Jake's murder?"

"Yes, it does. Jake and his friends made these disks. I think there is some kind of connection."

Linda then asked, "Will this be a danger to us?"

Charles thought for a few seconds. "There might be some danger. I just do not have any safer place to keep the disk except in the bank."

Everyone was silent; it seemed like it happened for a long time but really just a few seconds. Then a voice from the back came out. "Charles, I do not know you very well. I did know Jake real well. If we can help you find out how or why or who killed Jake, I tell you, go for it. We will be glad to help in any way."

All the employees looked at Susan. They knew something that Charles did not. Susan could tell he did not know. She told Charles, back in college, she and Jake were very close friends. Most of the ones at the bank must have known that. Susan started to yell, "One, two, three!"

They all yelled out, "Go for it!" Charles thanked each of them personally.

Then they all went to Kate and told her if there was anything they could do to help, just ask. Kate was very happy. She wondered how she would fit in; now she knew.

Andy went to the main door and opened it for business. Just like every other bank day, they all started to work. He thanked Charles for doing that. Charles told him, "No thank you and your workers for letting me intrude on you." Nate could not believe what he was seeing. People were willing to put their lives and work in jeopardy to help one person whom some of them hardly knew, Charles and Jake.

Charles told Tom and Kate, "Nate and I will leave now to go home and pack. Pick us up at eleven."

Kate said, "Do not be late."

"Do not worry."

As Charles and Nate were backing out, Charles asked Nate, "How long will it take you to pack?"

"About fifteen minutes."

"Good. I have a few stops to make. I want you to go with me."

"Do not forget."

"I know, we will not be late."

Charles drove to the Country Carloet Store at the edge of town. They walked in and went right to the manager. Charles introduced Nate to Connie. She asked, "What do you need?"

Charles told her, "Could you ask your employees to write down any names or license plate numbers that they feel is strange?"

"Strange in what way?"

"Well, if someone asks how to get to my house or a car that looks suspicious, out of the ordinary."

Connie told Charles, "For you, I sure will."

"Just give the information to Burt."

"No problem."

Charles thanked her, and then he told Nate, "Well, let's go."

Charles took Nate to Tire Company and Repair on the other side of town. There were five people in there drinking coffee. Charles asked all of them to do the same. They told him they would do that. Charles took Nate to several businesses; they all told Charles yes.

When they finally got back to the house, Nate watched Charles looking and fumbling through some cards. Nate asked, "What are you looking for?"

"I am looking up Mr. Martin's phone number." Charles found the card and started to dial.

After he dialed, a voice said, "Tran Oil." Charles asked if he could talk to Mr. Martin. This nice, friendly voice asked who was calling.

"This is Charles Appel, who is calling long distance from Coal City, Illinois."

She told Charles, "Just wait a minute. I will find out." Charles waited for about a minute. Her voice came back on. "Yes, Mr. Appel, I am putting you through now."

His voice came on. "Yes, Mr. Appel, how are you doing?"

Charles was not sure if it was Mr. Martin or not. "I am coming to Newark Thursday and leaving Sunday. I have something that you need."

"I am not Mr. Martin. He is out of town. I am his personal secretary. My name is Willium. I do know he would like to see you. What about Friday, nine thirty in the morning?"

"That will be fine." Charles then asked, "How are your computers doing?"

Willium did not change his voice and just said, "Well, we are having problems."

Charles told him, "After Friday, you will not." Then he hung up.

Charles looked at Nate. "You know, I think they knew I was coming to Newark."

Nate asked, "How do you know that?"

"I really do not know. I just have this feeling they knew. The way this Willium talked, he already had the time set. He did not ask to look at his schedule or nothing. Hell, he is a busy person. Also, the secretary put me right through. Hell, usually, that would take five to ten minutes to get through to a big wheel like Mr. Martin. This is going to be very interesting when I get to Newark."

Charles was wondering what Nate was going to say. Nate just told him, "Make sure you do not get over your head when you talk to big businesspeople."

"I will keep that in mind." He started look up a phone number in the telephone book.

Nate asked, "Now who are you calling?"

"I have to tell Burt what I am doing."

Charles dialed the number. The phone rang only two times. He could tell it was Burt's voice. "This is Charles Appel."

Right off the bat, Burt asked, "What the hell are you doing?" Charles started to say something, but Burt interrupted. "I am running this police department, not you."

He asked Burt to calm down. "I am going to explain."

"You better do it damn fast." Charles told Burt he hired the kids to watch his house and look for suspicious cars. Burt told him, "Hell, I know that. Plus, you went to all the businesses in town too."

"Yes, I did. Just do me this favor until I get back. I will tell you everything."

Burt hesitated for a few seconds. "You will tell me everything?" Charles assured him he would. Burt then told him, "You have a good trip, and you better be telling me the truth."

Tom and Kate arrived right on time. Charles and Nate started to walk to the trunk of the car. Kate got out and at the same time told Tom, "You get their luggage."

Charles asked her, "I did not know you were coming."

"Hell, if I did not go, you guys would never make it to the airport." By the time Tom was putting the suitcases in the trunk, Kate asked Charles, "You did bring your suit?"

Charles started to answer; even before he could say no, Kate said, "How the hell are you going to impress this lieutenant Steel with golf clothes on when you take her to this fancy restaurant?" Charles did not have a chance to answer. "Go get your suit and the cream-colored shirt, not the white one." Charles told them he would be right back.

As Charles was halfway, Kate yelled, "Do not forget your dress shoes!"

Charles turned around and yelled back, "OK, Mom!" He was back to the car in just a couple of minutes.

Kate told him, "Just lay the suit over the seat between Tom and me."

As Charles was shutting the door, Kate asked Nate, "Do you have everything you need?"

"Yes, and I do not have a reservation at a fancy restaurant."

Charles started to laugh. "Hell, Nate, where you are going, they have Chinese and French restaurants in the same building."

They were at the airport an hour early. They had no problem checking in. Charles told Tom and Kate, "You can leave, and Nate and I will go through the passenger gate and wait for the plane."

Kate told him, "Hell, we will wait. In fact, I am going to that store over there. You guys could go have a drink or two at the bar. Tom, remember, no more than two."

Tom told Kate, "All right, I will be good."

"Not with Charles around. It is impossible."

Kate came back to the bar. Charles noticed she had purchased something. "Kate, what did you buy?"

Tom turned. "What the hell did you buy?"

Kate told Tom, "The money you spend on golf. Do not worry about it."

"All right, just tell us what you found at the store."

"I found me a slick outfit and the grandchildren a few trinkets that I thought they might like. If you do not like it, too bad."

Charles told Kate, "I know Tom is real pleased with your purchases." Then he started to laugh.

By this time, they could see that their plane had arrived. Charles told Tom and Kate, "Thanks for taking us."

Kate said, "We are very happy to help." Nate thanked them too.

Tom told them, "Good luck getting through the metal detector."

Charles told him, "Why did you have to say that?"

Nate asked, "What is the joke?"

Tom said, "Just stand back and watch."

Charles went first through the detector. Right off the bat, all sorts of alarms went off. He took out all his change. Tom started to laugh. Kate asked, "What's so funny?"

"Just watch Charles."

Charles walked through it again. The alarms still went off. This time, he had something in his billfold. Charles put his billfold in the box. He told the guard, "I have a lot of money in there. Do not lose it." Charles walked through it again. This time, he had a dime in his handkerchief in his back pocket. The next time, he made it through.

Kate asked Tom, "Why does Charles bring so much change?"

"Remember, a few years ago, I brought him to the airport?"

"Yes, what happened?"

"Hell, it took Charles thirty minutes to get through that machine. In fact, the guard was getting mad and told Charles to shut up or miss the plane."

Kate then watched Charles take off his shoes. She could tell Charles was getting upset. He told the guard, "Hell, I know you guys are doing your job. But next time, I am not going to wash my feet and make you guys smell them." Finally, Charles was OK to go.

When Nate went through, no alarms; the guard never searched his shoes but just told Nate, "Have a good flight." Charles was shaking his head; he could not believe it. Then they both turned around and waved goodbye to Tom and Kate.

When Charles and Nate were finally out of sight, Kate told Tom, "Go get Charles's clubs." Tom went out to the car. Lucky for him, he parked at the two-hour parking. He only had to go a few yards. Tom came back with the clubs.

Kate told him, "Now we have to get to the counter. It will be closed." She was at the airline booth. "Put the clubs in the luggage place."

The attendant asked, "What can I do for you?" Kate told her she made arrangements to fly the clubs to Newark. She gave her some numbers and some identification.

The attendant told Kate, "You just made it. These clubs will go to Saint Louis on this plane. We had a little delay."

Kate asked, "Are you sure they will be in Newark at the Plaza Hotel by Thursday morning?"

"With the price you paid, they will be there tomorrow afternoon with no problem." Kate thanked her, and then they left.

Even before they were in the car, Tom asked, "How much did that cost?"

"Well, it was almost half a ticket price."

"Hell, Kate, you did good. Charles will be surprised."

"I just hope he does not stay any longer in Manchester."

"Hell, Charles assured me he will do just as you asked."

Charles and Nate made it to Saint Louis with no problem. They had time to go to the bar and had two drinks together. Charles asked Nate, "When are you going to tell your company you quit your job?"

"I will tell them when I am in Kansas City."

"Hell, I thought you should have done it a few days ago."

Nate told Charles, "Yes, I should have. I just did not know how to go about it."

"I hope you have done it before you get back."

"I will have it done."

"Well, good luck, and be careful."

"Same with you."

Charles walked with Nate and watched his plane take off. Then Charles went to his plane and checked in. He was on board in no time. Charles had a window seat, just as he asked Kate to get. He always liked to just make sure the plane was in the sky. Charles was getting situated very comfortably. He sat back and was thinking about what was happening at Newark since Jake's funeral.

A few days earlier at Newark, Mr. Martin was entering their computer department. He had his best computer personnel looking at the disk they took from Charles's house. Mr. Martin asked, "Well, let's see what is on the disk."

His computer specialist told him, "We have to check for viruses."

"Hell, they copy it off his computer. What is the problem?"

"Well, one thing we cannot believe is he still uses floppy disks. Hell, they quit making them years ago. Who knew he still uses them?"

Mr. Martin told them, "Just hurry up."

The commuter specialist said, "We have to find some old equipment that still have floppy disk. We have one in our old equipment room."

"Well, do it, damn it." In a few minutes, they were ready.

The disk was loaded up and running. The information was coming on the screen. At the same time, they were making a copy of the disk on the company's main computer. Just as it hit the last sentence on the page, the computer person just yelled, "Oh shit, stop it!"

Mr. Martin asked, "What is wrong?"

"Hell, I do not know for sure, but look, it is fading away. The damn thing is not erasing. It is moving into other files. Hell, we have to get out now." By the time he hit the Escape key, it was too late.

The computer person was running all over, shutting down computers. Mr. Martin asked in a worried voice, "What are you doing?"

"That disk has a virus in it, a virus I have never seen. Hell, our virus screen did not pick it up until it was too late. I do not know how he did that, but he had to give this virus on his on computer."

Then another person, out of the blue, said, "Just maybe he has a disk to clean it up. So after we spread the virus to his, he went back and cleaned his."

Mr. Martin said, "Well, what about the information? Can you save it?"

They looked at Mr. Martin. "No, we cannot."

Then one person told them, "I remember one or two things on the first page. It had Secretary of State John Douglas Jr.'s name on one of the lines." Another person told Mr. Martin he had seen *Johnson v. Tran Oil* and *Baker v. Middle Oil.*

Mr. Martin was really pissed off. "You mean to tell me this Mr. Appel let us break in his house and take a disk to give us some information so he could try to give us this virus?"

The computer person told Mr. Martin, "Yes, it seems that way."

Mr. Martin asked, "Why did you not print it out?"

"We did not think we had enough time."

Mr. Martin went out of the room. "You people better get this fixed. Why has not Nate called me yet? I am going to kill that son of a bitch if he does not call." He went back to his office. He could not believe what was happening. He told his people, "I want to know everything about this Mr. Charles Appel. I want to know every step he makes, especially when he comes back to Newark. You tell all our people to keep in touch with us if this Mr. Appel's name comes up anywhere anytime."

A few days went by, and Mr. Martin's computer team did keep the virus from destroying all their computers. They did, however, had severe problems. The computer specialist told him, "If we could have the disk that can clean the virus, there would be no problem in fixing the computers."

Mr. Martin's phone was ringing after they discussed the computer situation. He looked at the phone. No one used that phone unless they gave that number to them. Mr. Martin answered it. Right off the bat, he asked, "Who the hell are you?"

"I am the manager at the Newark Plaza Hotel. Your people told me to call this number if Charles Appel's name comes up for reservations."

"You did good. I will make it worth your while."

The manager explained about the reservation for Wednesday through Saturday night. "He will be checking out by eleven thirty, Sunday."

Mr. Martin asked, "What else do you have?"

"I need to get a tee time for him Thursday morning at around ten thirty."

"What golf course?"

"This woman made the reservations. As a surprise, she is sending his clubs in advance. She did not ask for a specific course, just to make sure he gets his clubs." Mr. Martin asked for his name. "My name is Henry Jacob."

"Henry, I will call you right back. I will have the tee time set up for you to give to Mr. Appel." Henry gave him his number at the hotel.

Mr. Martin started to dial; he told his aide, "Mr. Appel is coming here. I am getting him a tee time for Thursday at the club."

After he dialed, a voice answered the phone. "Newark Golf Club." Mr. Martin asked for the Pro Shop. The voice answered, "Pro Shop at the Newark Golf Club. Ben is at your service."

"This is Mr. Martin. I need a tee time for four on Thursday morning at around ten thirty."

"We are booked up until twelve thirty."

Mr. Martin was getting upset. He asked Ben, "I need this tee time. Who is the foursome at the ten-thirty-two tee time?"

"It is the Nelson group."

Mr. Martin asked, "Is Thomas out there somewhere today?"

"Yes, he is on number 15 or so."

"You have Mr. Nelson. Call me the second he is in the clubhouse." Ben asked for the number. "Hell, he has the number." Then he hung up.

Mr. Martin told his assistant, "You get a hold of Paul and Allen. Tell them they are playing golf Thursday at the club. We are going to give Mr. Appel a golf lesson he will never forget."

The phone rang shortly afterward. Mr. Martin answered the phone. "What is so important you call me at the club?"

Mr. Martin thanked Thomas for calling back so fast. "I need to use your tee time Thursday morning. I have a guest coming to town that wants to play golf."

"Who is playing?"

"I thought you, Paul, and Allen, plus my guest."

Thomas asked, "Is this guest of yours that good?"

"Hell, I do not know. I just want you guys to beat him. If this Mr. Appel wants to play for money, take all of it if you can."

"This sounds like fun. I will call the rest of my foursome and tell them the situation."

Mr. Martin thanked him and then told him, "See you later." He called his personal secretary. "If a Mr. Appel calls here, make an appointment for him Friday morning at around nine thirty or so. Whatever you do, I do not want to speak to him. Tell him I am out of town or cannot be disturbed. Just make sure I do not talk to him."

She told him, "Yes, Mr. Martin, I will do that."

Mr. Martin was talking to his aides. They were deciding what was on Mr. Appel's mind. Mr. Martin said, "I just wish that damn Nate would report in."

The phone rang again. Mr. Martin answered it. "Who is this calling?"

"I am Henry Jacob."

"I was going to call you. We have a tee time for Mr. Appel. Tell him he has a ten-thirty-two tee time at the Newark Country Club."

Mr. Jacob told him, "All right, I have that written down."

Mr. Martin then asked, "Why did you call?"

"I do not know if this is important or not. This woman called and made a reservation for the restaurant Thursday night for Mr. Appel. We told her we could not give her that reservation at that time. Well, she was very insistent. We finally gave her one, but it cost her plenty."

"Well, what is the big deal?"

"The reservation is for two. She told us Mr. Appel will have a friend meet him at the hotel. I thought you might want to know this."

Mr. Martin thanked him. "I will make sure you are treated very good." He hung up the phone and told them, "I want to find out who the hell he is having dinner with. Try to check it out. We have to stay on top of this Mr. Appel."

"Why not call Nate's company to see if he got a hold of them?"

"Surely, they would have called me. I have to leave for Washington for a few days. Keep me in touch with anything that you find out."

Mr. Martin spent the next few days in Washington. He talked to his people there. He told them to check out Mr. Appel on their end. "I want to know all his finances, income. I want to know when he eats, what he eats, even when and how he takes a sip." Mr. Martin was not very happy. He spent all his resources, and nothing came up on Mr. Appel that was out of the ordinary.

When Mr. Martin was back at Newark on early Tuesday morning, nothing had improved on the computers. The computer specialist still was at the same place where he left him. His secretary told him, "Mr. Appel is coming Friday morning at nine thirty."

"Good."

Then on Tuesday late afternoon, his private phone rang. He answered it. He thought it might be from Washington about Mr. Appel. Instead, it was Nate. Mr. Martin asked, "Why the hell have you not called before now?"

"I tried a few times, but Mr. Appel never sleeps. I did not want to take any chances. How bad are your computers?"

"You know about that?"

"Yes, Mr. Appel set up a virus he had gotten years ago from a computer wizard from Chicago. Did the virus hurt us very bad?"

"Yes, we still have not fixed it yet."

"Do not worry, Mr. Appel is bringing you the disk that will kill the virus."

"I have an appointment with him Friday at nine thirty."

Nate told him he already knew that. "Be careful. He has a date Thursday night."

Mr. Martin said, "Yes, we know about the reservation. Who is his date?"

"You will not believe this. It is Lieutenant Steel, who is on the case of his son's murder."

"Hell, we got her off the case. She was asking too many questions. We have one of our men on the case. It will never get solved."

Nate told Mr. Martin, "Do not underestimate Mr. Appel. This man has no enemies in his town. He has kids watching his house. He has all the businesses looking for strangers. He has the police checking out any strange car's license plate. Hell, he has the whole town helping him in anything he wants. Get this—the tapes, he has them, all right. He keeps them in the damn bank. He even has a friend working on the tapes as we speak."

"We have to get those tapes. We have to find the others as fast as we can."

"On that matter, I have a problem."

"What is it?"

"I am flying to Kansas City to check on Joseph. I cannot just go anywhere in Kansas City to ask questions."

Mr. Martin asked him, "Where are you staying?"

"I am staying at the Crown Center."

"Good, you can enjoy all the bars and restaurants without leaving the hotel. So when you arrive at the Center, call Danley and Wilson's law office. Tell them to get all the information you need. Do not leave the hotel."

"You got it." Nate then asked, "Is it wise to use them again?"

"Well, we do not have Kansas City all the way yet, but Danley knows all our people. We do not have that much choice. Besides, we do have most of the police department."

Nate asked in a different voice, "On that matter, is that lieutenant Wilson still on the case?"

"Yes, he is. That is why I do not want you to leave the hotel."

"When the hell can we get rid of him?"

"Well, not yet. Do not worry, if he gets too close, we have other resources to handle him. Just do what I told you to do. Everything will work out."

Nate assured him he would. "Two more things. The first one is I have to quit my job to live with Mr. Appel."

"Hell, that is good news. He must trust you."

"The other thing is he is going to Manchester, New Hampshire, to see the parents of his son's girlfriend. You might want to check that out." Just as Nate was ready to hang up, he remembered something. "Shit, I forgot to tell you the best. Mr. Appel is rich. That damn Jake had been playing the stock Carloet. Hell, he is worth two million. Mr. Appel does not trust no one. He already converted one million in cash through several banks. Like I said, do not take Mr. Appel for granted. This guy is smart and crazy. He wants to find out all about us and his son's killers."

Mr. Martin told Nate, "Just keep up the good work. When we know the rest of the players, we will handle Mr. Appel."

Nate asked, "What about the tapes?"

"Hell, if we have to, we will rob the damn bank. Just stay loose. We will get all the information you need, and then go back to Coal City and continue to keep the good relationship with Mr. Appel."

"Should I call you back before I leave Kansas City?"

"No. Danley or Wilson will fill me in. Just try to give us better warning on Mr. Appel if he screws with us."

Nate told Mr. Martin, "I will try, but it is hard to be alone in that damn town."

The second they hung up, Mr. Martin called Danley and Wilson's law office. He told them to have all the information on Joseph's murder case ready by tomorrow. "Go to the Crown Center, and give it to Nate. Whatever Nate needs, you make sure he has the information."

Danley asked, "Is it wise to have Nate back here?"

"We have no choice. Just do it. And make sure you make a list of the ones you know we cannot trust, like that lieutenant Wilson. Make sure Nate goes over the information with you so he is very familiar with it. I am beginning not to trust Mr. Appel. He has to believe Nate." Danley assured him it would be done.

Mr. Martin hung up the phone. He told his people to check out the parents of Jake's girlfriend. "Do not go to Manchester. Just find out what you can through our resources. This should be good enough for now. We will just have to wait and see what Mr. Appel does when he arrives here."

Charles arrived at Manchester, New Hampshire. At the airport, he went directly to the luggage pickup. The line was not very long; this took only a few minutes. As he picked up his suitcase, an airport employee showed, and Charles asked him, "Where is your bar?"

The employee asked with a smile, "Flying does make you want you to drink?"

Charles replied with a smile, "Yes, it does. Just tell me where the bar is." The man told him. Charles gave him a dollar for the answer.

Charles was surprised there were very few people there. He walked right to the bar, which was not very big. He asked the bartender if he could use the phone. The bartender told him, "No, we do not allow customers to use the phone. The public phone is outside the door on your left."

"Samuel told me it'll be all right."

The bartender asked, "Are you Charles Appel from Coal City?" Charles told him yes. "Well, there has been a change in plans. Samuel is waiting for you in the last booth by the wall. Hell, I am Russell, Samuel's friend. He told me you would be here. We did not know who to look for."

Russell took Charles to the booth where Samuel was sitting. Samuel stood up and reached out his hand. Immediately, Charles reached for it. With the strong grip they both had, Charles knew this man meant business.

Samuel thanked Russell for taking Charles to the booth. Russell left. Charles sat down. Samuel asked if he was hungry. Charles told him, "Well, I guess I could eat a hamburger or something."

Samuel raised his hand, and the waitress came at once. Even if she was busy, it looked as if she dropped everything to come to their table. Charles and Samuel ordered their sandwiches. Samuel explained that Janace would not be very happy to cook food at this time of night. "This is why I decided to meet you here. You and I can have a few beers and get to know each other before my wife has a million questions to ask, like why my daughter Amanda?"

Charles looked at Samuel right in the eye. "I do not have all the answers, but I will tell you this—Jake and his friends either through luck or smartness found out information that someone or some company or maybe our government does not want nobody to find out. I believe this is why Jake and Amanda were murdered."

Samuel looked Charles right in the eye. "I will tell you this—I have friends that will be glad to help."

Charles looked at Samuel. "You really mean if I let you help, then you will help us? If this happens, what will your wife say?"

"Janace and I already made that decision since you called. We both want justice done no matter what."

Samuel then ordered another round of drinks. When the other beer showed up. Charles started to pay. The waitress told Charles, "Forget it. This is on Samuel's tab."

Samuel looked at Charles. "You do not think I am going to let a guest of mine pay for anything, do you?"

Charles thanked him. "I do not know what you do for a living. What I am finding out might be very dangerous." Samuel started to laugh. Charles, with a bewildered look, asked, "What is so funny?"

"Well, what I did in the past was working for the CIA."

"You mean the real CIA?"

"Yes, in fact, so did Russell and a few others that live around here. The company wanted younger men, so they gave us an early retirement."

Charles asked, "What did you do?"

Samuel said in a smart voice, "If I tell you—"

"I know, you have to kill me."

Samuel started to laugh. "That was an old one." He then explained he was on surveillance mostly in the last few years. Charles was amazed. Samuel asked, "Could this be of some help?"

Charles thought a moment. "Well, with what little I know, yes, this could be real big help."

Samuel told Charles, "Well, Russell and I will be glad to. We already have our equipment ready."

"I will tell everything. I just do not know if you want Janace to know everything."

"Yes, we lived all these years being up front with each other. That is the way it will be."

"Well, I will tell both of you together."

"Good, we will talk tomorrow when we are all more awake."

"Good. Maybe we should go to your house."

"Hell, we can have another beer or two."

Samuel and Charles had a few more beers, and then they went to Samuel's house. The house was big but not huge. It had four bedrooms, a basement, a living room, and a large kitchen. As they walked in from the garage, Janace was at the side door. Samuel introduced her to Charles. Janace was just as good looking as Amanda. Charles told her, "I know where Amanda got her looks from." Janace thanked him.

Samuel told Janace, "Charles is going to tell us everything tomorrow morning over lunch."

"No, he will tell us, say, during a big brunch. Food will be ready at ten thirty."

"That is fine. Can I take Charles to the basement before we go to bed?"

"Well, do I have a choice?"

Samuel told Charles, "Follow me. You have to see this."

As he turned on the light going down the steps, Charles could not believe what he had seen. The first thing was the light on a doorbell. "You have the same system as Amanda and Jake." Jake set it up at his house.

When Charles was to the floor, Samuel turned on the ceiling light. The train engine was already running.

Samuel told Charles, "I have it turned on immediately when I turn the upstairs light on."

"Jake told me about your train engines. I really did not believe Jake when he told me how big your layout is." Charles still had his eye on all the buildings and train track. "This had to take you years to build."

Samuel turned on some switches. "Watch this." The train went around a small curve, and then when it passed a certain point, all the lights went off except the ones on the layout. This was the best night scene Charles had ever seen. He was amazed at all the detail of the bushes and buildings.

When the train moved forward a few feet, the lights were getting dimmer on the set. The ceiling lights were getting brighter like it was daylight. Finally, all the lights were off on the layout. The room lights were all like they were when they first went down the basement.

Samuel showed Charles a few engines that Jake had given him. Charles told him, "This is what Jake asked me a few years ago. He handed me this train book and asked, 'What engine would be the best for the birthday of Amanda's father?' I picked out this one and one or two more."

Samuel went to a shelf. "Are these the ones?"

Charles looked at them. "Yes, they sure are."

"These mean so much to me not just because Jake gave them to me. These two are hard to find and very expensive."

"I did not know the price. The book said 'call for a price.'"

"You might have shit if you knew how much."

"Hell, they could not have been over a hundred apiece."

Samuel laughed. "What if I told you they cost at least three thousand apiece?"

"Hell, I probably told Jake he was crazy."

"That is what I told him. Amanda told me to keep quiet and take them. Jake had the money. So I took them with great pride."

Charles, while he was looking at the setup, noticed the trees did not look very real. Samuel noticed Charles was looking at something. He asked, "What is wrong? I can tell you noticed something."

Charles looked at him. "You know, I used to have a train set."

"Jake told me that." Samuel went on to say, "You were real good at landscaping."

Charles smiled. "Well, I was not that good. I was just stubborn until it looked real."

Samuel asked, "All right, tell me, how can you help my set?"

"Well, your trees are not quite right. Some look too fake. Some are too big in some areas and not big enough in others. I tell you what, I have several trees. I will mail them to you."

Samuel looked at Charles and then his trees. "You are right. How do you make yours?"

"Well, I never bought a tree. I go to a friend's house who has a privet hedge. I take small twigs at different lengths. I then spray glue on them and sprinkle this flaky green stuff on the twigs. After they are dried, you just shake the twigs. What stays on is your tree. Do not worry, I have torn down my set years ago. I have probably a few hundred trees in a box. I will be glad to give them to you."

While Samuel was showing Charles the wiring and all the special switches, Charles asked Samuel about the doorbell light. Samuel told him, "Yes, that was my idea. Jake noticed that one time he was down here. I noticed the light was red. I asked Janace who was down the basement. Jake asked, 'How did you know?' I told him about the doorbell. Jake asked if I could make him eighteen to twenty. So I made him twenty."

Charles told him, "Well, I know where three are."

"Well, I know Jake had one, and Amanda had one."

"Jake gave me one. I know where at least ten to fourteen are. Or should I say I wish I knew where the rest are." Charles asked Samuel, "At the airport bar, you said you and your friends. How many are we talking about?"

"Besides me and Russell, I have three more."

"Suppose I need some phones tapped or some surveillance cameras or, say, I want a bank to be real secure, could you and your friends do this?"

"We can do whatever you need. If we need to, we can even kill a target for you and not get caught. Please do not let Janace know that."

Charles asked, "What would this cost?"

"Well, I am not rich, but we could probably come up with the money. A good surveillance system and alarm system is around fifteen to twenty thousand. It just depends on the location."

Charles started to laugh and then quit laughing. Out of the blue, he asked, "Did anyone from Newark came to Amanda's funeral and gave, say, a hundred thousand dollars to you?"

"No, but a stranger did give us fifty thousand because Amanda was Jake's girlfriend."

Charles asked, "His name was not John Martin, was it?"

"It sure was."

"Did anything strange happen to your house that same day?"

Samuel asked, "How did you know that?"

"Well, was your doorbell light red that day?"

"Yes, both of them. I have one in the computer room too."

"What about your surveillance? Was it working?"

Samuel told Charles, "Yes, but that day, we were coming in and out. We turned it off."

"Do you think some stranger could come in and drop flowers or food to your house and check out your computer?"

Samuel said in a shaking voice, "If they were good, they could have done that."

"This is what happened at my house. This Mr. John Martin and his friends made me a visit. He gave me a hundred thousand." Charles asked, "Did you or Janace know Jake saved over a million dollars?"

Samuel looked at Charles and almost fell over. "You mean your Jake has over a million?"

"Well, yes. I did not know it until after his funeral."

"Hell, I did not know it. In fact, Jake told me he just makes seventy thousand or so. Hell, he never drove big or expensive cars."

"You got that right. Talking about cars, did you help Jake put his computer in his car?"

"I do not know anything about that." Then Samuel said, "Wait a minute, Jake asked me if it was possible to run a computer to phone from the car. I told him, 'Sure. You need a computer person to do it for you.'"

Charles told Samuel, "Well, he found one. While you are sleeping or wondering, just think about other situations you might remember. Tomorrow I will tell both of you all I know. Just maybe, with Janace's permission, you can be a big help to me."

Samuel went to the refrigerator and took out two beers. He handed Charles one; while he was opening his, he told Charles to plan on that. "I am going to bed after this beer. You can stay down here and help yourself to the train or anything you want. I will leave your bedroom light on so you will find the room. You will not miss the bathroom, just the next door down."

"I will go with you. It is getting late. I need a good night's sleep." So they finished their beer.

Charles went up the steps first, and Samuel followed. When they were standing on the main floor, Samuel turned off the lights to the basement. He told Charles, "Thanks for coming. We appreciate this visit very much."

"I believe I am the one who is glad. I just hope Janace is not putting herself out."

Samuel laughed. "Do not worry about that. Just make sure you are not late. Janace does mean ten thirty, not ten thirty-five."

Charles laughed. "I will be up and ready in plenty of time."

Samuel showed Charles to his room and the door to their second bathroom. He then walked down the hall to their bedroom. Charles could hear Janace talking to Samuel. He could not make out the words.

Charles went to the bedroom. He could tell Janace kept good care of the furniture and the house. There was not one speck of dust in the room. He did notice that some pictures on the wall were missing because the ring on the wall. Charles wondered for a few seconds, *What were the pictures?*

There was a note on top of the bed; it said, "I put some extra towels in the bathroom. Help yourself—Janace." While Charles was in bed, he wondered how much he should tell them about Amanda and the way she died. He started crying while he was trying to fall asleep.

Charles woke up early; he knew he would. The clock said six ten. Charles went to the bathroom and took his shower. He was dressed and ready to go by six forty-five. He could not tell if Samuel was up yet. Charles went down the basement and turned on the light. He could still not believe how the train worked, but he played with it.

Charles went to the refrigerator; there was the beer. He thought about it, and then he noticed a Coke. He told himself he better behave and reached for the Coke. While the train was going around, he was wondering what Nate was up to. Then he said out loud, "I wonder if I can trust him."

Just as he said that, Charles did not realize Samuel was down the steps. Samuel asked, "You do trust us?"

Charles said in a very surprised way, "No, I am very sorry. I was thinking out loud about Nate. I sent him to Kansas City to check on Joseph. I believe he was murdered. I just, in some way, think he is my friend yet maybe my enemy."

"In my experience, first instinct is what I go by. I trust you with my life. I can tell that."

Charles replied with his Coke in his hand, "I know I can trust you." He raised it and took a drink.

Samuel went to the refrigerator and reached for a beer. He handed it to Charles. "Jake told us you like Coke in the morning with company, but at your home, you have a beer since his mom died. So here, this is home from home." Charles took the beer. Samuel told him, "Well, this is my house. It is just too early for me. I already had three cups of coffee."

Charles asked, "What time did you get up?"

"I get up at around five thirty every day, go to the coffee shop to have a cup of coffee or two, and then come home. You were not up yet, so I did not wake you."

"Hell, if I knew that, I would have been glad to go with you."

"Hell, I will take you next time." Charles told him he would not forget that.

Samuel said in a serious note, "You do trust us, don't you, Charles?"

"Yes, Samuel. In fact, I am concerned with Janace."

"In what way?"

"Well, my friend Tom and I found Amanda dead. I do not know how to hide what we have seen from Janace or just tell you or what."

Samuel said in a hurried voice, "You tell me in detail right now. I will tell Janace after you leave."

Charles thought for a second. "OK, here it goes."

Samuel went back to the refrigerator; he grabbed two beers this time. Then he told Charles, "Come over here at the table. Now tell me."

Charles sat down and opened the other beer. "The night before I called Amanda, she gave the address, and we set up a time the next morning. Just like your house, the light was red. I told Tom something is wrong. The door was ajar. We walked in. The apartment was a mess. You could tell someone was looking for something. I walked in Amanda's bedroom. There she was, tied to her bed, all bruised up. You could tell they beat her."

Samuel started to cry. "We know they raped her."

Charles also started to cry. "This is what I do not want to talk about in front of your wife." Samuel thanked him for telling him. "Well, that is not all. Before the police came, I waked in her computer room. I could tell they were looking for something. I believe if she did not know Jake, she would still be alive today. I hope you can forgive us."

Samuel looked at Charles. "Do not blame Jake or yourself. Amanda had never been so happy meeting Jake. I know Amanda told Jake to proceed with his idea. It is important to both of us. I just wish they told me what they were up to."

Charles grabbed his beer. "I wish I knew what they were up to. I tell you this—I need your and Janace's help, but without it, I will find out the truth."

Samuel looked at Charles's eyes. "After you tell Janace and me what you know, we will be right with you."

By this time, Janace yelled down the steps, "I want both of you up here! It is my turn to talk to Charles!"

Samuel finished his beer, and Charles already had his done. Samuel yelled up the steps, "We will be there in a minute!"

On the way up, Samuel told Charles, "Do not tell Janace how you found Amanda's body unless she presses you."

"Do not worry."

Charles never paid much attention to the kitchen when he first arrived at the Tulmans'. Their kitchen was of a nice size. The kitchen table was at least five feet from anything. You did not have to worry about bumping into cabinets or the refrigerator. Janace had real good solid cabinets. Charles did notice again that a few pictures were missing on the wall. Besides that, the kitchen was in immaculate shape.

Janace had the plates on the table. She showed Charles where his plate was. To save time, Janace had the food on the cabinets, counter, and stove. Charles could not believe all the food. She had eggs over easy, bacon, hash browns, biscuits and gravy, sausage links, pancakes, and all sorts of toasts—white and brown. Janace even had Heinz ketchup.

After Charles loaded up his plate, he sat down waiting for Samuel and Janace to do the same. Samuel told him, "We do pray at each meal at our house."

"That is fine. So do I." Janace smiled after Charles told them that. Samuel gave his prayer. He started to eat, so Charles did not waste any time. After a few bites, Charles looked at Janace and told her, "You know, if I did not know better, I bet you called Kate and asked what I liked, or Kate called you."

Janace said with a smile, "Well, I was wondering what to cook for you, so let's just say I had some help. Your friends are right, you know."

Charles asked in a different tone of voice, "What about?"

"You should have more of a different eating pattern."

Charles replied with a smile, "You are right. I am just too picky to change."

Samuel told him, "Well, at our house, I love this meal. So if Janace cooks for us like this all the time, you just come by anytime."

Janace told Samuel, "Well, you are not starving."

Samuel looked at his stomach. "Well, I just I could probably lose a few pounds."

Charles said, "Hell, you just look like you're twenty pounds over. That's not that bad." Then he realized he used the "hell" word. Charles immediately apologized.

Janace told him, "Well, in this kitchen, it is not the worst word ever said."

Janace was done with her plate. She took some dishes to the sink. On the way back, she opened the refrigerator and had a bottle of wine and two beers. She told Samuel, "Get some glasses while I finish clearing the table."

Charles started to help. Janace told him in a stronger voice, "You just sit down. We will do this. You start thinking on what you are going to tell us. I have to get this done, even though I already know I will be very sad."

Charles did not know what to say. He drank some of his beer. As Janace was sitting down, she told Samuel, "Bring some more beer for you and Charles." Then she took a big swallow of wine and asked Samuel to pour her some more. Samuel did exactly what he was told. Samuel and Charles both knew, at this point, Janace controlled this gathering.

Janace looked right at Charles. "You have the floor. Just start wherever you want. Samuel and I might butt in to ask a question or two, if you do not mind."

"You can ask me anything." Charles told them, "Well, to me, I am going to tell all of you what I know. Just like you, the police got a hold of me late at night and told me about Jake's murder. I went to Newark the next day. I have seen Jake's body." Charles started to cry. "I could not believe how they beat him up."

He went on. "We went to his house, you know. It was funny in a way. I have only been in that house three times—once when Jake moved in; another time on his birthday, where I met Amanda; and this to see if anything I could tell was missing. The only good thing about the trip is I met this lieutenant, Ciara Steel, whom I sort of have a date with when I arrive at Newark."

Janace's eyes lit up, but she did not interrupt yet. Charles told them, "Well, anyway, I did not tell the police, but I could tell they were searching the computer room a lot. That is when it hit me. Just maybe they were looking for the disk."

Janace asked, "What disk?"

"I will get to that in just a minute. I asked the police if they had Amanda's number since she found Jake's body. Amanda was upset. They told me, 'Here is her number. Call her tonight. She wants to see you tomorrow morning or something like that.' So Tom and I ate supper and had a few beers. I called Amanda. We were to be at her apartment. I forgot what time, around nine thirty or so. I had to talk to her about the computer. I thought she could answer my questions without the police.

"When Tom and I got there, I noticed the doorbell, which was just like Jake's and mine. The red light was on, and the door was ajar. Tom did not like this, but we went in. This is where we found Amanda has been murdered."

Janace started to cry. Samuel was sitting beside her, holding her hand. Charles asked, "You just tell me if you want me to continue."

Janace said in a shaking voice, "You can continue."

"I told Tom to use the phone to call the police. I went in the back room to see if Amanda had a computer. There it was. Tom told me I should wait. I told Tom, 'I have to do this. Do not tell the police nothing. I will explain on the plane.' I only noticed the same at Jake's house. They were looking for information that I knew I had.

"When the police arrived, we stayed around. Then finally, Lieutenant Steel took us back to our hotel and then to the airport. I told her I will be back after the funeral. She told me to be ready to answer some questions. I told her likewise. At the airport is where she gave me your address, so I thought after we buried our children, I better come here and talk to both of you."

Janace was crying and thanked Charles. Out of the blue, she asked, "Did they hurt Amanda before she was killed?"

He looked at Samuel. Janace said, "You son of a bitch, you told Samuel."

Charles told her, "Yes. I did not know how to handle it, so I told Samuel to tell you in his own way after I left."

"Well, one of you tell me right now." Then she took a big swallow of wine. Charles did not realize it, but Samuel already had more beer on the table.

Samuel started to cry. "Amanda was beaten up and raped."

Janace still was crying; she just cried harder. She looked up at Charles. "What is your plan now?"

Charles took a few more swallows of beer. "Well since Jake's funeral, I found out Jake left me around two million dollars. I am going to spend all of it to find out what is going on and who killed our kids."

Janace looked at Samuel and then at Charles. "Well, we want to help too."

Samuel told Janace he told Charles what he did in the past. "I told Charles if you will let me, I know I can help."

Janace looked at Samuel. "I know this will very dangerous to all of us. They took our only children. They took part of our lives. Anyway, they might as well try to take the rest of it."

Samuel took his beer and told Charles, "Here's to war."

Charles told them, "This could be to our death."

Janace filled her glass of wine. "Here's to death. Let's hope it is the murderer's death, not ours.

Charles thanked them with a smile. "I do need your help. Here's to death."

After a few more beers, the three just had small talk. It was time for Charles to leave. Janace told Samuel, "Let's take Charles back to the airport."

Charles was already packed. As he and Samuel were walking out, Janace told them, "You are leaving me."

On the way to the airport, Janace wrote down Charles's address and phone numbers. She already had Tom and Kate's. She then asked, "All right, you guys, what is your game plan? I am not stupid."

Samuel told her, "In a few days, I and Russell are going to Coal City to secure the bank. Charles has to get the OK from the banker. Then we will set up some surveillance for Charles's house. We will come back to our house and wait till Charles needs more help."

Janace told them, "Well, I am coming too." Samuel told her no. "I am going to make this trip. Your friends can make our house safer while we are gone."

Charles told them, "That makes sense. I will give you the money when you arrive in Coal City."

Samuel looked at Janace. "We have not left our house since Amanda's murder. Maybe it is time. You let us know."

Charles told them, "I will call you after I set it all up." Samuel and Janace agreed.

When they arrived at the airport, Charles's plane was there. He still had an hour before takeoff. The three went to the bar. Russell was just getting there. Samuel told him, "It is on."

Russell brought over the drinks. In a hurried voice, he asked, "What do you want from me?"

Samuel told him, "Get the guys and buy our surveillance equipment for a bank and for our house. Make sure they cannot trace it, and do not trust nobody from this day on. I will talk to you later tonight."

Russell reached over for Charles's hand. "Thanks for helping. We will get the son of a bitch." Charles thanked him.

Samuel could tell Charles was uneasy. "Believe me, we can trust him. In fact, on this end, it will be just you and me. My team will not do nothing until you tell us what you need. I have a hunch you will have a long and hard list."

"I will keep you all busy." Charles stood up shook Samuel's hand, gave Janace a hug, told her, "Thanks, and I am sorry."

"No thank you for being honest and wanting the truth."

Charles told them, "I will get in touch in a few days." He turned around to Janace. "By the way, when you put the pictures back of Jake and Amanda, make me some copies, please."

Janace asked, "How did you know?"

"I just noticed the empty spots on the wall."

"I sure will." Then Charles went to his plane.

CHAPTER 5

Starting the War

As Charles was getting in the plane, he did not realize how long he had been with Janace and Samuel. Charles knew he did not answer all the questions Janace had. Then he thought Samuel was telling her as he did.

As the plane was taking off, he decided to just sit back and try to come up with the right plan for Ciara. Then he thought, *Hell, just hope for the best.* He had not spent time with a woman for a long time. He then started to grin. He lived with his wife, Rose, for all those years and still never figured her out. Charles decided he would spend the time thinking on Mr. Martin. This could be life-and-death to someone.

Charles lay back and started to think. He could not get Ciara out of his mind. He wondered what Ciara found out about Amanda and Jake. Should he tell her the truth? Maybe she knew the truth and wanted to see if Charles would tell her. Then he wondered what Nate had been up to, if he was with him or not.

Charles just started to fall asleep when the pilot came on. "Please fasten your safety belts." He noticed he never unfastened his since takeoff. Charles was very nervous on this trip. *Let's just see what happens.*

After the plane landed, Charles started for his luggage. He noticed this tall guy was going in the same direction, so he asked the man, "Where is the luggage area?"

The stranger he asked just gave him a dumb look, like, *You cannot read?* Then he told him, "Follow me." The guy did not say a word. Charles could not stand for that. By the time they got to the luggage, Charles knew the stranger's first name was Ralph. Ralph knew Charles's name and even knew he was from Coal City, Illinois.

Charles found his luggage; he noticed Ralph was not in sight. He started to laugh. He was probably the only idiot who talked to a stranger. He decided he would try not to. For him, though, he knew that was not his character.

Kate told him the hotel had a van or transportation for him. "Just go to the nearest desk, and ask where the ride to the Newark Plaza is." While Charles was walking to the desk, he noticed a sign through the glass door that said "Newark Plaza." The arrow pointed to the right. Charles walked through the electric door. He turned right and noticed several hotels had a sign at certain locations. Charles walked a few yards, and there was the stop for his hotel. There was also Ralph standing.

Charles, without a thought, asked, "You going to the Plaza?"

Ralph again did not want to talk. You could tell Charles did not leave much choice. "Yeah, if you are going there, the limo will be here."

Charles told him, "Yes, so I guess we will ride together." He could tell Ralph was not that gung ho about the situation. Charles thought it was funny.

In a short time, the limo pulled up. On the side of the limo, there was a sign that said "Newark Plaza." The driver got out and asked, "Is this all?"

Ralph told him, "I guess me and this guy."

Charles told the driver, "You can call me Charles. The other guy is Ralph."

The driver took their luggage, put it in the trunk, and then opened the door for Ralph and Charles. Just then, as Charles was getting in, he heard a voice. "Wait, I need the ride." Charles could tell the driver did not hear the voice. He thought, though, Ralph should have but did not say anything. Charles told the driver, "Wait, here comes another."

Ralph told the driver to go on. Charles told the driver, "Hey, who is this guy telling you what to do?"

Ralph asked, "Do you know who I am?"

"You are a smart-ass, Ralph, who does not give a shit about others."

The driver could not keep from grinning. Ralph told Charles, "I am Ralph Nugen. I control part of that hotel."

"Well, I am a guest of your hotel, and this person must be too."

By this time, this young girl was at the limo. The driver had no choice but to put her luggage in the trunk and open the door. This nice-looking brunette thanked him. The driver told her, "Do not thank me. Thank Charles over there. He heard you." She looked at Charles and thanked him.

Charles told her, "No problem, and my name is Charles."

"My name is Nancy."

Charles, who usually did not pay that much attention, asked her, "You weren't a stewardess on the flight from Manchester?"

She told him yes. Then she looked at Charles again. "You're the one that slept on the plane." Charles told her yes, and she started to laugh. He asked, "What's so funny?"

"Well, the rest of us could not believe how fast you fell asleep. We have never seen nobody fall asleep on a short flight."

Charles told here, "Well, Nancy, I take short naps, but I do not sleep much."

By this time, the driver was out of the airport, going down the road. Charles was looking out the window. Nancy told him, "It takes thirty minutes to the hotel."

"I have never been to this part of town, or I do not think so."

Ralph was looking at Nancy's legs. While she was talking, her skirt caught part of the seat on the edge. You could see her long legs and her panties. Charles did not really know what to do. Nancy just started to talk to him. Charles thought it was maybe just because he helped her get the ride. He, in a hasty way, asked Nancy, "You mind if I sit beside you? The view from the window is better." Nancy told him no. As Charles moved to the other side, he pulled Nancy's skirt toward her. Ralph did not say anything, and then Nancy figured out what kind of show she was giving.

Without being embarrassed, she asked Charles, "Hey, after we get settled in, what about a drink at the bar?" Charles told her he would be glad to. She looked at her watch. "Say, down at the bar, thirty minutes after we get there." He told her that would be fine.

Charles noticed Ralph turned his head and did not say a word for the rest of the trip. He also knew nothing was coming out of this. Hell, she was probably twenty-five years younger. Then he thought, *Hell, Ciara is probably fifteen to twenty years younger.*

The limo pulled up to the hotel. The driver opened the door for Ralph first, and then he opened the trunk. He came around the other side to open the door for Nancy and Charles. Nancy right away got her things and yelled back, "See you in thirty minutes, Charles!" Charles told her OK.

The driver told Charles, "Boy, it does not take you long."

Charles just smiled. "No, we're just having a few drinks, that is all." He asked the driver, "That Ralph guy, is he really a big shot?"

"Yes, he is part owner of this hotel, plus a few others."

"I guess he did not tip you."

"You are right there. He is too good for that."

Charles told him, "Here, take this twenty. That is for Nancy and me." The driver took the twenty and thanked him. Then he told Charles where to go to get checked in.

By the time it was his turn, he did not see Nancy anywhere. Charles gave his name to the woman who worked on the computer. "Mr. Appel, first of all, here is a message for you. We have your golf clubs in the storage room. We have a tee time for you at nine thirty in the morning." Before Charles could get a word in, this girl told him, "Be down here no later than eight fifteen."

Charles asked in a bewildered voice, "What are you talking about?"

"Your friends from Illinois made the arrangements when they made the reservation."

"Yes. Is there more?"

"Well, Mr. Appel, your suite is already taken care of. Any other expenses you have, we will just add it to your card." Charles told her yes.

The girl had a real nice smile all this time. Charles told her, "You know, for this time of night, you have a good attitude, and it's nice to see a nice smile."

The girl thanked Charles, and then she turned her head. She looked at the bellhop and asked, "Bill, could you take Mr. Appel to his room?"

Bill told her, "Yes, no problem."

As he picked up his bag, Charles asked, "Would it be possible to take my clubs with me so I can practice my putting?"

"No problem." He went behind the desk. He tried to open the door. He asked for Susan to give him the key.

Susan turned around. "Here, catch." Charles could tell they worked well together.

Bill went in the room and came out with the clubs and shoes. When he came back to Charles, he asked, "Sir, are these yours?" Charles could tell right away they were. Bill had no problem carrying them and his luggage.

On the way up the elevator, Bill asked, "What kinds of clubs do you have?"

Charles laughed. "Well, not the best. I made them myself or, should I say, put them together."

Bill looked at Charles. "Well, I have Golfsmith."

Charles laughed. "So do I. It is an old model, Tour Model II."

"Mine are Tour model IV."

"Hell, I have a set of those two." Charles could tell Bill was worried about a tip. *Here is a guy living in a suite and then playing with old clubs.*

As he opened the door, Bill turned on the lights. Charles could not believe the room. It was huge. Hell, it was bigger than his main floor. He had a big bed, a nice bar on the side wall, and a really big TV screen. Charles asked, "Bill, you sure this is my room?"

"Yes, Mr. Appel. Is there anything else you need?"

"Well, I want some ice, and is there any whiskey in that bar?"

Bill showed Charles where the ice was and how to operate the bar. Charles asked if he wanted a drink. Bill told him, "Yes but not while I am on duty."

"Hell, if you catch me in time sometime, I will buy you a drink." Then Charles handed him a twenty.

Bill told him, "Thanks. Good luck on your game."

Charles took a few minutes to unpack. His suit was wrinkled. Charles remembered Kate told him they had clothing service. He made himself a drink. He knew it was late, but he called down the desk. A voice came on. "Yes, Mr. Appel, can I help? This is Susan."

"My suit needed ironing before tomorrow night."

"Well, Mr. Appel, I can have somebody take it now, or you can bring it down with you in the morning."

Charles asked, "Will it be ready in time?"

"No problem, Mr. Appel."

"I make you a deal. I call you Susan. You call me Charles."

Susan said in a nervous voice, "We are not supposed to do that unless you mean it."

"Susan, you call me Charles, and tell Bill to call me Charles too." He started to hang up, and he could hear Susan say, "OK, Charles."

Charles was cleaned up, enough for him to go find the bar. He realized he did not even notice how nice the hotel was at the lobby. Charles came down to the lobby. He was surprised he made it without getting lost as was usual. Susan was standing at the desk. Charles walked up to her. Right when she had seen Charles, she walked up to him. "Can I help you, Charles?"

"Yes. Tell me how to get to the bar, could you, please?" Susan went on the other side of the desk and went right to Charles. Then she explained in detail. Charles thanked her. He started to walk away.

He did not know why, but he turned around. Here was this Ralph giving Susan a hard time. Charles could not help it. He turned around and went right to them. Before Ralph or Susan had seen him, Charles said in a sharp voice, "Is there a problem, Ralph?"

Ralph looked up. "This does not concern you. This is between an employee and myself."

Charles could not stop himself. "I believe Susan is getting in trouble because of me."

By this time, Ralph was getting red in the face. "Well, I overheard Susan calling you Charles. We have a company policy that says nobody calls our guest by their first name unless they tell them to."

"Well, is that what Susan told you?" Ralph, in a weak voice, said yes. Charles then went on. "You have a company policy saying you could call your employees liars?"

"Well, no."

"I did tell Susan to call me Charles, just like I told Bill and probably everyone I meet in your hotel." Charles knew he overstepped his grounds, and then he said, "What the heck, in fact, Ralph, until I leave your hotel, all your employees can call me Charles except you. I gave you your chance. You call me Mr. Appel." Ralph was really mad. He did not know what to say. Charles told both of them to have a nice night and then turned around and went toward the bar.

Charles was smiling a little bit; he was wondering what Ralph was doing. Charles did not turned around; he would ask Susan or Bill later. Charles was noticing how nice the main floor was. It had a bar sunk down in the middle of the room. It was closed at this time of night. Charles had seen a sign that said they served brunch from nine thirty to one thirty during the day.

Charles kept on walking; he could not believe how nice the ceiling was. It had glass fixtures and fancy mirrors everywhere. The drapes around the windows were long and very new looking. Charles noticed everything looked new and expensive. By the time he was paying attention, he walked past the bar by a few feet. As he turned around, he heard a voice. "Charles, here we are." Nancy was coming out of the bar with a glass of wine. Charles did not realize he was walking fast to get to her.

Nancy told him, "Follow me." Charles followed her to the back. There were three more girls and a couple of guys. Nancy introduced everybody with their first names. Then she told them, "Hey, you all know how big that Ralph Nugen thinks he is, the ladies' man." The girls said yes. "Well, my skirt was caught. I did not know it. Ralph was looking up my skirt, and Charles here moved over to spoil his fun." Nancy asked Charles what he liked to drink.

"Well, I started with CC and water at my room."

Nancy must have known the people there. The waitress was there in a minute. Nancy told her, "Give Charles here a CC and water, and give us another round."

Charles found out that they were all off tomorrow but would fly out late the next night. So at a very short time, they were ready for another round. Charles asked the waitress if he could charge the drinks to his room. The waitress came back with the drinks and then told him, "Just sign here, sir."

Nancy looked at the waitress. "Gail, just call him Charles. Is that right, Charles?"

Charles looked at Gail. "That is right. Just call me Charles."

"My name, as you already know, is Gail."

Charles found out the other two guys were male stewards; they all worked together. The guys were not very talkative. A few minutes went by. Gail came back with a round of drinks. Then she sat down. She told the guys, "Hey, listen to this, you are not going to believe this." Charles told her to put these drinks on his tab. Gail looked at Charles. "You are crazy. I heard this from Susan at the desk and Bill." Nancy looked at Gail. "Your Charles here put Mr. Nugen in his place. He gave Susan a hard time, like he usually does. Charles here told him to call him Mr. Appel and all other employees to call him Charles. They're going nuts. Nobody talks to Mr. Nugen like that."

Charles had a few drinks by then. He knew sometimes things come back to haunt you. "Hey, it is not a big a deal. He is probably nice. It's just that he had a bad day."

They all laughed. "Mr. Nugen always has a bad day."

Charles drank his drink and told them, "Have a nice time."

He found the way back to his room. When he opened the door, there were some flowers. The note just said, "Thanks—Susan and Bill."

Charles just wondered what was going through Mr. Martin's mind for the next few days. He did not even get undressed; he just fell on the bed and went to sleep.

During this same time, Mr. Martin kept track of Mr. Appel. He had his people to watch and see what he was up to. Since Nate told them he was going to Manchester to talk to Amanda's parents, Mr. Martin told them to check them out. This did not take long since Mr. Tulman worked for the CIA. His personal secretary told Mr. Martin Mr. Tulman retired nine years ago.

Samuel and Charles did not realize that, the second his plane landed at Manchester, there was a person already there waiting for him. They knew when Mr. Appel's flight left Manchester and arrived in Newark.

Mr. Martin called the Newark Plaza and asked for Mr. Ralph Nugen. After a few minutes, Mr. Nugen answered the phone. Mr. Martin told him, "We already know Mr. Appel is staying at your hotel. We already know he is going golfing at our golf course. We do not know for sure what he is going to do between the second he arrives and the appointment he has with us. I want you to be at the airport, ride the limo to the hotel, and see if he meets anyone. My people will watch him from Manchester to Newark."

"No problem, I will call you by Friday at ten in the morning."

"That be great. We will tell you what we need you to do after that."

Mr. Martin followed Charles all the way to the Tulmans'. They were not ready to set up bugs. They did think about that when they made their visit during Amanda's funeral. They decided the Tulmans were not a player for the tapes.

Mr. Martin was pissed off. "Who the hell would think this damn Mr. Appel would be a millionaire and go see the Tulmans? Who would think this guy would give our computers a virus?"

Out of the blue, his secretary told him, "Maybe we should eliminate the Tulmans and Mr. Appel, Mr. Martin."

"We probably will, but at this stage, we need the tapes. We really need to know who the hell was on that damn Jake Appel's team. We have to wait and just keep a close eye on the Tulmans and that damn Mr. Appel."

Charles woke up on Thursday morning at five thirty. He showered and went to his suitcase; he noticed he was a little low on money. Kate told Charles he better put some in an envelope and to not lose it. "Maybe you should put it in the safe or something."

Charles was laughing and then praying that nobody took his money. As he searched for the envelope, he wondered that whoever bought the flowers checked out his luggage. To his dismay, the envelope was still there.

Charles was ready to go down to the main floor by seven. *Why bother anyone?* He took his suit on one arm and picked up his clubs on the other. As he went to the elevator, a woman walked by. She asked, "Mr. Appel, I will help you."

Charles told her, "Thanks. Just hit the elevator button. How did you know my name?"

She stood there laughing. "Mr. Appel, after what you told Mr. Nugen, we all know who you are."

"Just call me Charles."

She turned around. "Well, you call me Isabel."

Charles just smiled. "Well, Isabel, you have a good day." Isabel turned around with a smile on her face.

When the elevator door opened, there were just a few people around. Charles went right to the desk. This tall blond guy was standing there. He asked, "Mr. Appel, what can I do for you?"

Charles did not know how the hell he knew who he was. "I need this suit ironed or steam-cleaned by the time I get back at, say, six o'clock this evening." This young man told him no problem. Charles then asked, "By the way, can you look up my reservation? I do not even know when I am playing, or I forgot."

The blond guy turned to his right. Charles was glad he had seen the guy's name. When he came back, he said, "Mr. Appel, you are playing at the Newark Country Club."

Charles was going to ask for directions but did not bother; he could see he was writing it down. Charles told him, "Thanks, Steve." Before Charles left, Steve started to leave. "Wait a minute."

Steve asked with a bewildered look, "You need something else?"

"No, just call me Charles. I do not like real personal names."

Steve started to laugh. Charles asked, "What is so funny?"

Steve, trying to be polite, just said, "Well, what happened to Susan must be true."

"As long as all of you do your job and treat me nice, I feel as though it is only fair I treat all of you nice."

Charles noticed, looking through the glass door, there was this taxi outside. This driver was cleaning his windows while waiting for a customer. Charles did not have a watch, so he looked around. There was a clock on the wall behind the desk; the time was seven fifteen. Charles decided to go to the golf course. As he was walking out, this other cab pulled in front of the cab that was already there. The bellman took Charles's clubs and told him, "Here, sir, this cab will take you." Charles was not sure what was going on. In his earlier experience, the cab that is first is first, and then the bellman goes to the next cab.

The other driver yelled in a disturbing voice, "Hey, I was here first!"

The bellman told him, "Mind your own business, or you will never get a passenger." The driver knew the bellman was right, so he dropped the argument.

Charles thought for about two seconds or so. He took the clubs from the doorman. "I will take this cab. It is only fair." The doorman still had his hand on the bag, like, *You cannot do this.* Charles asked him in a very nice way, "Will you let go of my clubs, please?"

The other taxi driver asked, "What is the problem?"

Charles told him, "Nothing against you, but it was this other driver's turn, that is all."

The young person who gave up the argument decided that if this stranger was going to argue for him, he would too. So he got out of his cab and walked up to Charles. "Mister, I will be glad to take you anywhere you want at half the price."

Charles told him, "Well, if I can get this person to let go of my clubs, I will miss my tee time, and that will really piss me off."

The driver told the bellman, "Let go now." The bellman was turning red and getting a mean look. Before Charles could realize it, the cabdriver hit the bellman in the stomach. The guy dropped to his knees. "Let go of the bag."

As he picked up the clubs, he said, "Mister, we better get going." Charles jumped in the front seat of the cab. The cabdriver threw the clubs in the back seat. Charles thought for a minute—his shoes. Through the excitement, he held on to them.

The cabdriver sped away. As he was entering the street, he said, "Well, I will not have that as a stop for a while." Charles thanked him.

The cabdriver asked, "Where to?"

"I have a nine-thirty tee time at the Newark Country Club. The address is—"

"Hell, I know where that is, no problem. It will be forty minutes or so."

"That will be fine. Should I be in the front seat?"

"No, but just buckle up." Charles did, and the driver thanked him.

Then he said, "You mind if I ask you a question?" Charles told him no. "How did you get a tee time at the country club? This is not normal." Charles explained how his friend arranged the time.

The driver told him, "Hell, you are lucky. I used to belong to that course. There was no way a stranger can make a tee time without knowing somebody."

Charles started to think. "Well, I might know someone who just wants to keep an eye on me." Then he thought maybe that was the deal of the other taxicab.

Charles looked up on the visor; he noticed the cabdriver was Carlo Donnley. The picture looked bad, but it did look like him.

Charles asked, "Carlo, can I ask you a question?"

Carlo turned his head just a second. "Well, if you call me Carlo, what should I call you?"

"That is fair. Call me Charles."

"Well, Charles, what is the question?"

"How did you belong to the country club?"

Carlo told Charles, "Well, I was working with a large company. They got greedy through the stock. Carloet made some illegal deals. Some went to prison. I got probation. I was really innocent. Believe it or not, the ones who did it never went to jail or probation. So here I am, driving a cab."

Out of the blue, a semitrailer swerved to Carlo's lane. In an instant, Carlo maneuvered the cab where you could hardly tell a wreck almost happened. Charles was a little nervous. Carlo was laughing. "Hey, I will look after you."

"Good move. That damn semi was just a few inches from us."

"That is nothing. I used to be an amateur race driver for years. I won some, but after I lost my big job, I ran out of money. My wife left me and took the house. Just glad we did not have any kids."

Charles told him, "That is too bad."

"Hey, that's the way it goes."

Carlo turned his head for another second. "Just suppose I help your golf game. Will it be any interest to you?"

"Hell yes, I will make it worth your while."

Carlo handed Charles a notepad. "Here, write this down. I will save you some strokes, especially if you are playing for money." Charles told him he was ready. "This course has good and bad holes. As long as you play your game, do not force nothing too much. You can score. A new player has a big disadvantage because of the layout of the course."

As he was telling Charles about the par threes, Carlo noticed that the cab that butted the line was following them. Carlo asked Charles, "Do you know that cab that wanted your ride at the hotel?"

"Yes, what about it? Well, that cab has been following us ever since."

"That is why they wanted me in that cab."

Carlo said quickly, "Do you want me to lose it?"

"Hell, they know where I am going. Just keep going. I'd rather know about the course."

"Like I was telling you, all par threes are straightforward. There is water or sand all over the place. On the first one, all you need to do is keep it in the middle of the green. If the pin is in the back, putt a little harder against the green. If left of center, the ball breaks more than you think. If the pin is right of center, just aim a little higher, say, no more than an inch above the hole, say, every ten feet. If the pin is below center, run faster. Play no break.

"The second par three on the front is easier. For some reason, the green runs through. Even though it might not look like it, it does not play much break anywhere. The back nine par threes are faster greens than the rest of the course. So do not overhit the ball. It will roll. On number 13, if you can fade it in, the ball works better than a draw. The draw, it seems to me, rolls too far past the hole. On number 16, use one less club unless the flag is blowing straight across, and then use the regular club. The distance is set on the gold Carloers for the white tees on all holes."

Charles told him, "Well, what about the distance on the rest?"

"Well, if the wind is blowing that flag straight across, add two clubs on all holes except that par three sixteen and par four eighteen. I do not understand it, but them two holes play that way. Just use the distance from that gold plate." Carlo told Charles, "That cab is still behind us."

"Hell, they know where I am going. If it makes a move, that is dangerous. Just try not to let that happen."

Carlo assured Charles, "No problem." He went on. "The par fives, I believe it is three, nine, twelve, and seventeen. On three and twelve, use three-wood. Or if you can, hit a good long three-iron. You need to hit it straight and, I say, 220 yards. You have to go over a creek on both of them. On your second shot, use something that goes straight around 170 yards. That leaves about 160 out. I hope to land it on the green and get out with par.

"If you try any harder, you're out of bounds or in big trouble. The other two, you can go for it. The drive is open. On both of them, no matter what you think, your best shot is left. You're better off far left than right. If your drive goes right, just take a club that you can hit out of the rough. You need just 150 yards. Just aim left, and do not go right. If your drive is good and to the left, just take a three-wood or something that goes around 220. You should be only 30 yards from the green. If you can hit a ball extra 30 yards, you're on in two. The trick is if you go right and go for it, there is trouble all over the place. Just go left and take your par. You might luck out and still get a birdie.

"All the par fours play like they are, except eighteen. Play the yardage as the gold plate tells you. Number 1 green is straight and fast. Number 2 green is, for some reason, slower, so be aware of it. The rest of the par fours green is like the first hole. The break is normal. Just use common sense. I do not get greedy on them. If you hit the ball solid, use your driver on the par fours. If not, take three-wood. Use something that goes around 220 or so. You should still par them, except eighteen. On your second shot, play the distance you think."

By the time Carlo told Charles everything he knew of the course, Carlo was pulling in the drive. Carlo stopped the cab. "Here is one of the par threes. Here is the first one on the front nine. See all the sand and water? The pin is left today. Just keep it in the middle. To close to the pin be a perfect shot, but it will roll in the water or sand. Just go for a par. Even a bogey is better than five or six."

Carlo pulled up to the clubhouse. A person was there already to take Charles's clubs. As Charles was getting out of the car, he reached for his billfold. He pulled out a hundred. Charles tore it in half. He gave Carlo one half of the bill and said, "Come back here in four hours or so. I will give you the other half.

Carlo told Charles, "Well, I will miss some rides. My shift will not be over yet."

"I will make it worth your while."

"You got a deal." Carlo forgot to tell Charles something. He jumped out of his cab. "Hey, Charles, I forgot to tell you, the flag is not blowing yet, but it will."

Charles walked toward Carlo. "What are you talking about?"

"The flag, it is this flag you go by, not the hole flag." Charles looked up at the flag. It was an American flag. Carlo told him, "This is the flag you go by. You can see this flag on the whole course. Do not use the pin flags. Use this flag."

Charles looked at Carlo and asked in a nonpositive voice, "Are you sure about this?"

"You're damn right. The hole flag is misleading. Whatever this flag is blowing is the way you play your game. Trust me."

"Well, I will. For some reason, I believe you." Then Charles told him, "Be back here. I will tell you what happens."

"Well, for the hundred, I will." Then Carlo added, "I want to come back just to see how you did."

While this took place, Carlo noticed the cab that followed them was parked a few yards away. Carlo told Charles, "You better keep an eye on your back." Then he turned his head toward the other cab.

Charles looked around and notice it too. "Thanks. I really need your ride back."

"I will be here for sure."

Charles walked in the clubhouse. He could not believe how nice and big it was. A man was at the door and asked, "Can I help you, sir?"

Charles told him, "Yes. Where is the check-in counter?"

The tall man told him, "Right over there. Your clubs are at the driving range right out the back door a few feet from the desk."

Charles thanked him and handed him a five. He thought, *Hell, for that little bit, it was not worth that. It might be a good gesture.*

Charles walked to the desk. This person was dressed real sharp. He asked, "Can I help you, sir?"

"Well, I think so. I am supposed to play a round at around nine thirty." Charles noticed his name on the wall. This sign just said "Ben is your pro for today."

This Ben looked for a few seconds. "Well, Mr. Appel, you are a little early. Your tee time is at ten thirty."

Charles told Ben, "That is fine. I will practice."

Ben looked around the room. "You are playing with Mr. Thomas Nelson, Paul, and Allen."

"How good are these guys?"

"They are fairly good, all in the low eighties or so." Then Ben asked him, "How do you shoot?"

"Well, I am in the mideighties to low nineties."

"Good luck." The driving range and practice green were right through that door. "If you want a drink, the bar is through the archway down a few yards."

Charles thanked him and then was just looking around the pro shop. While he was looking at some clubs, he watched Ben reaching for the phone. Whoever answered it, Charles thought, was talking about him. Ben was staring at Charles while he was talking. Charles could not hear what was said.

Charles went outside; they had piles of golf balls at each area to practice. The club also had a bucket of tees where you could just help yourself. He thought, *This is a real nice place. Where I golf, this does not happen.* Charles was not upset of the wrong tee time; he knew he would be back in plenty of time. He just wondered if Carlo would be waiting for him.

Charles went to the practice green; he noticed his putter was working well. Maybe with Carlo's help, he could shoot a good round today. Charles looked up at the tall flag. At this moment, the flag was hardly moving. After a few more minutes, Charles decided to have a drink. He always had a couple of beers before he started, if possible.

Charles found the bar. This nice-looking woman asked if she could help him. He noticed her name was Charon. Charles told her he would like to have a Budweiser with a glass. She came back with his beer. Charles gave her a twenty. He did not have any idea what the charge was. Charon came back with fourteen dollars and fifty cents. Charles told her, "Keep the dollar and half." Charon thanked her.

He stopped her as she was about to leave. Charon asked, "You need something?"

Charles asked, "Will you be here between one and two this afternoon?" Charon told him yes. "I have a cab coming to get me. The driver's name is Carlo. Tell him to stay around until I am done. I will pay for all his drinks."

Charon looked at Charles, like, *Who do you think you are?* He could notice Charon was wondering what to say. Charles gave Charon a hundred. "This should pay for his drinks. You keep the change."

She took the hundred and told him, "Mister, I will keep Carlo very happy."

"Thanks. Just call me Charles from now on."

Charon looked at him. "I will not forget your Carlo." Charles thanked her.

Charles was having his second beer. Charon asked, "Charles, do you know your group?"

"No, they just put me in with some guys."

Charon was looking over his head. At same time, she told Charles, "If this guy here is your group, be careful. They will try to get all your money."

Charles did not even have a chance to turn around. This tall, slender man sat beside him. He asked Charles, "Are you Mr. Appel?" Charles told him yes. "I am Thomas Nelson. You are going to golf with my group."

Charles introduced himself, reaching out his hand. While they were shaking hands, he told him, "You just call me Charles."

"Well, call me Thomas. I will introduce you to the others at the tee."

"That will be great, Thomas."

"Finish your drink. We are getting on a little earlier." Charles finished his drink and followed him.

Thomas went out to the driving range. His clubs was already in Charles's cart. Thomas told him, "Since I am familiar with the course, I thought it will be better if I drive."

"That will be great."

They drove to the number 1 tee. The other two was already there. Thomas introduced Charles to Paul and Allen. Charles noticed he did not give their last names. Probably just as well; he would forget them anyway. Allen asked Thomas, "Did you explain to Charles how we bet?" Thomas told them no.

Charles told them, "Hell, whatever you guys do will be fine with me."

Paul turned around. "Well, we play for fifty dollars a hole, one tie, all tie. The low person gets a hundred."

Charles knew he had to say OK, so he just told them, "That will be fine with me." In his mind, he was about to shit. Hell, they never played for that kind of money. Charles just hoped he can hold his own.

Thomas led off. His drive was right down the middle. Paul just went a little left but in good shape. Allen went right almost in the wrong fairway. Charles could tell they were all wondering how he would do. He wondered the same thing. He hit the ball good. For Charles, it was not bad; the ball went straight, not as far as Thomas. Charles figured he probably bogeyed. When they were waiting for Allen's shot, Charles asked Thomas, "How good is Allen?"

"Hell, he is a lot better than that." When Allen hit the ball, he landed only three yards or so off the green. Paul hit his next; he reached the green and ended up six feet from the pin. Charles walked up to his ball; he knew he would be lucky to get it there. Hell, he hit it fat. It landed twenty yards from the green. When Thomas hit his, he landed five feet from the pin. Charles chipped to the left for a twenty-foot par. Allen almost made his chip. Paul was farther away. He missed his putt. Thomas put it straight in the hole. Charles thought, *This is not good.* He knew he was playing out of his league. Then if Carlo told him right, just maybe he can win a few holes anyway.

The next hole, Charles hit a biggie this time, Allen birdied, and Thomas and Paul parred. Charles was hoping that just maybe he could birdie this par three. When he was getting a beer out of the cooler, he noticed the three of them were talking. Charles knew they probably wanted to beat him, but since he teed off last, they all had to go for it.

Allen's shot went just like what Carlo said. The ball landed near the pin but rolled off the green, almost in the sand. Thomas's shot landed in the middle of the green and left a long putt. Paul shot landed on the green but on the left side. Charles knew he had a chance to do it. He left at the flag. The flag was not moving. He picked his club and hit the ball. The ball landed right of Thomas's but left a ten-foot putt. They all missed their chance for a birdie.

Charles remembered what Carlo told him. He aimed it higher and hit it harder than the other greens. It was a good thing that it almost rolled short but just had enough to go in. Charles was thrilled inside but did not try to show it on the outside.

Meanwhile at the hotel, Mr. Ralph Nugen was upset that the cab they wanted did not pick up Mr. Appel. He called Mr. Martin, who he could tell was waiting for the call. Mr. Martin told him he already knew about the cab deal. That did not matter. Mr. Nugen told him, "Well, besides that, Mr. Appel did not do too much except all the employees like him. Then Mr. Nugen noticed a note in the reservation. "He does have a reservation at the restaurant. Do you want me to accidentally lose that reservation?"

Mr. Martin was mad. "Ralph, I already know how Mr. Appel got you pissed off. We need to know who he is eating with and what they talk about. So do this. Leave the reservation. In a few minutes, a team is coming to you. Make sure they set up the devices in his room and as close to the table as you can. Do not screw this up." Ralph assured him he would not.

The team that Mr. Martin was talking about showed up in just a few minutes. Ralph took the hotel main cards. He went with them to Charles's room. They told Ralph to stay outside. The maid was just going toward Charles's room. Ralph told her, "Skip this one until we are done in here." The maid knew this was strange; never before was Mr. Nugen even around.

The team was in the room only for ten minutes. As they were leaving, they walked by the maid. Ralph told her, "You can do that other room now."

"I will do it right away."

Mr. Nugen told them, "We will go to the restaurant now before we open." The maid did not think too much about it. She was busy doing her job.

Back at the golf course, Charles was holding his own. In the past three holes, he managed to tie, or they tied to make sure Charles did not win. They were on seventeen, tenth now. Charles remembered what Carlo told him; on the other par five, he bogeyed. Thomas and Paul hit their drives middle to left. Allen went right like he planned to. Thomas asked him, "Taking the shortcut?"

Allen told them, "That is the only way to birdie the hole."

Charles asked, "Can you get to the green from there?"

Thomas answered, "Yes. Really, it is not that bad of a shot."

Charles was next to hit. He remembered what Carlo told him. He took out his five-iron. He aimed it left and then turned the club a little toward the green. He knew he had to go far left enough to carry and then hoped it would fade right in the middle of the fairway. Right before he was setting up, he could tell by Thomas's reaction that their plan did not work. Charles hit the ball solid. The ball landed about 140 yards out, just like what Carlo told him.

Allen went to his ball and hit it. The ball went short and in the sand. Thomas's and Paul's balls landed about 120 yards out. Charles knew his distance was perfect for his favorite iron. He pulled it out and landed the ball by three feet from the pin. Charles could not believe it; neither could the others. Paul's ball landed twenty feet from the pin and Thomas's fifteen feet. Allen hit his sand shot fat, and it landed on the fringe. He could still make a birdie if he could chip it in. He missed by three feet. Paul putted; he missed his by just three inches. Thomas was putting good; Charles could tell he was confident in his game. Thomas putted the ball; it was going right at it and then just broke left, just enough to rim the cup, but did not fall. Thomas told Charles, "There you go. You can really make up some ground."

Charles knew he was trying to shake him up. He went right up to the ball, made his quick look, and then hit it. *The ball is going to short*, Charles thought.

Thomas told him, "It will be short." They all thought the same. But sometimes you just do not know. The damn ball went in, just barely got there. Charles could hardly keep his emotion.

When they got to eighteen, Charles had to tee off first. He could not believe how you can see that American flag from all the tee boxes; the wind was blowing against them. The flag was blowing but not straight out. Charles took his three-wood. He could not believe what Carlo told him: "When the wind is against you, do not use more club." Charles hit the three-wood solid and straight; it landed about 140 yards out. Thomas and Paul smashed theirs; they were only a hundred or so out. Allen hit his solid; it landed by Charles's.

As Charles was lining his shot. Thomas asked, "Think you can hit that club that far? You are against the wind."

Charles told him, "Well, you know, for some reason, I believe this hole is in a gully or something that the wind does not matter that much." He took his standby iron. He hit it better than he did on seventeen. The ball landed by two feet from the pin. Allen landed his on but real long on the edge of the green. It looked like 45 feet or so.

Thomas used a wedge; the ball landed 3 feet past the pin and rolled back about ten feet. He was pissed off. Paul landed his three feet short of the pin, and it rolled six feet past it. By this time, they all knew there was nothing wrong with Charles's putting. Allen missed his long putt and just tried too hard. Paul thought he had a chance and just pulled it. Charles could tell they did not want him to win. Thomas lined his up. Charles could tell he was still thinking of the last hole. Thomas hit the ball solid, and it just went left, about an inch. Charles knew he had this short putt. He started to putt, and then Allen told him, "Hell, pick it up."

Thomas told Charles, "Hell no, putt the damn thing." Charles started to smile a little. He had gotten them to argue with themselves. Just too bad it took eighteen holes.

Charles lined his putt up. The ball went straight in. Paul and Allen told Charles, "Not too bad of a round for not playing this course. Thomas just went straight to the cart. He never said a word to Charles all the way back to the clubhouse.

Charles knew he did good twelve holes that one seven put him at eighty-seven. He was happy he kept himself in the game. Charles wondered if Carlo was at the bar. After all, they got off a little earlier. Since the tee time was different, just maybe he would be there. When Thomas was more sensible, he invited Charles to join them to settle up at the bar. Charles told him, "That will be fine. I am supposed to meet my ride there anyway."

As they walked in the bar, Charles noticed Carlo was talking to Charon. He went right toward Carlo and asked, "Is Charon taking care of you?"

Carlo laughed. "Oh yes, and thanks for the drinks."

Charon was smiling all the time. Charles could tell he was missing something. Charon started to laugh. "Carlo and I know each other very well. When he was a member here, we had a good time together."

Thomas was sitting at the table; he yelled at Charles, "Come over here! Let's settle up!"

Carlo turned around and looked at Thomas. He jumped up. "Do not tell me you played these guys." Charles told him yes. Carlo, in a very fast-forward motion, jumped up and went right to the table. He asked Charles, "Did they take you for much?"

Paul told Carlo, "Settle down. Your friend beat us in holes."

Charles told Carlo, "With the help of you, I won twelve holes. I lost total stoke. I had a seven on number 5, I think. You know these guys?"

"Yes, it is a long story. I do not trust them at all."

Paul told Carlo, "Hey, that's the way it goes. Just get over it."

Charles did not know what to do, so he threw out a hundred. "Here is to the one where I got a low score." Paul took the money. Then they handed Charles his money. Carlo could not believe it. They subtracted the difference, and each gave Charles three hundred dollars.

Thomas told Charles, "Now I know how you knew the course. Carlo told you all about it."

"Well, it just so happens he gave me the ride in the cab. While I was riding, Carlo and I became friends. He just so happens to tell me about the course." Carlo was smiling. You could tell he wanted to be there, especially when it was these guys.

Charles went over to the bar and asked Charon, "Before you bring us another round on me, I have a quick question."

"Ask away."

"Just how good is Carlo in golf?"

Charon started to laugh. "Go over the plaques by the wall over there."

"So what?"

Charon told Charles, "Every time you see a Carlo, that is your cabdriver."

"Bring the drinks over. I will pay for them." Charon did not hesitate.

Charles went right to the wall; he could not believe what he had seen. "Hell, this Carlo Donnley has the course record of sixty-two. He has the longest-drive plaque." Charles went on down the wall; he had seen Carlo's name on three hole in ones. He won four amateur tournaments on this course. Charles was so amazed; he wondered, *Why the hell is he a cabdriver?*

Charles walked to the table. Carlo was watching him looking at the plaque. Charles had seen Carlo looking at him and asked, "Why did you not tell me?"

"I do not like to brag. I just thought I'd help you out."

Charles thanked him and said, "We have to talk on the way back to the hotel. I might have a deal for you."

"That will be great. I am off duty now since somebody is trying to get me drunk."

Charles laughed. "Do not worry, I have a date tonight. I am not going to screw that up."

"Hell, good luck."

By this time, Charon was over with the drinks. Charles gave her a hundred. Charon told him, "Hell, I will by these from that big tip."

"Hell no. Here, take this." Charon thanked Charles.

Carlo looked up at Charon and told her, "Thanks for telling Charles about my golf."

"You are welcome," she replied with a kidding voice.

Thomas told Charles he and Allen had to leave. They got up and asked Paul if he was leaving. Paul told them, "No, I will have another drink, and then I will go home." Charles could tell Thomas really was not very happy with that but did not argue at that time. Charles wanted to see how Carlo knew them. He also wondered if any of them knew Jake.

Charles did not pay that much attention about his drink at that time. He did notice Paul was looking down Charon's low-cut top. Charles had to figure a way to keep Paul there for a few drinks longer. At the same time, he had to figure a way to let Carlo know. Charles, in a quick move, spilled Carlo's drink on the table. As he was getting up with his napkin to keep the beer from getting on Carlo, Charles whispered, "Just play along. I will explain." Carlo did not answer and just got up from the table.

Carlo told Charles, "I am going to get a bar rag."

"I will go. I spilled the drink."

Paul was just sitting there looking at the score card. He hardly noticed the drink was spilled. Charles and Carlo both went to the bar. Carlo asked Charles, "What are you doing?"

"I need to find out all I can from Paul. You think you can ask Charon to flirt with him to keep him here for a while so I can ask Paul some questions?"

"Hell, she'll do it for you. Might need some more tip."

"Ask her for me. I am going back to the table."

When Charles went back, Paul was still wondering where his bad shots were at. Charles told him, "Hell, Paul, you did great. You just missed a few putts, and you were off line on your chipping. No big deal."

"I guess you are right."

Charles did not notice Carlo was already back. Charon came over with a towel and Carlo's drink. As she was cleaning up the table, Charles could tell Carlo talked to her. Hell, her nice round breasts were almost falling out. Paul could not help but watch. Carlo told them, "Hell, Charon, bring Charles and Paul another drink." Paul did not say a word; he was so busy checking out Charon.

Charles asked Paul, "Do you work for Thomas and his company?"

"Well, we work with Tran Oil. We both work for the same boss."

Charles asked, "Do you guys play golf together a lot?"

Paul still was watching Charon walking away. "No, not that much, just on company business."

Carlo told Paul, "No, tell him the truth."

Paul said in hasty voice, "What do you mean?"

Carlo told Charles, "Hell, Thomas, Allen, and Paul play together whenever their boss wants to beat someone in golf. For some reason, their boss did not want you to win."

Charles knew he should take his time, but he could not stand it any longer. "I have a question for you, Paul."

Paul looked at him. "I do not think I should be talking to you anymore. I am going to leave." He stood from the table.

In a not very loud voice but loud enough that he had gotten Paul's attention and Paul turned around, Charles asked, "Did you know my son, Jake Appel?"

Paul's mouth dropped; he was shocked. Charles knew he had gotten his attention on that; so did Carlo. Paul came back to the table. "Jake was your son?"

"Yes, and I am going to find out who and why he was killed." Paul told Charles he did not have anything to do with Jake's murder. He went on, saying, "I cannot believe our company had anything to do with Jake's murder either."

Charles asked Paul, "What do you do for Tran Oil?"

"I work on the shipping end of the company. I make sure that the oil is delivered on time throughout the country. Hell, my office is in New York. I just come to the main office when we cannot solve the problem over the phone or when they have special meetings. I never knew Jake.

"Jake's name only came up once in our meetings. Thomas had a problem on a court issue. Mr. Martin just told Thomas to use Jake on that matter. I asked Thomas who Jake is. Thomas just said, 'We use Jake on court issues. In fact, I did not even known his last name until his murder.' One of my secretaries was talking about it. I overheard her and asked who Jake Appel is. She told me he worked for Mr. Martin. Jake called us for information every once in a while."

Paul went on to say, "A few days ago, I was playing golf. Thomas asked if I wanted to play some. I told him sure, so Thomas set this golf outing out. I was just told to try to beat you. Well, you are better than what we thought."

Charles told him, "Hell, I was lucky today. You better get going now. If I were you, I would be careful on what you tell Thomas and Mr. Martin about what you told me."

"Again, you have to believe me, I do not know nothing."

Charles told him right now he did not know what to believe. "It is too early to point fingers at any one person."

After Paul left, Carlo did not know what to say. They just finished their beer. Charles was just sitting there thinking what to do next. Carlo told him, "We better get you back for that date."

"Yes, I better." Charles walked up to Charon and gave her a fifty. "I appreciate what you did. Thanks."

Charon told Charles, "For you and Carlo, I will help you anytime."

Carlo was going toward his cab. He did not see that other cab around. Charles was waiting for him and did not realize Carlo put his clubs in the car. Carlo could tell Charles was still thinking about his son. Charles looked at Carlo and said, "All right, Carlo, tell me how you came from a well-to-do person to a cabdriver."

"I wondered when you are going to get to that." Carlo told Charles, "Well, I did not work for Tran Oil. I worked for this investing company.

Tran Oil was one of our major clients. Thomas and Allen were the spokespeople I dealt with for Train Oil. They were the ones who told me when to buy some stock or sell. Hell, they had the fingers in all sorts of businesses. Hell, some of them were their competition.

"I asked a few questions on some of the decisions my company made. I felt like it might be illegal. I knew it was very unprofessional. The next thing I knew, our company was investigated for stock trading. Hell, I and another guy ended up with probation. One of our vice presidents, Mr. Jack Hamel, was going to prison for three years. He ended up killing himself. I know he did not do nothing wrong. So I had several opportunities after that. I just did not trust nobody after that. Hell, like I told you, my wife left me with the house. So I am just driving a cab until I get myself back together."

Charles asked Carlo, "Do you know this Mr. Martin very well?"

"No, I do not. I do know that this man does not take no for an answer. In fact, after he finds out what Paul told us, I got a felling he will be gone."

"You have to promise me you will not tell anyone what Paul told us. He might be able to help me down the road."

Carlo told Charles, "Hell, I do not want to get involved anyway. I will keep my mouth shut."

Charles noticed Carlo was looking in the rearview mirror a lot. He asked, "Is everything all right?"

"You know, I think someone is following us again. This time, it is a black Ford."

"Just keep an eye on it. They are just seeing where we are going."

Carlo asked, "What are you going to do?"

"Well, to make it simple, I am going to find out who killed Jake. Right now, I am just causing some people to be nervous."

"It is not smart to get the wrong people upset."

"Well, hell, it makes it interesting anyway." Charles then told Carlo, "I have time. Pull over a nice quiet bar where we can talk without worrying about anyone overhearing us." Carlo told him he knew a place not far. "Keep an eye on our friends. See if they are following us."

As Carlo made some turns to go to this quiet bar, he told Charles, "They are still with us?"

"Just see how good you are. Lose them without killing us."

"Tighten your safety belt." Just as he said that, Carlo took off. Charles could tell there was some power in his cab. Carlo made some quick right and left turns. Hell, on turn, his hubcap came off.

Carlo then went through an alley. There were small parking spaces in the back. Carlo told Charles, "Well, get out here." Carlo led Charles through the back door. "Hell, this is Jake's Bar."

As they went through the small kitchen, the cook said hi to Carlo. Carlo told him, "Tell us if a stranger comes looking for us, Joe."

"No problem. I will cover for you."

Carlo went into the bar area. He told Charles to sit at the corner table. Charles went to the table, and Carlo moved to the bar. He was talking to the bartender for a second and then came back with two beers.

Carlo sat down. "All right, we can talk here. If a stranger comes, we will know about it."

Charles told him, "You know, I am a person who does think on impulse and gut feelings. So I am trusting you. Even though I hardly know you, I believe we can work together. I am involved a little more than I told you. I have these computer disks that I believe Mr. Martin needs. My son and his friends have been collecting data for several years. I believe some of this information is what killed Jake. The only reason I am alive is that I have the tapes. I know who the rest of Jake's friends are—well, sort of. Jake left me a message and just said, through the years, I met all of them. I just have to figure out who they are before Mr. Martin finds them."

Carlo asked, "What does this have to do with me?"

"Well, Jake left me around two million dollars. I'm spending all of it to find out who killed him. I need a driver that I can trust. So I thought when I need you, say, in New York, you could fly out with me or meet me there. You pick out a car, not from the airport but somewhere."

Carlo told Charles, "You mean a car that is not bugged or have a bomb in it?"

"That is exactly what I mean." Charles told Carlo he would pay all expenses, plus about fifty thousand a year.

Carlo did not know what to say. *Here is a complete stranger I've only met less than ten hours ago, and he wants to hire me as a driver.* He asked Charles, "Are you nuts? Hell, I could be working for them. This could all be a setup."

Charles told him, "Well, I thought of that. Sometimes you need to trust people."

"Let me think about it. I will tell you tomorrow."

"That will be great. I need a ride to Mr. Martin's office tomorrow morning at nine thirty. If you are at the hotel, say, eight o'clock in the morning, you can give me the ride and tell me."

Carlo's eyes got big. "You mean you have an appointment with this Mr. Martin?"

Charles told him, "Oh, I forgot to tell you I made a computer virus on a disk they took from my house. I have a disk to clean their virus up. I told them I will bring it tomorrow. You might not want to miss this meeting. It might be interesting."

"Hell, you might end up dead."

Charles laughed. "Well, if you take the job, it might be the shortest job you'll ever have."

"Well, if I am not there by eight, that means take another cab. I am out."

"That is fine. Let's get back to the hotel."

When Carlo and Charles arrived back at the hotel, the black Ford was sitting outside. Charles told Carlo, "Hell, you did a good job. Thanks. If you want, we can go to the bar and have another drink."

"No. I have some serious thinking to do."

"Be careful. Watch your back."

Carlo asked Charles where to put the clubs. Charles told him, "Here, I will take them. See you tomorrow."

"Do not count on it." Then he pulled away.

The doorman came up to Charles and asked if he needed help. Charles told him, "Here, put my clubs over the corner somewhere. Tell Bill to put them in my room for me." Charles handed the doorman a five.

"Bill won't be on duty for another hour."

"That is all right. I just want Bill to go to my room."

Charles noticed that, as he was walking through the door, the black Ford left. He was hoping Carlo caught that too. Well, Charles did not have to worry. Carlo noticed the black Ford as he was to the intersection. Carlo took a right. The black Ford kept on following.

Carlo was a six-footer and 245 pounds. He worked out all the time. Charles did not know yet, and Carlo never brought it up. Carlo thought it was funny. He was not broke. Through the years, he managed to save three hundred thousand after the divorce. He was just a cabdriver trying to come up with what to do. Carlo knew he could never belong to the club since so many of them were assholes.

Carlo kept on going through wide roads and made some turns, just enough to keep the black Ford close but not out of reach. Then he found the road he was wandering to. The road went straight just a few yards; the only other road turned left to a dead end. Carlo sped up so the black Ford would have to. As Carlo passed the first left, he slowed way down. The black Ford, which did not want to be too close, decided to turn left. Carlo immediately backed up. He blocked the road with his cab. Carlo was out of his car in no time and beat the driver out. Carlo grabbed the driver and asked, "What the hell are you doing?" As that happened, the driver's gun fell to the ground.

The passenger was out and had his revolver pointed at the driver and Carlo. Carlo told him, "You just get in the car while this man tells me why he is following me." The passenger refused.

Carlo grabbed the driver and knocked them both to the ground. He reached for the driver's gun. The passenger ran on the back side of the car. Carlo already had the gun at the driver's head. He told the passenger, "Now let's do this again. You drop your gun, or I will shoot this driver. Or maybe I'll shoot you first and then the driver. It is your choice."

The passenger dropped his gun. Carlo made the driver put the passenger in the trunk. As that was done, he told the driver, "Now tell me who hired you to follow me."

"Hell, we were told to follow Mr. Appel. Since you two seemed to get along, they wanted us to keep an eye on you."

"Well, you made a mistake." Then he shot holes in the two side tires. Carlo told the driver, "Thanks for the guns." Then he hit the driver over the head but not very hard, just enough to make sure Carlo made his way back to his cab. He figured it would not take long for them to find him. So he went to Jake's Bar.

Carlo called the Newark Plaza and asked them to page Mr. Charles Appel. The man at the desk said, "Just a second." He went to the bar. "I will connect you to the bar." After a few minutes, Charles was on the phone. He was wondering who was calling him. Then he hoped it was not bad news about Carlo.

Charles said in a nervous voice, "This is Charles Appel. Who is this?"

Carlo just said, "This is your cabdriver who just had a gun pointed at him."

Charles immediately asked, "Are you all right?"

"Yes. The black Ford and I had a disagreement. You and I have to talk tomorrow. I am safe at Jake's Bar. I am not promising nothing. I will be there at eight o'clock."

"Good. I will see you then."

"Have a nice time tonight."

"Since you are all right, I will."

Charles left the bar and went to the desk. There was still no one there he knew. He asked the clerk, "Is my suite ready by any chance?"

The man went to the back room. "Here it is, Mr. Appel."

Charles noticed his name on his coat this time. His name was Henry Jacob. Charles remembered that Kate telling him to ask this Mr. Jacob about his reservation. Charles was staring at Jacob to see his name tag. He asked, "Can I help you again, Mr. Appel?"

"Call me Charles. Are you the one who made my reservation at the restaurant for tonight at around seven thirty?"

Henry looked at Charles's reservation. "Yes, I am, Mr. Appel. Your friend and I made a deal."

"Yes, I know. I owe you some money."

"Yes, you do." Henry was looking around.

Charles noticed no one was around. "You want it now?"

"Well, this will be a good time."

Charles handed him a hundred. "That was the deal I was told." Henry took the money and then thanked him. Charles turned around and told him, "I believe in tipping for good service. I understand the situation. You can still call me Charles." Henry was still smiling as he thanked him.

Charles then remembered something. "Tell your friend Joseph I will settle with him after we eat." He started toward the elevator and turned around. "Two more things, Henry."

"Yes, what can I do now?"

"When is Bill on duty?"

Henry looked at his watch. "In forty minutes."

Charles told him, "Tell Bill to bring my clubs up to my room."

"I will do that for you. What is the other issue you have?"

"Well, if you are day shift, Susan is night shift. What does Ralph Nugen do?"

Henry started to laugh. "You're the one."

Charles said, "What?"

"You're the one that pissed Mr. Nugen off."

"Yes. I thought that was over with."

"Hell, Ralph made a phone call to someone. He was thinking to cancel your dinner reservation. Whoever he talked to told him no. I was worried about losing my money. Since it was you, hell, I would have gotten you in that restaurant for nothing. Nobody cares for Mr. Nugen. To answer your question, somehow or another, he is actually part owner of this hotel, or he has a backer that wants to be out of the picture."

Charles thanked him and then went to the elevator. When he was walking out, going toward his room, there was a voice not really loud but just enough that he could hear it. Charles turned around; it was Isabel. He asked, "Can I help you, Isabel?"

Isabel put her finger over her lips and whispered, "Follow me."

Charles followed her to the laundry room. Isabel told him, "I was told by Frances, who is the day shift maid, that Mr. Nugen and three others were in your room for a few minutes. Frances was told not to clean your room until they left. Well, we all need our jobs, so she did what she was told. So when I came to work, she told me what happened, so I am telling you. You will not raise a stink to get Frances and me in trouble, will you?"

Charles smiled. "No, I will not. Here, take this money. You take half. Give Frances the other half. Isabel, keep me informed if any other things happen."

Isabel said, "Do not worry, Charles, your room will be watched like it was a bank."

Charles went to his room. Hell, he did not know what to look for, so he just took his shower and made himself a CC and water. Charles noticed he had an hour to kill, so he thought he would take a nap. He looked at the directory and could not figure it out. He dialed zero. The operator answered. Charles said, "Could you make sure I am awake in an hour?"

"You really need to call extension 55. I will be glad to take care of it for you. We will wake you up in an hour, Mr. Appel." Charles thanked her and then lay down.

He was more tired than he thought. The phone was ringing. He answered the phone. "This is your wake-up call, Mr. Appel." Charles jumped off the bed; it was six thirty. Charles thought he would be down the bar early just in case Ciara came before time.

As he was getting dressed, he walked by the big mirror on the dresser. He noticed his clubs were in the room. Charles, at first, did not like that; then again, maybe Bill knocked on the door, and he did not hear it. Charles was as dressed as he could be. He wished Kate were here to check him out.

Charles was going toward the elevator when he noticed Isabel was working in an empty room. He stopped to look at her. Charles knocked on the door just so he would not startle her. Isabel looked at him. "You need me, Charles?"

"Well, I am meeting someone. I thought you could tell me if I have this suit on right.

"You men, sometimes you guys cannot get dressed without a woman."

Charles laughed. "Well, I do not wear a suit very often."

Isabel said with a polite smile, "I can tell." She laid down her duster and came toward Charles. She straightened up his tie and moved his coat around. "There, now try not to mess with it. This is fine." Charles thanked her and then went to the elevator.

When he was walking out, Bill noticed him right off the bat. "Charles, I knocked on your door. I did not think you were there. I put your clubs by the dresser." Charles thanked him and handed Bill a five. "Hell, keep it. We will do anything for you."

"I know. Thanks for the flowers. It made the room look nicer."

"That was Susan's idea."

Charles went down the lobby toward the bar. The time was around six thirty, so he had plenty of time. Charles noticed a pay phone near the bar. He walked up to the phone and knew they would find out whom he called, but he did not think they could tell what he was saying. So he took a chance.

Charles went through several numbers. He was slow as he did not use his phone card very often. After a few minutes, a woman's voice came on. "This is the Tulmans'. Can I help you?"

"Janace, this is Charles Appel. Can I speak to Samuel?" Janace asked how he was doing. Charles told her, "Fine. How are you doing?"

"Thanks for coming. You really helped us out. Here is Samuel."

Samuel asked, "Charles, how are you doing?"

"Well, I started to make some noise. Can you tell me how to find bugs in my hotel room? I was told four men were in my room for around ten minutes or so. I am very sure they bugged my room. I do not even know where to start."

"Hell, it is hard telling. Look under the phone by wall fixtures. Look for little holes in the wall."

Charles asked, "I wonder if I get my date in my room. In the movies, they turn on the water to prevent the bugs from working."

"Well, that would work, but you want to talk to her in the bathroom."

Charles thought just for a short time. "What about a Jacuzzi? We could turn it on and sit inside the Jacuzzi."

"That would work. Still, be careful what you say, unless you want them to hear you."

Charles thanked Samuel. Right before he hung up, he asked him, "Maybe you and Janace could come to Coal City to do what we talked about earlier than planned, say, next Wednesday or so."

Samuel paused a minute. "You got a deal. We will be there."

Charles gave Samuel Tom and Kate's number. "Call this number, and tell them when and where to pick you up. We will be there."

"All right. I might bring a friend or two."

"Hell, bring whoever you need."

"See you Wednesday." Then he hung up.

Charles went in the bar. Gail was watching him on the phone. She already had his drink ready sitting on the bar as he walked in. Charles put his money on the bar and drank. Gail asked, "You want another?"

"You are good."

"You are looking good tonight."

Charles thanked her and then told Gail, "If a woman around five foot five with black hair asks for me, make sure she finds me."

Gail looked at Charles. "Well, if you do not move, you will see her first."

He did not really paid that much attention. Gail was right. "Well, just in case. I do not want to miss her."

"I am just kidding you. I am a little jealous you are not waiting for me."

Charles knew that was a joke; to him, he never felt he was good looking at all.

A black-haired woman was walking through the door. Charles could not believe how nice she looked. For a second, he was not sure if that was Ciara. Gail asked Charles, "Is that your friend?"

Charles said in a really nervous voice, "Yes, that is Ciara."

When Ciara was just a few feet from him, Charles stood up; no words came out of his mouth. Ciara was laughing. Charles finally started to talk; his first words were not the best. "I cannot believe how nice you look."

Ciara told him, "Thanks. You do not look bad yourself."

Charles was still looking at her black dress. The top was not cut really short, but he could notice how nice and round her breasts were. As Charles was watching Ciara sitting down, he was looking at the slit on her dress.

She did not show all her legs but just enough. Charles could not believe he did not notice how nice looking she was a few weeks ago.

Ciara asked Charles, "How are you doing?"

"I am doing better."

"I am glad."

"I cannot believe you said yes."

"I told my friends the same thing, so here we are."

Charles told her, "We have a few minutes yet. You want a drink?"

"I will take a plain margarita."

Charles looked up. Gail must have heard her. She was already making it. Gail set the drink in front of Ciara. Charles thanked her.

Gail handed Charles the phone. "Isabel wants to talk to you."

Charles did not know what to say to Ciara. He asked, "What do you need, Isabel?"

"I forgot to tell you. Frances is real sure they went up to the restaurant where you are eating too. She did not know what they were up to, just that they wanted to get there before the restaurant opens." He thanked Isabel and then hung up.

Charles told Ciara, "I am sorry about that."

"No problem." Ciara looked at Charles. "It does not take you long for everyone to know your name."

"I told everyone here except Ralph to call me Charles."

Ciara said with a slight smile, "Yeah, I know. I asked the woman at the desk where the bar was and said that I was looking for Mr. Charles Appel. This person told me, 'Well, Charles is at the bar.'"

They finished their drink and walked toward the express elevator to go to the restaurant. Bill was just accidentally walking by and asked Charles, "Hi. Is everything all right?"

"No problem."

Ciara started to laugh. "Is there anyone here who does not know you?"

"I will tell you the story on how this happened." Ciara told him she could hardly wait.

When they entered the restaurant, Ciara's eyes opened up. Even Charles was amazed at the big doors and nice floors. The glass and mirrors all over the restaurant were fantastic. A man was at a nice desk or booth. Charles noticed it was made out of walnut. He asked, "Can I help you? I am Mr. Joseph Madigan."

"Joseph, I am Mr. Appel. I have a reservation for two."

Joseph's eyes lit up. Charles thought either he remembered or he was all ready for them. He told Charles, "Follow me."

Charles let Ciara go first. As they were walking, he noticed this table for two by a window. Joseph started sit Ciara down, and Charles asked him, "You know, Ciara has never been here before. Maybe she wants the table by the window."

Ciara was caught off guard, but more importantly, so was Joseph. He explained that the table was already reserved. Charles handed him a hundred. Come on now, you can do this."

Ciara could not believe what she had seen. Through her experience, she felt something was up. She told Joseph, "You know, that table over there is better." So reluctantly, Joseph took them to the other table. Ciara could tell he was not happy at all.

As Joseph sat her down, Charles was almost seated. "Your server is Max. He will be here shortly."

Ciara was not mad. Charles knew, though, that she did not have her smile like it was. After Joseph was out of hearing range, she asked, "Charles what the hell was that about?"

"Do you believe in gut instinct or feelings?"

"Yes, I do."

"Well, Ciara, I want you to promise, no matter what happens tonight, you will go out with me two weeks from today. You pick the restaurant, and I assure you that date will just be us."

Ciara thought for a few seconds and still had no words. Then she told Charles, "I pick the restaurant with no intrusions and no bullshit. Tell me the truth."

Charles replied with a big smile, "That is right. I will tell you everything I know, plus our next date."

"Well, I have something to tell you tonight also. Deal, two weeks from tonight, I will meet you at the airport."

"I will call you and let you know the plane's arrival."

Ciara was feeling better now. Then Charles told her, "No matter what happens tonight, right?"

"Right."

By this time, Max was there; they ordered their drinks. Charles ordered a CC and water and Ciara a glass of white wine. After Max left, she asked, "Well, when are you going to tell me something?"

"Well, that phone call I had at the bar was Isabel. She is a maid here. Some men went in my room. I believe they bugged my room. She forgot to tell me they went up to this restaurant right after they left my room. So in the movies, I have seen this one scene where, at the last second, he switched tables. So I tried that."

Ciara asked, "Well, I wonder if they figure you would do that, then they bugged this one."

Charles said in a very nervous way, "I never thought of that."

"Relax. The way that Joseph looked, he was not happy at all, so I think we are safe."

Charles looked at Ciara; he still could not believe how nice she looked. "You know, I have an idea. We will enjoy our meal and just have small talk. Then we will go to a place of my choosing, and we will talk about what I have been doing and what you want to tell me."

"That sounds like a good plan."

Ciara told Charles while they were eating that she had a sister who died of cancer. Both of her parents passed away in the last three years. Charles told her he was sorry. Ciara said, "Well, what do I know about you?"

"Yes, we both lost a lot of loved ones through the years. I lost my wife, grandchild, and daughter-in-law and then my son."

"Hey, life still goes on."

Charles looked at Ciara. "Especially when I meet someone so beautiful as you."

Ciara thanked Charles and then reached over and gave him a little kiss. He could not believe that. Ciara could not either. She turned a little red. Charles told her that was the first kiss he had for years. She started to laugh. "You mean you have not been on a date for years?"

"Well, you see, in the big city of Coal City, I never could just ask anyone out that reminds me of my wife, so I just never dated after she died."

"That's the reason you have been acting so nervous."

Charles asked, "You can tell?"

"Hell, you need another drink." So they had a few more drinks and then were getting ready to leave.

Charles asked Max for the bill. Max took a few minutes and then handed Charles a little tablet. Charles left him enough to pay the bill, plus gave him another fifty. Ciara noticed how much Charles left out. She could not believe that. "Hell, the last time I have seen you, I did not figure you have that much money to throw around."

Charles laughed. "Just wait. I will tell you."

As they walked by Joseph on the way out, he handed Joseph another fifty. "That was the deal, right?" Joseph took the money and said thanks.

Ciara said as they were near the elevator, "He is still pissed off."

"That makes me feel good."

When they were on the main floor, Ciara asked Charles, "Well, where are we going to talk serious?"

"Well, I never thought about it yet." Just then, they walked by the gift shop. Charles noticed this two-piece swimsuit. He looked at Ciara. "I know now." Charles walked in the shop and bought the suit.

Ciara asked, "What are you doing?"

"Well, will it fit?"

She told Charles, "Yes, but do you think I am going to wear that?"

"Well, either that or nothing." So Charles bought the suit.

Ciara was not sure if she should ask, but she did. "Now where?"

"Well, we are going to my suite. Hell, I have never been in it no more than a few hours, so we are going to use it."

"I thought it was bugged."

"Hell, you are a policewoman. Between you and me, we will figure something out."

Ciara could not believe what she said next. "Well, let's go for it."

Charles opened the door for Ciara; she could not believe the room, the nice view, the Jacuzzi, the bar. Charles was making his CC and water and asked, "Wine or what?"

As she was still looking around, she replied, "Wine will be fine. How much does this cost?"

Charles laughed. "Kate would not tell me. She told me to splurge to make a good impression with you."

Ciara smiled. "Well, that worked, but how did you afford this?"

"Well, since I met you, Jake was worth a little over two million."

Ciara about fainted. "You mean two million dollars?"

Charles told her, "Yes. I am going to spend it on finding out who and why they killed Jake."

Ciara, while Charles was talking, was walking around the room. To Charles's dismay, she found a bug by the lamp and one behind a picture. Ciara went to Charles real close. "You better watch what you say."

"Hell, they already know that." Charles then told her, "Why not go change into the swimsuit and I will put on mine?"

Charles had his suit on in no time. To him, it seemed like he was waiting an hour for Ciara. It was actually just three minutes or so. When Ciara came out, Charles could not believe her body. Her breasts were just like he thought. They were not real big but just nice and round. Her waist was not twenty-four, maybe a twenty-six or twenty-seven. Hell, he could not tell anyway; his eyes were on her legs. For a five-foot-five woman or so, her legs looked perfect to Charles. This was the first time he was this close to a woman whom he never knew for years.

Ciara knew Charles was staring at her. To break his mind's thought, she asked, "You think there are more bugs in the rooms?"

Charles looked at her. "What bugs?" He knew he was busted, so he apologized for staring at her body. Ciara was, in a way, embarrassed, but this was the first time she could remember that someone really checked her out like Charles did.

He told her, "Hell, you know, I really do not understand this Jacuzzi."

"Here, my friend has one." Ciara turned on the faucets and pushed some buttons. There came out streams of warm to hot water.

Charles told her, "Samuel was right. It did make enough noise."

Ciara was in the Jacuzzi in no time. Charles took a little longer. As he was all the way in, Ciara went toward him and asked, "How close should we get so we can talk?"

By this time, her breasts were against his chest. Charles could see her nipples protruding from the suit. As she moved her legs around Charles's, he could feel her thighs rubbing close to his body. Charles told Ciara, "Maybe this was not a good idea."

"Hell, I think it is working very well."

"You go first. What have you found out?"

"Well, one thing, no more than what you told us."

"No kidding? What about Jake's murder?"

Ciara told Charles, "I have to be honest. We still have no leads whatsoever." Charles told her he was not surprised. "They did spent all the time in Jake's computer room. There were hardly any unusual things in the rest of the house. You already knew that."

Charles asked, "What about Amanda's apartment?"

"In our opinion, they just wanted to make sure Amanda did not have a disk or information on her computer. We feel they used Amanda's murder to give someone a message."

"You mean things like this will happen to me or the other ones who have the information?"

"That is exactly right."

Ciara started to rub Charles's chest. He started to move his hands all over Ciara's body. She did not seem to mind. Charles started to kiss her. Ciara could not wait either. They both started to enjoy each other's bodies. Charles had not had practice whatsoever. Ciara hurried up the situation and put her hand down his trunks. Charles's eyes lit up; he was kissing her, and he had his hands all over her breasts. By this time, Ciara was completely naked. She had Charles's trunks off. Ciara lay back in the sexiest position and told Charles, "Hell, you can tell me in a few minutes."

Charles started to be really close and looked up at Ciara. "You sure about this?" She pushed Charles's body as close as she could toward her body. He started to kiss her while they were making love.

After Charles and Ciara made love, he did not know what to say. Ciara put back on her suit. Charles was just lying in the Jacuzzi, still naked. He was out of words. Ciara found his trunks and told him, "Put these back on before we get carried away again." Charles did what she asked. Ciara sat beside him and had the nicest smile Charles had ever seen on her. He knew he was smiling. "Your turn to tell me what you know."

Charles went out of the Jacuzzi and made another drink. Ciara told him she would take another wine. He came back with the drinks. They were sitting on the edge of the Jacuzzi. Charles turned up the jet streams of water just to make sure there was more noise. "Today I met a cabdriver that I believe I can trust. I met you while you were doing your job. Then I really met you tonight. I feel as though I could trust you with my life. So because of my feelings, here is what I am trusting you with. Please do not tell your partner or your supervisors, all right?"

Ciara told Charles, "Tonight what you say is between us. Tomorrow will be another day."

Charles thanked her and then went on. He told her about the disk at his house and explained they were going through them starting a couple of days ago. Ciara stopped Charles. "Is there anyone you do not trust?"

"Well, Nate. I sent him to Kansas City to check out Joseph. I just have different feelings toward him."

Ciara looked at him very differently. "You mean you're having a person stay with you that might be against you?"

Charles said with a smile, "I have an answer to that. On Mafia movies or somewhere, I heard you should keep your friends close and your enemies closer."

"That could get you killed."

"What happens, happens."

As they were getting dressed, Charles told her, "One more thing."

"What is it?"

Charles asked, "Tomorrow morning, I have an appointment with Mr. Martin. Would you like to go?"

Ciara asked with a dumb look, "As a friend or a police officer?"

Charles said in a strange voice, "As Ciara. I have never heard both. This might put you in trouble with your bosses. This Mr. Martin has big friends in this town, I believe even in your police department."

"Hell, why not?" Ciara asked, "Well, what is this meeting?"

"I forgot to tell you that. In the morning, I will tell you as we go."

Ciara asked in a very sexy way, "Well, are you going to take me home, or should I just stay the night?"

Charles knew what he wanted. Before he could get a word in, Ciara already was down to her underwear. "I believe I will sleep here." Then she jumped in bed. "Well, are you joining me?"

Charles could hardly wait. He was in bed in no time. Ciara told him, "You were good earlier. Let's just see how good you are in bed." They made love again. Charles could not believe what was happening. He had not been with a woman for years whom he cared for. Then all at once, he was doing it twice. Charles just wondered how Ciara was feeling. He knew, with her job and knowing all the people she knew, he was probably not the most satisfying sex partner she ever had.

Charles woke up in the morning at his usual time. He did turn around and notice Ciara was not in bed. He got out of bed and went to the bathroom. There was Ciara still taking her shower. Her body still looked as good as last night. Charles was looking at her when she was coming out of the shower. Ciara was surprised that Charles was standing there. She asked, "Enjoyed the view?"

Charles was embarrassed; he just said, "You look just as good if not better than last night."

Ciara replied with a smile, "You just keep that thought. We have other things to do today." She stepped out of the shower. "It is your turn."

While Charles was taking his shower, Ciara was getting dressed. He opened the shower door and yelled at her, "If you are hungry, just order room service!"

Ciara was walking toward the shower. There was Charles, naked. She was staring at him. Charles said, "Keep that thought. We have things to do."

She was just in her underwear. He watched her taking off her bra and panties. Ciara said, "What the hell, this is better than room service." She went in the shower. They made love. Charles could not get over her nice breasts and body. He figured no matter how good or bad he was, he must have something.

When they both finally were done in the shower, Ciara asked, "You do not have to tell all your friends everything, do you?"

"I will only tell my friends what you tell yours."

Ciara smiled and told Charles, "You are a dirty dog."

Charles and Ciara finally were ready to leave. He picked the bugs from the tabletop. He then went to his suitcase and took out the disk. Charles told Ciara, "We can leave now."

When they were walking toward the elevator, Charles noticed a hotel maid was walking by. He noticed the name tag said "Frances." Charles stopped and turned around. He was looking at Frances's back and, out of the blue, yelled, "Frances, wait a second!"

Frances turned around and asked, "Are you speaking to me?"

Charles walked toward her with his hand in his pocket. He pulled out a twenty. "If you are the Frances I think you are, thanks." And he gave her the money.

Frances could not believe what happened; neither could Ciara. Frances walked toward Charles. "Thank you, Mr. Appel."

"You just call me Charles."

Frances started to laugh. Ciara asked, "What is so funny?"

"That is what Isabel told me Mr. Appel would say." Frances turned around and went back to her job.

Ciara looked at Charles and told him, "You know, there is probably no one like you in Newark or, for that matter, the world."

"We better get down to the lobby and see if Carlo is there or not."

As the elevator door opened, Ralph was standing right there. Charles thought, *This is odd. A person who is part owner will not be here at this time of day.* "You know, Ralph, you have one of the best hotels I have ever been in." Charles went on to explain, "All your employees speak English. I have been in hotels in Chicago, New York, and other places.

Their maids and other workers either speak Spanish or God knows what."

Ralph did not know what to say. Charles caught him off guard; he could tell he shocked Ralph. Charles reached out his hand to shake Ralph's. As a reflex, Ralph reached out his. Charles had the bugs in his hand while they were shaking hands, and he knew Ralph could feel them. "You know, I change my mind. You can call me Charles."

Ralph still did not know what to say, especially when he was feeling the bugs in his hand. Charles made sure Ralph took them. Ralph was watching Ciara all this time. He was trying to think if he should make a big deal about what Charles told him or about the bugs. He took the bugs and said, "Mr. Appel, thanks for the compliment."

Charles told him what he said was the truth. "Tell all your employees to keep up the good work. Remember, you can call me Charles."

Ralph was in the elevator by this time. As the door was closing, he said, "Thanks, Charles." Ralph was mashing the bugs in his hand all the time Charles was talking. He was hoping Charles and Ciara did not find the rest of the bugs.

Ciara could not wait and asked, "What was that about?"

"While I was shaking his hand, I gave him back their bugs."

"That pissed him off. You know, what you said about the employees speaking English is right. They all speak English at this hotel. The others in town do not."

"That's what bothers me in our great country. We let all these people in our country, and then we do not care if they speak English. That is bullshit. Do not get me started. I will show you my bad side. You might not like me no more."

"Hell, I do not think you have a bad side, just a fair and honest side."

Charles laughed. "That is what I always told my wife. Just be fair and honest."

They were at the main doors. Charles had seen a cab outside; it was not Carlo's. He was disappointed. Ciara could tell. To cheer Charles up, she said, "We are early. Maybe Carlo is a right-on-time person."

"You might be right. We are early."

"This will give me time to call my partner and the station." Ciara pulled her cell phone from her purse. She told Charles, "Hell, I have ten messages."

"When I get back home, I am going to buy a cell phone."

Ciara laughed. "You mean you never had one before?"

"Hell no. I do not like to be bothered when I golf, so I never messed with it."

Ciara used her speed dial; her partner answered on the first ring. Charles could hear his voice where he was standing. George asked, "Where were you last night? I tried to call you."

Ciara answered with a smile, "I was having my date, remember, George?"

"You must like this Charles."

"Well, we had a very good first date. George, I am going to be late. I am going with Charles on business."

George asked, "You mean on police business?"

"I will tell you later." Ciara then called the station. Charles did not have any idea whom she was talking to. She just said, "Captain, I am going to be a few hours late." Ciara knew he would not mind; she never was late or missed work unless it was important.

Charles asked, "Who is your captain? Is he or she as nice as you?"

Ciara laughed. "Well, Captain Armstrong is nice, but Arthur tries to be tough with all the pressure he has on him." She could tell Charles had something on his mind. "OK, what is it?"

Charles asked, "What are you talking about?"

"Hell, I am not stupid. You are thinking about something."

"Can your captain be trusted?"

"I think so."

"Do me a favor. Do not tell your partner or captain what happens today until I leave town. Is that fair?"

Ciara told Charles, "I can live with that."

"Good. Make sure you keep your eyes and ears open. It just might be important when I come back in two weeks. Promise me you will be very careful from now on." Ciara assured Charles she would be. He can tell Ciara thought he was making too big a deal out of this.

Ciara was looking through the door. "Here comes another cab. Is this your friend Carlo?"

Charles looked up. "Hell," he told her, "my eyes are not that good. Wait till the cab is closer."

By this time, they were outside. The bellman asked if they wanted a cab. Charles told him, "No, not yet."

Ciara could tell this must be Carlo's cab because, as it was getting closer, Charles was smiling. He told Ciara, "This is it." Carlo parked the cab and was getting out. "Let's go." Charles dragged Ciara toward Carlo.

"All right, slow down." Charles stopped and told Ciara he was sorry.

He introduced Ciara to Carlo. Carlo told her, "Charles here was very nervous meeting you. Now I understand why."

Charles asked him, "Well, you with me or not?"

"Do not get impatient. Let's see how this meeting goes, and then I will tell."

Ciara told Carlo, "That makes sense. I do not know if this is the right way to do this."

Charles told both of them, "This is the only way I am going to do this."

Ciara was looking at Carlo, who was looking at her. At the same time, they told Charles, "This time, we will. Next time, we might decide what is best."

Charles told them, "Deal. Let's get going."

As Charles let Ciara in the back seat, Carlo was already starting the car. Carlo told him, "Hell, they fixed the tires on that black Ford."

"I wondered if that was the same car."

Ciara asked, "What are you guys talking about?"

Carlo told her, "Well, that car and I had a few words yesterday. I shot the driver's side tires out after I took their guns from them."

"Did you report it to the police?"

Charles told Ciara, "Well, he just did."

Carlo started to laugh. "You know, I could work for you. Hell, I better tell you the truth before we get to Mr. Martin's business office."

Charles asked, "What are you talking about?"

"Well, if I work for you, I am not as broke as you think. I am worth just around three hundred thousand after my divorce. I just cannot figure out what to do."

Charles was a little amazed, and then he told Carlo, "You know, you could be a great help to me not only as a driver. You could also figure out what companies own what. You also could help me find the others Jake had helping him."

Ciara told both of them she thought Charles should have told the police about Mr. Martin breaking in his house. She went on, saying, "You should have called the police yesterday."

Charles and Carlo both looked at Ciara. She had never seen that look from Charles. Everything was quiet all at once. Charles was trying to say something but just could not put it together. Carlo thought it was Charles's place to say something. Ciara told them, "All right, I am with you guys today. I promised Charles I will not do anything until he leaves town. I will keep my word."

Charles smiled and told Ciara, "We will have something to say for sure on our next date."

Carlo told her, "Well, you two must have had a good time."

Ciara was getting embarrassed and just told Carlo, "Mind your own business."

Carlo started to laugh. "That is fair."

Charles was smiling all the time while Ciara and Carlo were talking. She told Charles as she was smiling, "Take that smile off your face."

"Well, we did have a great time."

"Yes, we did." Then she kissed him.

Ciara asked Charles if he had some kind of game plan when they arrived at Mr. Martin's office. He told her, "Well, not really. I was just going to play it by ear."

"Well, I wonder if they have guns there."

"Hell, I am giving them the disk. They do not have to use guns." Ciara gave Charles this stare. He admitted, "Maybe we should have a plan. Hell, you're the policewoman. You tell us."

"Leave me alone. Give me a few minutes."

Charles told Carlo, "Hell, you have any ideas?"

"Hell no. Someone better have one quickly. We have three blocks to go."

Carlo pulled the car in a parking spot. Ciara told them, "Well, how's this for a plan? Carlo, you stay here. If we are not back in thirty minutes, call the police." She handed him her phone. "You do know how to use one?"

"Hell, I have my own. Keep yours."

Ciara told Charles, "Hell, you better hire Carlo. At least he is in the right year."

Carlo asked, "What is that about?"

Charles told him, "Hell, Ciara cannot believe I do not have a cellular phone yet."

Carlo was laughing. "Hell, I cannot believe it either." Charles told both of them to leave him alone.

Charles said in a more serious tone, "Well, what is your next step?"

Ciara said, "Maybe you could hide the disk before we get to Mr. Martin's office, say, in a garbage can or something. At least if things get messy, they will not have the disk right away."

Charles asked, "Well, I have a question."

Ciara sat there for a minute. "Well, what is it?"

"If they want the other disk, they will be very disappointed." Carlo and Ciara could tell Charles was thinking. Charles asked, "Well, do you have your weapon on you, just in case?"

Ciara told him, "No, I left it at the department. I really did not think I needed a weapon on a date." Carlo started to laugh again. Charles could not help from laughing either.

Charles told Ciara, "Maybe you should stay with Carlo."

She started to jump all over Charles. "What do you mean? We had a very good time last night. We decided I'll go with you just so you have a witness, which is a cop. Now you change your mind. If I do not go, we will never have another date."

"All right, you and I will go together. I just do not want you to get in trouble with your captain."

"You let me worry about my captain, and you worry about the disks."

"Fine. You will go out with me again, won't you?"

Ciara looked at Charles. "Yes, I will be glad too."

Carlo interrupted them; he reached over to the glove box. When he opened it, he reached for his .38 pistol. "Here, you might need this, Ciara."

She was dumbfounded. Right away, she asked, "What the hell are you doing with this weapon?"

"After yesterday, I decided to put my gun in the car instead of underneath my pillow."

Ciara took the pistol; she made sure it was loaded. She thanked Carlo and turned her head toward Charles. "I hope I do not have to use it. I will have a lot of explaining to do. When we enter the office, we can tell the situation. If it seems right, you will ask to go to the restroom or something, get the disk, and give it to them. We will get the hell out."

Charles told her, "Hell, that sounds good enough for me. What about you, Carlo?"

"Hell, I better call the police now."

Ciara told him, "Very funny."

Charles and Ciara stepped out of the car. He told Carlo, "Remember, thirty minutes."

"Do not worry."

As they were walking toward the building, Charles asked Ciara, "Maybe you should go back. I do not want you to get fired or in trouble."

"Hell, let me worry about that."

"These people are big. I believe they control a lot of people, even police departments."

Ciara again told Charles to let her worry about that. "You just give them the damn disk, and then we will get the hell out."

By this time, they were at the main door. Charles opened the door for Ciara. The inside looked beautiful, like an entrance to a nice hotel. It was even better than the Plaza. Charles went to the middle of the entrance, about twenty feet from the door. There was this tall well-built man standing at the counter. The man asked, "Can I help you?"

"Yes. I am Mr. Charles Appel. I have appointment with Mr. Martin."

The man looked at his notepad. Ciara and Charles both knew he knew who they were; he was just putting on a show. The man looked up. "You may go to the elevators. Take the one on your left. It will take you straight to the top. There will be someone waiting for you." Charles thanked him, and then they walked toward the elevator.

When they were on the top floor and the doors opened, there was another well-built man. He told them to follow him. Charles noticed there were several computers lined up by the wall. He could not help himself and asked the man, "Did you have computer problems?"

The man turned around and told Charles, "Very funny." Charles knew right then the man knew who he was.

As they were getting closer to this big office door, Charles noticed a flowerpot. He walked to Ciara's right and slipped the disk in it. Charles pushed Ciara's arm and pointed to the flowerpot. He could tell she understood what he did.

The man knocked on the door. There was another person opening in from the other side. The man told Charles and Ciara, "Come on in." Charles let Ciara walk in first; he was right behind her.

Charles could see Mr. Martin on the other side of a huge walnut desk. The office room was very large. On Mr. Martin's left, there was Thomas standing. Charles told Thomas he had a good round yesterday. Thomas said he had a good time. Mr. Martin told Charles, "Yes, I heard all about that game." Charles asked if he made a bet.

Ciara went to her right while Charles was making small talk. She decided not to sit in a chair; she just stood there. Charles noticed she had her hand real close to her purse without looking suspicious.

Mr. Martin looked at Charles. "Well, where is the disk?"

"It is close. I just do not want to bring it too close in case someone does something stupid." Charles looked Mr. Martin right in the eye. "Like breaking in my house."

Mr. Martin apologized for the house break-in and explained, "We thought you might have something of ours that Jake gave you."

"Why not just ask me? I would have told you."

Mr. Martin did not want to call him a liar. Charles even knew he was not telling the truth. He was testing Mr. Martin's nerves. Mr. Martin told him, "Well, I want the disk now."

"There will be no harm coming to us?"

Mr. Martin told his man at the door, "Search the woman." The man started to walk toward Ciara. Mr. Martin told him to stop. The man stopped right in his tracks. "Let's have some fun out of this. Take off your clothes. We will see if you have the disk."

Ciara knew she was being tested now. They did not even search them as they entered the building or the office. She knew Mr. Martin knew she was a policewoman. Ciara told him, "You are crazy. I am not taking off my clothes for you or anyone."

Mr. Martin told her, "You leave us no choice. Either you take them off or my men will rip them off."

Charles knew this was not going to happen; he started to tell Mr. Martin, "The disk is . . ." He could not finish his sentence. Ciara started to take off her clothes. She had her dress unzipped and pulled down to her waist where you could see her sexy bra. Ciara pulled down her dress clear to the floor. They all could see her panties very well.

Ciara asked Mr. Martin, "Well, you want to see more?"

Mr. Martin did not want to push her anymore. He told Charles, "Give me the damn disk. I will leave your lady friend alone."

Charles went toward Ciara and told her to put her dress back on. He, through the excitement, realized they were not searched. Charles did not have Ciara's experience and did not realize Mr. Martin was testing her.

Ciara could sense Charles was pissed off. He reached in her purse and pulled out the revolver, aiming it right at Mr. Martin. By this time, Thomas had his gun out. Mr. Martin told everyone to relax. Charles told Ciara, "Get that damn disk now." She went toward the door. "If anyone bothers Ciara, you're dead." Mr. Martin told his man to let her go.

Ciara was being followed by one of Mr. Martin's man. She walked to the flowerpot and found the disk. She handed it to the man. They walked back in the room. Ciara went toward Charles. He could tell Ciara was mad. He sensed she was mad at him instead of Mr. Martin.

Mr. Martin was laughing. Charles asked, "What's so funny?"

"You think we'll let you walk in without searching you? We know who your friend is. We were testing both of you. She knew that. You did not." Mr. Martin told Charles, "Now get the hell out before someone gets hurt."

Ciara grabbed Charles. "Well, I think it is time to go." Charles walked behind her. As they entered the elevator, Ciara told him, "You idiot. We were set up. They were seeing if I would go for my gun. They knew if I did, I would be in big trouble. So I went along."

"Well, I should have let them see all your body."

"Thanks for stopping that. I felt Mr. Martin would tell me to stop."

Charles laughed. "Well, if I were in his shoes, if a woman was going to take off her clothes, I would have not stopped her."

"Thanks for that thought."

As they were leaving the office building, Charles asked, "Well, did I hurt your job?"

Ciara said in a sarcastic way, "I do not know. Time will tell."

They were almost to Carlo's cab. He was already out. He could not wait to ask how things went. Ciara told Carlo, "Well, they got the disk. Charles did not handle the situation very well at all."

Charles told him, "I will tell you later."

Ciara was on her phone. She asked George to pick her up at her apartment. Ciara gave Carlo her address. He asked, "Should I lose the black Ford again."

Ciara told him, "No, they already know where I live."

On the way to Ciara's apartment, Charles apologized for not handling the situation well. Ciara told him to forget it. "You are not used to this kind of work."

As Carlo pulled up to the duplex, Charles noticed Ciara lived in a very fine neighborhood. He got out of the car to open the door. Ciara stepped out. Charles started to walk her to the door. She told him, "This is fine. I will see you later."

Charles thought for just a few seconds. "What about tonight?"

"No. I have to get some rest."

"Well, I do not leave till Sunday, maybe tomorrow."

"Do you not get it? I am mad at you."

"Well, sorry. What about in two weeks?"

"We will see. Call me."

Charles went back to the car. Carlo asked, "What did you do to her?"

Charles told Carlo how she had to take her dress off. Then in some way or another, he pulled Ciara's pistol out. "Mr. Martin was just testing us. He found out Ciara is a cool person and I am a hothead."

Carlo started to laugh. "Hell, just relax. You will see her tomorrow."

"You are right." Charles looked at Carlo. "Well, what are you going to do?"

"What do you mean?"

"Well, you can work for me starting now, or you can take me back to the hotel."

"Hell, let me think some more while I take you back to the hotel." Charles did not say anything all the way there. Carlo pulled up. "You know, that black Ford is still following us." Charles told him he did not give a shit right now. "You know, I need a day off. What about a round of golf on me? I know this nice course. We can play."

Charles told him, "Well, that is the best idea yet." So Carlo waited for Charles to get his clubs. He was back in no time.

Carlo said, "Hell, we will stop at Jake's first just to have a couple of drinks." He and Charles went at the bar and had their beers and then went to the golf course.

Ciara ran in her duplex crying. She knew she really liked Charles; she just did not know how to handle this kind of situation. She had not felt this way toward anyone in a long time. While she was running around getting ready, she looked out the window. There was George, right on time. Ciara hurried up and finished getting dressed.

As Ciara was walking to George's car, he could tell she was mad. Ciara entered the car and turned her head. "I will tell you what happened when I am ready."

George started his car and told Ciara, "The captain wants to see us."

"Well, that did not take long."

"Should I know something before we go in the captain's office?"

Ciara knew she made the promise to Charles. She and George had been partners for two years now. "Well, on Jake Appel's case."

George looked at Ciara, "Well, what about it?"

"Well, Mr. Appel has more information than we thought. In fact, he has more information than we do."

George asked in a hurried voice, "You better tell me so I do not look stupid to the captain."

"You promise not to tell anyone?" George promised. Ciara told him about the virus that Charles put on a disk; in some way or another, the disk ruined some computers of Mr. Martin. "Well, Mr. Appel has some other disks at his house or somewhere in Coal City. Mr. Martin wants them very bad. He also wants some names that he thinks Charles has."

Ciara started to cry. George asked, "Well, do you like this Charles?"

"Yes, I do. I just do not know how to handle this. It has been a long time for both of us."

"Hell, he will call you before he goes back."

"I told him not to call me."

George said with a grin on his face, "Hell, if he likes you, that will not stop him from calling."

"I hope you are right."

George and Ciara pulled into the police station. Ciara told him, "Remember, this is between us, not the captain."

George assured her he would not say a word. "In fact, you do the talking to the captain."

"That will be fine."

They were at the captain's office. The captain had seen them coming and motioned for them to come in. Then as they entered, he told George to shut the door. Captain Armstrong did not give Ciara time to move no more than a foot. He asked her, "What the hell are you doing?"

Ciara asked the captain, "What are you talking about?"

The captain was getting mad. "What the hell I am talking about? That Mr. Appel is getting in the way of your investigation. I want him out of your way."

"Wait a minute, this Mr. Appel has more evidence and more facts than we do. How come all our leads are dead? How come all our evidence is nothing. Then this Mr. Appel comes in town and stirs the pot, and all hell breaks loose."

Captain Armstrong was getting red in the face. George and Ciara both knew what she said rattled his cage. Armstrong asked George, "You know anything about this?"

George looked at Ciara and then told the captain, "No, sir. Whatever Ciara found was between after work last night and this morning."

Captain Armstrong looked at Ciara. "I think either you or Mr. Appel is hiding something. You better let me know very soon."

Ciara, in a very disturbing way, asked the captain, "How come you called us in now? Hell, we have not had a solid lead since the murders. Then Mr. Appel comes to town and had a meeting, and then you called us in. Who the hell is talking to you?"

The captain was furious. He told George to leave the room. Ciara told him, "You stay. I might need a witness just to keep this situation calm."

George asked the captain, "What do you want?"

"You can stay. Sit your ass down." Captain Armstrong looked at Ciara. "What was that supposed to mean?"

Ciara was still mad. "Well, sir, this is very funny. Mr. Appel has a meeting with this Mr. Martin, and then after less than an hour, you call us in."

Captain Armstrong lost his composure. "Jesus Christ, Mr. Appel pulled your revolver on Mr. Martin. That could have been a very bad situation for this department if he pulled the trigger."

Ciara walked toward the captain's desk. "Who the hell told you about the damn gun? I did not bring it up. Who told you?"

The captain was mad by now. "Well, Mr. Martin has a lot of powerful friends in our city. He knows the chief. Hell, he runs around with the damn mayor. You do not think something like that will not get to me?"

Ciara asked, "Well, what do you want from me?"

"From now on, George and Henry are on the case. You go back to your desk and start on the last case you were on. Do not get involved with Jake Appel's murder or his girlfriend's. What's her name?"

"It was Amanda Tulman, sir."

"You know anything about some disk Mr. Appel has?"

Ciara kept her cool. "No, sir. Why?"

"Mr. Martin thinks Mr. Appel has some disk of theirs that will help the investigation. We are thinking of a way to get them." Ciara knew the disk was not actually Mr. Martin's. But the information on the disk might have come from Mr. Martin's people. Ciara decided to keep her mouth shut.

Captain Armstrong told Ciara, "You can leave now. Tell Henry to come in."

She looked at George and gave him a look that said, *Keep your damn mouth shut.* George nodded that he understood.

Ciara walked by Henry's desk and told him, "The captain wants to see you."

Henry asked, "What about?"

"Hell, let him tell you."

Ciara went to her desk. She knew she had to find Charles to tell him what the captain told her. She called the hotel. When the person answered, Ciara said in a hurried voice, "I need to speak to Charles Appel. It is very important."

"Mr. Appel just left a few minutes ago with his golf clubs. Want me to leave a message?"

Ciara asked, "Who am I speaking to?"

"This is Henry Jacob. I am the day shift manager."

"Tell Mr. Appel he has to call me as soon as possible. I am Ciara Steel."

"You want to leave a number?"

"No, he knows my number." Then she hung up.

Ciara was trying to figure a way to find Charles without being too noticeable. She left the station and drove to the hotel herself. She asked the doorman if he remembered Mr. Appel leaving with his golf clubs. He told Ciara he sure did. "He went with his taxi driver friend."

"Do you know where they went?" Ciara thanked him and then left.

For once, Ciara wished she golfed. She only knew one golf course in the area. The problem was there were at least twenty golf courses in a forty-mile range. Ciara's second problem was Charles introduced her to Carlo but did not give his last name. Hell, for being a policewoman, she did not even know his cab number. Then she remembered that the cab company name was Donnley Cab Service.

Ciara was driving toward the golf course she knew. On the way, she called George. He asked, "Where are you? We need to talk."

"Never mind now. Give me the number of Donnley Cab Service."

George went through the phone book. "Well, it must not be that big of a cab company. Here is a little ad in the yellow pages."

Ciara did not hesitate. "Well, what is it?" George gave her the number. Ciara thanked him.

George yelled, "Wait, do not hang up! I have to talk to you!" He heard the click before he said the last word. George tried to call back, but the line was busy.

Ciara dialed the number immediately after George gave it to her. There was no answer. She arrived at the golf course in a very short time. Hell, she did not even know the name of it before. The sign said "Country Air Golf Course." As she went up to the drive, she was looking for Carlo's cab. She did not see a cab anywhere.

Ciara walked in the clubhouse to the pro shop desk. This tall slender man asked, "Can I help you?"

"Yes, maybe. I need to know if two men are playing golf here." The man looked at Ciara.

"Well, we only have a hundred or so here. Could you give me a name or something?"

"Charles Appel or a Carlo Donnley." Ciara noticed there was this name on the wall: John Jones Pro. She asked, "Are you John?"

"No, that is the pro. I am just assistant pro. My name is Dan Wilson." Ciara had seen his name on the wall a few feet from where the pro name was.

Dan looked up at her. "Hell, I know Carlo. He is not here today. He plays our course during the week.

"Does Carlo play much?"

"Does he play? Hell, we cannot figure out when he makes any money driving his cab. Wait a minute, I will call a couple of courses where I know he plays." Ciara thanked him. While Dan was on the phone, she was walking around the clubhouse. She did not realize the money in golf clubs. She thought it was a waste of money.

Dan walked where Ciara was looking at the clubs. He asked, "You want to buy a set?" Ciara told him no. Dan handed her a piece of paper. "Here you are. Carlo is playing at the Oaks Golf Course." Ciara was just going to ask how to get there when Dan told her, "I wrote the directions on the back. It is not too far from here."

Ciara thanked Dan. "If I ever start the game, I will give you the first chance."

"That will be great," he replied, even though he knew the odds of her playing golf was slim.

Ciara, while walking to her car, checked if she had any messages. George left several. She decided she did not want to talk to anyone in the department and just turned her phone off. Ciara followed the directions that Dan gave her. She had never been on some of these roads. She never went golfing either.

When Ciara found the golf course, she was disappointed. The sign needed a paint job; it looked very run down and old compared with the other course. As she was approaching the clubhouse, Ciara noticed how the fairways looked greener, and the trees seemed to look better taken care of. *This is the second golf course I have ever been on. Who am I to judge one from another?*

Ciara parked her car. She only had fifty feet or so to walk. This course had a smaller clubhouse. When she walked in, the pro counter was to her right. Just as she was going toward it, Ciara noticed this old man standing behind the counter. She also noticed there were no pictures or sign to tell who the pro was. Just as she was walking close to the counter, he saw a tall heavyset man. She decided this man must be in his seventies or so. This man asked Ciara, "Are you the one looking for Carlo and his friend?"

"Yes, how did you know?"

"Well, Dan gave a very good description of you. He was right. You are very good looking."

Ciara thanked him. Even before she started to ask where Charles and Carlo were, this old guy yelled, "Samatha, I am going to take this lady out on the course! Take care of the place!"

Samatha yelled back, "OK, Keith!"

Ciara asked Keith, "What are you doing?"

"Hell, I thought we go out and find them. They should be on number 7 or so."

Ciara followed Keith to the golf cart. She asked Keith to slow down. Keith turned around and saw she was several feet behind, so he waited for her. Keith asked, "How long have you known Carlo?"

"I just met him. I really want to speak to Carlo's golf partner."

Keith told her, "This is the first time I have seen that person. Get in."

Ciara lifted her leg to get in the cart. Keith noticed how nice looking she was, even though she was short. She just had this nice look on her. Ciara could tell he was checking her out. She asked, "Well, you like what you see?"

Keith started to laugh. "You are one of the better-looking women who have ever been here. Usually, women stay away from my course. It's not the best looking one from the buildings and driveway." He did tell her his course was one of the hardest playing course around.

As Keith was driving the cart, he told Ciara, "If you see someone hitting the ball, tell me if it is coming toward us."

Ciara said in a very nervous way she had never played golf before. "How the hell am I supposed to tell you if the ball is coming at us or not?" Keith was laughing while she was talking. Ciara looked at Keith and asked him, "What is so funny?"

"Well, lady, I cannot see that good no more. I was hoping you could watch out for both of us."

"This is great—on a damn golf course in a golf cart when the driver cannot see."

Just as they were toward the left rough, about two hundred yards from the number 9 tee, Ciara heard someone yelled four. She did not know what that meant, so she asked Keith, "What does four mean?" Then at that second, a golf ball bounced and hit the cart.

Keith asked Ciara, "What did you say? My hearing is not that good either."

Ciara, in a louder voice, asked, "What does four mean?"

Keith stopped the cart and told her, "Turn your heard around."

She, in a surprised voice, asked, "What for?"

"When you hear four, that means someone has hit the ball toward your direction."

Ciara told him to go on. "Hell, you idiot, it already happened about thirty yards ago."

Keith had finally seen the golfers; there were four of them. He went on by them. Ciara asked, "Why did you not stop them and ask if they had seen Charles and Carlo?"

"Hell, this is my golf course. I know what I am doing."

Ciara said in a very loud voice, "You cannot see or hear, but you can find Charles and Carlo without asking someone?"

"Carlo and Charles should be the next two golfers." Keith approached the eighth green. He stopped and asked Ciara, "Do you see anyone yet?" She told him no. "One of them had a bad hole." Ciara did not know what he meant. Keith just kept on going.

She told him, "There are two golfers riding toward us from the other tee box, I think."

"Well, there they are." Keith was getting closer. Ciara could not tell; they both had on golf hats.

When Keith was just ten yards away, she told him, "That is them."

Charles was not paying attention to the golf cart coming toward them. Carlo noticed Keith; he was not sure who was with him. As Keith was getting closer, Carlo could tell it was Ciara. Charles was setting up his shot. Carlo told him, "You better wait."

Charles stopped his stance and looked up. He could not believe he was looking at Ciara. Carlo said with a smile, "Hell, she came to see you." He could tell Charles was happy about seeing Ciara.

Ciara jumped out of the cart and ran up to Charles. "We have to talk now. It is important."

"Hell, I never quit in a middle of a round unless it rains." Charles looked up to the sky and then at Ciara. "Hell, it is not raining, so why not just ride along?"

Keith overheard Charles and told Ciara, "That will be great. We will follow you and Carlo, and then on the back nine, I will play with Carlo. You two can ride together."

Carlo told her, "Hell, that sounds good to me. I need to win some more money from Charles anyway."

Charles hit his ball solid. Carlo told him, "Hell, when your friend comes, you start hitting the ball better."

Charles, with a big smile, told Carlo, "I think my game is going to change."

Ciara was not very happy. She tried again to tell Charles what happened at the police station. He told Ciara, "Hell, it cannot be that bad. I need to finish in low numbers to win my money back."

"How much are you behind?"

"Hell, I forgot." Charles asked Carlo, "How much do I owe you?"

Carlo turned around. "You owe me five dollars."

Ciara said in disbelief, "Hell, what are you playing for?"

"A dollar a hole and first on for a dollar."

Carlo was laughing out loud now. Ciara asked, "What is so funny?"

"I bet you thought we were playing for big bucks."

Ciara looked down to the ground. "Well, I thought it will be a lot more than that."

Keith told her, "Get in the cart. We will watch from a distance."

Ciara did what she was told and told Keith, "Hell, he is a stubborn person."

"Hell, for not meeting you two before, I say you both are stubborn."

"Well, I think you are right. I still have to talk to Charles. It is very important."

"Hell, it can wait for ten more holes."

Charles and Carlo tied the next holes. Carlo was closer to the pin on eight, and Charles was closer to the pin on nine. They both parred each hole. Keith was surprised of Charles's swing. He told Ciara, "That boyfriend of yours has a good stroke."

"He is not my boyfriend, just a friend."

"Well, the way you two looked at each other, he is your boyfriend or lover." Ciara did not say a word.

By this time, all four of them were at the clubhouse. Carlo led the way in the side door where the sign said "snack shop." Ciara was right behind Carlo and then Charles. Keith went to the main door, where he kept his clubs. Ciara asked Samatha, "Where is the bathroom?" She noticed Samatha had a cooler waiting for Carlo.

"Go to your right. You will not miss it." Samatha asked Charles, "Do you want some beer too?"

"Yes, just give me the same as Carlo. That will be fine." Charles did not realize until Samatha reached in the big cooler and pulled out a twelve-pack. He told Carlo, "Hell, you drink just as much as I do or more."

"Well, we did not have any on the front, so Samatha knew I will drink my twelve beers one way or another."

Carlo went outside to help Keith move the clubs around. Keith told him, "This will be a very interesting back nine."

"Hell, since Ciara came, Charles is hitting the ball good."

"Are you worried you are going to lose?"

"Hell, what happens, happens."

Charles and Ciara were walking out. She was still trying to get Charles to stop so she could tell him what happened. Charles told her he was sorry. "Maybe we better just start a new day now."

Ciara told him she was sorry. "I have to talk to you. It is important."

"Hell, we will talk at the nineteenth hole. I want to beat Carlo." Charles could tell he was upsetting Ciara. He also knew whatever happened must be important for her to find them. Then Charles figured a few more hours or so would not hurt. "Just sit back and watch us play. Maybe you might want to play sometime."

"In your dreams." Charles laughed just at the same time Ciara was laughing.

Ciara noticed Carlo and Charles were drinking a can a hole. Charles was so interested in his game that he forgot to ask Ciara if she wanted a beer. When he turned around, he did not even notice Ciara had a beer in her hand. She told Charles, "Thanks for asking."

"Just help yourself."

"I will thanks."

Carlo and Charles were still tied, going in the eighteenth hole. Charles told Carlo, "Hell, I still owe you five dollars. I bet you ten dollars I'll beat you in this hole."

Carlo, without hesitating, told Charles. "You got a bet."

Keith told Carlo, "Are you going to tell him about the creek?"

"Hell no. You do not either."

"Hell, the way he is hitting the ball, he will drive it right in the creek."

"No shit."

Carlo was teeing off first. Charles was standing by the cart, looking at Ciara. She was looking at the score card and told Charles, "You know, I do not know nothing about this game, but what does this line on the score card mean?"

Charles looked at the card and asked her, "What are you talking about?"

"This line that went through the fairway."

Charles said with a dismayed look, "Well, that son of a bitch, he was not going to tell me."

Ciara asked, "Tell you what?"

"Thanks. Just watch."

Carlo hit his drive really good. Charles noticed he used his driver but choked way down on the club. Charles went to the tee box. He was smiling at Carlo. Carlo was sure Charles had his driver; he knew Charles would be right in the creek. As Charles brought his club back, he only took it three-quarters back and then hit the ball solid. Carlo told Keith, "Hell, he figured it out."

Keith was laughing. "Well, your plan did not work."

Carlo asked Charles, "How did you know?"

"Hell, I did not. Ciara figured it out." Charles's next shot landed three feet from the pin. Carlo's was closer to the green by ten yards; his next shot landed fifteen feet from the pin. Carlo missed his birdie try. Charles told him, "Hell, pick it up for par."

"Hell, do not choke."

"Hell, for trying to set me up, I will not miss this one." Charles walked right to the ball. He told Carlo, "You know, this hole is mine." Charles hit the ball; it rolled like it had eyes and went straight in.

Keith was laughing and told Carlo, "Well, lose some, and win some."

Charles was not paying any attention on Keith's game. Keith told them, "Hell, you guys never waited for me at all." Charles told him he was sorry. "Well, for your information, I'll beat both of you guys on the back nine."

Charles and Carlo looked at each other and then at the score card. Keith shot thirty-three. Charles shot a thirty-five and Carlo a thirty-six. Charles told Keith, "Hell, good nine."

Ciara looked at Keith. "For not seeing or hearing, you are not bad at all."

Keith told all of them, "Hell, it helps when you own your own course."

Ciara picked up the cooler while Charles took his clubs. She noticed all the beer was gone. Hell, she only had one. Carlo was finishing his last beer as he was getting out of the cart. Ciara asked, "Do you guys always drink that much beer?"

Carlo told her, "I do not know about Charles, but I do."

Keith asked them if they wanted to have one more before they left. Carlo told him, "No, I am going to take Charles and Ciara to Jake's."

Keith told them, "Thanks for letting me play with you, even though you more or less forgot about my score." Ciara thanked Keith for a very nice time. "Hell, you saved the round for Charles. He should take you out to eat."

Charles overheard what Keith said. He looked at Ciara. "Well, what about it?"

Ciara told him, "Let's do one thing at a time. I have to talk to you. After that, you might not want me to be with you."

Carlo told her, "You and Charles follow me to Jake's. You two can do your talking as we go there."

Charles told him, "That is a good idea. Why not take my clubs in your car just in case Ciara and I end up together?"

"Sure, follow me."

Ciara started her car. Charles told her, "All right now, follow Carlo, and tell me what is so important for you to come and find me."

"Captain Armstrong knew what happened in Mr. Martin's office before I arrived at the station."

Charles was not surprised when Ciara told him Mr. Martin knew the chief and the mayor. "Hell, that's not big a deal."

"Well, wait a minute, let me finish. The captain took me off the case. It is George and Detective Henry Strafis."

Charles asked in a very nervous tone, "You did not get fired, did you?"

"No, I am not fired. The captain just took me off the case."

"Well, will George keep you in touch about the case?"

"Well, a few hours ago, I would say yes. Now I do not know. I have this funny feeling now. I still have not told you why I found you. The captain overreacted about Mr. Martin. I believe the captain might know more than we do."

Charles asked, "What are you talking about?"

"The captain is trying to get the prosecution to get your tapes in Coal City. He feels you have evidence for the case."

"What are you saying?"

Ciara pulled off the road and stopped the car. She noticed this black Ford passed her and then hit the brakes as Carlo pulled off the road about a quarter of a mile ahead of Ciara. "You know, I think that black Ford is following either us or Carlo."

"Well, get back on the road. We will try to keep the car between Carlo and you."

Ciara pulled back on the road in no time. Carlo, by either luck or instinct, pulled on the road before the black Ford could pass him.

Charles told Ciara, "That was great driving. We can see what happens now. All right, what are you trying to tell me?"

"I am trying to tell you if the captain gets your disk, then Mr. Martin will have your disk, and the case of your son will be dropped."

"When we get to Jake's, I will make some phone calls. I do not see a problem at this time."

Ciara was surprised. "You mean those disks are not important? Then why are you going through them?"

"The disk is the key. I just feel, with a phone call, I can protect the disk and make Mr. Martin very disappointed again. Just trust me. I will explain."

"You are crazy. This is not a game. They are killing people."

"Do not worry, I am not taking this as a game. Just at this stage, I feel we have to play on what Mr. Martin does."

The black Ford was still following Carlo's cab. Charles asked Ciara, "What would happen if we box that Ford in at Jake's? Is there anything you can do as a police officer?"

"Well, I could think of something."

"Well, if Carlo goes in the back of Jake's, there is not that much room. We could block the black Ford in, then you could do whatever you can do."

Ciara, in a surprised way, told Charles, "You know, you are getting better at this."

Charles told Ciara he remembered this street. "Carlo will take a left here and then turn in the alley. If the car follows Carlo, speed up. We will have them." Sure enough, the black Ford turned in the alley. Ciara sped up. Carlo must have been playing really close attention. As Carlo pulled into Jake's, he purposely blocked part of the alley so the black Ford could not pass him. Ciara was right on their bumper and then stopped. She was out of the car in no time. She had her pistol in her hand as she hurried up to the driver's door. Ciara showed her badge and told the driver to show his driver's license. Charles could not believe how fast Ciara did that. Hell, he was just getting to the back of the car. Carlo was already at the passenger door.

The passenger could not decide what to do. Carlo just told him, "Well, here we are again. You might need more tires."

Charles told Carlo, "No, not this time. Let Ciara handle it."

The driver told Ciara, "You do not know what you are getting into."

She looked at his license. "Well, Mr. Larry Gillett or whatever your name is, you were speeding and following too close." Then Ciara went on. "I believe you were driving in a reckless manner as you pulled into this alley. Have you been drinking?" The driver told her hell no.

Ciara made the guy get out and walk a line. Larry was as sober as could be; he walked the line really straight. All the time, he told Ciara, "You might need to find another job."

Ciara asked, "Mr. Gillett, are you threatening me?"

"No, I am telling you, you are messing with the wrong people. You better let us go."

"OK, get the hell out. I do not want to see this car again today."

Ciara told Carlo to move his car. He looked at Charles, who shrugged in a way that said Ciara was handling the situation all right. Carlo parked his car in the proper parking place; the black Ford took off. Ciara told Charles, "I will park my car beside Carlo's."

Carlo and Charles were really impressed on how Ciara handled the situation. Carlo told him, "Hell, she can take care of herself. You better be careful. She might beat you up."

Charles was laughing. Ciara was walking toward him and asked, "What's so funny?"

"You impressed Carlo so much he told me I better be careful around you."

Ciara told them, "I need a drink after this. I have a feeling this is not the end."

Charles led the way and opened the door for them. Carlo told Ciara, "There is a table over there. What kind of drink do you want?"

"I will drink a beer same as Charles." Charles and Ciara were already seated as Carlo went to the bar and ordered the drinks. She told Carlo she had never been here before. "The outside is rough looking, but the inside is nice looking."

Carlo started to laugh. "Hell, Ciara this is a dump compared with where you go."

"You ever heard of Old Joe's?"

"Yes."

"Well, for your information, my grandpa ran that tavern while I was growing up."

Charles asked, "Old Joe's?"

Carlo told him, "Hell, that tavern is a dump compared with this one. Hell, there used to be fights in that tavern all the time."

Ciara told Carlo, "And my grandpa kicked them out."

While Ciara was taking a drink, she asked Charles, "Give Carlo and me your plan on your disk."

"Well, I am going to call my friends Tom and Kate and tell them to make copies of what Kate had done. Then I was going to tell Andy to put some old bank disks in the safety-deposit boxes and let them have them. I am going to call Samuel."

Ciara asked, "Samuel? Who is that?"

"Hell, Samuel is Amanda's father, Mr. Tulman."

"Hell, he is helping you too."

"Hell yes, he is. Do you know he worked for the CIA?"

"Hell, we cannot find anything out on the Tulmans. It is all top secret."

Charles told Ciara, "Hell, he is going to be one of my aces in the hole, just like you."

"What makes you so sure I will help you?"

"Hell, you went out of your way to find me, even when you are mad at me."

"Well, I guess."

Carlo interrupted, "Hell, the way you handled the black Ford, you have to be on Charles's side."

Ciara started to have another drink, and then she reached out to make a toast. "To the future, whether I have a job or not." Charles and Carlo picked up their beers, and they hit their glasses together.

Charles then told her, "Hell, you can always work for me."

Ciara said with a smile, "I think I am working for you now. It's just that the police department is paying me."

Carlo handed Charles his cell phone. "Here, use my phone. It is more private than the pay phone."

Charles wrote down the numbers and then asked Carlo to dial them. "I still do not understand those small phones." Carlo dialed and handed the phone to Charles. The line was busy. Charles told them, "Hell, if Kate is on the phone, we will be drunk before I get through." He handed the phone back to Carlo.

Carlo and Ciara were laughing. Charles asked, "All right, what did I do now?"

Ciara told him, "Hell, just hit that button by Send. It will automatically redial."

"You are a smart-ass."

Carlo raised his hand. His friend brought over three more beers.

Charles pushed the Redial button; this time, it was ringing. Kate answered the phone. "Kate, how was the disk going?"

"Hell, Jake and his friends are in deep shit. Hell, they have bits and pieces about senators getting killed to judges. You name it, they have it."

"Slow down. I need you to hide your disk and tell Tom to destroy the computer."

Kate asked, "What? Destroy the computer?"

"Yes. Make sure all the memory is destroyed. Hell, let Tom take it to Dingers. They can use it for target practice. I will be back as planned. Get the disk out now."

"I will do it right after we hang up."

Charles asked, "Is Tom playing golf today?"

Kate said in a smart-ass voice, "What do you think?"

Charles started to laugh. "He is playing." He asked Kate to give him the bank number. "I need to talk to Andy." Kate gave Charles the number. "One more thing, make sure Andy can get to the safety-deposit boxes. Do not forget to take all the stuff out. Just give it to Andy. He will help us."

"Do not worry, I will take care of it."

Charles handed the phone back to Carlo and then told him, "Here, dial this number now." Carlo did and handed it back to Charles.

Ciara's glass was empty. Charles raised his hand with three fingers up. Carlo told him, "Hell, that is my job."

Charles was glad the phone was ringing. A voice said, "AJ Trust." Charles knew it was Diane.

He asked, "Is Andy in?"

Diane told him, "Yes, he is, Charles." He could not believe she knew his voice that well.

Andy picked up the phone. Charles told him he needed a favor. Andy asked, "What is it?"

"I need you to put disks in the safety-deposit boxes that Kate will show you. Then I need you to make copies of the disks. Put them in another safety-deposit box of your choice."

Andy asked, "What is going on?"

"Ciara believes the government is going to take those disks. I cannot let that happen. So you let them have everything in the safety-deposit boxes that are in my name. Just make sure you switch the disks and take out all my important papers. I will be back Sunday to fill you in." Andy told him he would do that. Charles asked one more thing. "You have an empty apartment above the bank?

"Yes, I do."

"I want to rent that from you. Is that all right?"

"That will be no problem."

Charles then told Andy, "One more thing, you remind Tom to destroy that computer I have. Make sure the memory is destroyed."

Andy told him he would do that. He then asked, "Is there anything else?"

"No, I will need that apartment Sunday."

"I will give the key to Kate." Charles thanked Andy and then handed the phone back to Carlo.

Charles then gave Carlo the last number. Carlo told him, "Hell, this is going to cost you."

"I will pay whatever it is."

"I am just kidding." Then Carlo dialed the number.

Mrs. Tulman answered the phone. Charles asked, "Janace, is Samuel there?"

"Yes, just a second."

Charles wondered how come everyone knew his voice. Samuel answered the phone. "What do you need, Charles?"

"Samuel, instead of Wednesday, could you and your people be in Coal City, say, Sunday? Something came up."

Samuel yelled at Janace, "We are going to Coal City Sunday instead of Wednesday!"

Charles could hear Janace's voice saying, "That will be fine."

Samuel told Charles, "That will be great." Charles told him he heard Janace's answer.

"Be careful. They are getting closer to home."

"Do not worry."

Charles handed the phone to Carlo. "Here, it is all taken care of."

Ciara started to jump on him. "You mean, in this short time, you have the disks taken care of where nobody will find them?"

"Hell, I did better than that. I am getting copies made. I am having the disks moved to other customers' safety-deposit boxes. Hell, they cannot get a warrant for all the bank safety-deposit boxes. Plus, I have another set of disks hidden somewhere else."

Ciara asked, "What is Samuel Tulman going to do for you?"

"Well, he is going to install a very elaborate alarm system in the bank where we can videotape what is going on in the bank and just see who is doing what when they go to the safety-deposit boxes."

Ciara explained to Charles, "This could be illegal."

"Andy is the president of the bank. I am installing this system to back up his other system. I promise, if Andy says no, then we will not do it. I will have to figure out another way, that is all."

Carlo stepped in and told Charles, "You know, I am leaning toward helping you. I am very concerned that you do not know what you are doing."

"You are exactly right. I am not at all experienced in noticing someone is following me. Nor do I know how to tap phones. Hell, I have four guns at home. I only know how to use one of them. So I need good help. I need people I can trust. I believe I can trust you, Tom, Kate, and Ciara. Nate is in the middle. I also have a lot of friends in Coal City who is helping me in some way or another. There are ten or so people who trusted Jake. They all have a bullet aiming at them. I have to try to save them. I have to try to find out what is going on. I have the disks, which they want very bad. I just pray to God that I can do what needs to be done without any more of my and Jake's friends getting murdered."

Carlo told him, "I will make you a deal. I will help you in any way. If I want to quit at any time, I will walk out. If I feel you are being reckless and not worrying about me and your friends, I will walk out. This is not a game. You might have to kill someone yourself."

While mostly looking at Ciara, Charles told him, "Ciara told me basically the same thing. I promise both of you I am going to learn how to shoot a gun. I am going learn how to protect myself, but most importantly, I do worry about all my friends that are helping me. You both just have to trust me."

Carlo stood up; he reached out his hand. Charles stood up and reached for it. As they were shaking hands, Carlo told him, "Hell, I will give it a try not because of you as much as whoever is after you is already after me anyway. I want to know what is going on too."

Ciara stood up. "You both are crazy. There has to be some agency or police department you can trust."

Charles told her, "The only police officer I trust is you. Your own captain took you off the case. Your own captain, I believe, is working with them."

Ciara said in a whisper, "I really believes I love you. I cannot see you get killed. You promise me you will watch your back."

Charles sat down. Carlo went to the bar and ordered one more round. Ciara was crying as she sat down. Charles told her he thought he loved her too. *Hell, this is the first woman I have been with since my wife died.* "You think I want to lose you?" Ciara reached over and gave him a hug.

Carlo was back at the table and asked, "Well, I missed something?"

Ciara smiled. "Well, I think we can make this work one way or another."

When the waitress brought the drinks over, Charles told Carlo, "You know, you never introduce me to your friends."

Carlo hit himself on the head. "Damn it, I am sorry. I never realize it. I am slow on that kind of stuff."

The lady sat the beers down. "My name is Mary. The bartender is my husband, Jake. We own the place. The cook is Jonathan. He is a friend of the family. The other waitress at night is Marie. She is our daughter. Her husband bartends for us. His name is Roger. The other person in our family is Carlo. He is our son."

Charles and Ciara both dropped their glasses of beer on the table. At the same time, they asked, "Why did you not tell us?"

Carlo was laughing. "I just wanted to make sure I could trust both of you before you found out. Hell, my apartment is on top of the tavern. My grandfather owned it first. He had two boys with both Jake as the middle name. That is how they came up with the name Jake's. My dad's other brother died a few years ago. So Mom and Dad took over the tavern."

Charles was upset with Carlo for not telling him; he was without words. Ciara just slapped Carlo and told him, "You know, you could have told us." Carlo was still having his smile on his face.

Charles finally looked at Carlo. "You know, you think this is funny, but I just wondered I did not like this place. I probably would not come back. Then I would most likely not even want to know you at all."

Carlo was still laughing. "Well, I figure if you did not like me or this tavern, you would not even come back in the first place."

"Well, that is true. I just feel like an asshole for not asking your parents' names before now." Carlo was still laughing; even his mom and dad were laughing.

Mary told Charles, "Hell, Carlo was talking about you the first time you took his cab. He could not believe how a person would stick up for a stranger."

Charles told her, "Hell, if I knew he was an asshole, I would take the other cab." Then he picked up his glass of beer and raised it. "Here is a toast from one asshole to another."

Carlo picked his glass. "Hell, I say to new friends." He then looked at Ciara. "Hell, that means you too."

Then Ciara picked her glass up and just said, "Well, hell, to good friends." They all took a drink.

Charles sat his glass down and asked Carlo, "Well, is there any other surprises you have?"

"No, the rest I told you about myself is true. I am divorced. I do have a lot of money. I'm just in a situation I do not know what to do. Mom and

Dad had this apartment not in use, so I've been living here for that past year or so."

Carlo's dad must have been eavesdropping; he yelled back, "Hell, if you want him to move with you, that is OK with me!"

Mary turned around and told Jake, "He can stay as long as he wants as long he pays his rent!" She started to laugh. "Hell, let us buy this round."

Charles told them, "We will drink one more, and then I have to get something to eat."

Mary told him, "Hell, just eat here."

Charles looked at Ciara. "Well, I thought maybe Ciara and I can go where she wants to go."

Carlo told his mom he would stay here and eat. Ciara told Charles, "Well, hell, I can eat here. We are with new friends."

Charles looked at Mary. "All right, we will eat here as long as I pay the bill."

Carlo told his mom, "Get the menus before Charles changes his mind." Mary brought them over.

Charles asked Ciara if she would give him a ride back to his hotel. Ciara, with a very pleasant smile, told him, "Well, I guess I will."

Carlo looked at him. "Hell, I have your clubs. What should I do with them?"

Ciara told Carlo, "Why not keep them and you and Charles go golfing tomorrow but not until noon?"

Carlo told Charles, "Hell, I just so happen to have a tee time. I have two groups teeing off at eleven thirty. Usually, there is always one or two not showing up. Either way, I know I can get you on with us." He looked at Ciara in a way that said, *Is that all right?*

Ciara looked at them. "Well, I can be gone by ten. Will that work out?"

Charles was embarrassed and asked Ciara, "You sure that is all right?"

"Hell, if it was not, you probably would pout the rest of the day. Hell, I have to go to the station to straighten out what happened today. I better be at the station by nine thirty or so anyway."

Carlo and Charles both looked at her and at the same time asked, "You think you are in trouble?"

She looked at her phone. "Well, since the incident in the parking lot, I have three messages from the captain and two from George. So I say yes, I probably am in trouble."

Charles told Ciara, "Well, hell, call George first and just see how bad it is. Maybe we should go to the station now."

"Are you crazy? I have been drinking in a way on the job. Then I bring you and Carlo in? That will look really cool."

"Well, what are you going to do?"

Ciara dialed George's number. He answered on the second ring. George knew it was Ciara and asked, "What the hell are you doing pulling over that car?"

"Calm down. I had my reasons."

George told her the captain was not pleased. "You better talk to him."

Ciara asked, "How long has it been since you found out?"

"Hell, about an hour and half ago."

"I will be in tomorrow at around nine thirty. Tell the captain I am not feeling very good. I took the afternoon off."

George told her, "Hell, I already told him that. I do not think he believes me, but he did not show any emotion. I think he will go along with that. Just be in tomorrow."

"I will be there. Trust me." Then she hung up.

Charles did not wait for Ciara to put her phone away. "Well, how much trouble are you in?"

"I will tell you tomorrow night at supper at my choice of restaurant."

Charles said with a smile, "You have a deal."

Ciara said as she was looking at Carlo, "You better be sober and on time."

"You have a deal. I will make sure he will be there. Just tell me where."

"I will tell Charles in the morning, and then you make sure he is there on time and sober, or I will arrest both of you for something."

Charles said with a smile on his face, "You have a date."

Carlo's mom took their order. Ciara and Charles had steak sandwiches with baked potatoes. Carlo must have been hungry; he ordered the biggest T-bone they had, plus a salad and baked potatoes. Charles was looking at Mary while Carlo was ordering. He asked if Carlo always ate that much. Mary said with a smile on her face, "Just when someone else buys."

"I asked for that one."

Carlo told his mom, "I will go over and get the other beers." Mary thanked Carlo and then went back to the kitchen.

As Carlo got up, Charles told him, "Why not have your dad come over to the table and sit with us?"

"You are crazy. Dad will start telling his stories. Hell, you and Ciara will never get out of here."

Carlo's dad must have good ears. He was halfway down from the bar and told Charles, "Thanks for inviting me." Jake sat down. "Hell, this is a special day. Give me one of those beers."

Carlo came back with the drinks. Ciara told him, "No more for me until the food comes."

"That would be smart. You already have enough trouble for the day."

Charles noticed right off the bat that Ciara and Jake were talking about Old Joe's. He was laughing when Carlo's dad told Ciara how her grandpa kicked him and his brother out many of times. Jake was telling her how, one time, her grandpa had three mean guys come in. "Your grandpa knew he could not handle the situation without help. He came down to where we were. Your grandpa told us if we would help him. We told him sure. So in a short while, the three guys were beginning to get real rowdy. Your grandpa told them to either settle down or get out. The tallest one asked, 'Who is going to do it?'

"I do not know how your grandpa did it. He put one hand on the bar and used it to pivot himself on the other side of the bar. He told that guy, 'Well, you are looking at him.' Your grandpa swung and hit the guy right in the jaw. The guy was startled. The other two were just as surprised. They jumped on your grandpa. Your grandpa swung around, got the one off his back, and got one or two hits off. Then all three of them were on your grandpa."

Ciara asked, "Well, did you help my grandpa or not?"

"Well, just listen to the story. After a few seconds, we could tell your grandpa was in trouble. So my friend told me, 'Well, it is time.' My friend Henry lunged toward your grandpa. He told them, 'All right, it is time to leave.' Your grandpa was standing there pretty bunged up.

"Henry noticed that the guy on his right had his hand in his pocket, like he was getting something out. That damn Henry nailed him before he got his hand out. Then the other guy swung at Henry. Henry took the hit. The sound of it had to hurt. So I naturally came over. I told the guy, 'That is my friend you hit.' The third guy told me, 'Like this.' He swung at me. I ducked and hit the guy right on the chin. Henry grabbed this man and hit him real hard.

"Hell, your grandpa had gotten recharged. He had the guy on the floor that really started the whole thing. He was beating the shit out of him. That poor guy yelled out, 'All right, we will leave!' So Henry and I stopped fighting. Your grandpa picked the one on the floor up and told them, 'Leave now. Do not come back unless you are respectable.' Henry and I looked at each other. We both heard that before.

"So the three guys left. Your grandpa, with a smile just, told us, "Thanks. It took you long enough.' Henry replied with a smile, 'Well, hell, you can handle Jake and me. We just wanted to see how you can handle three.' I told your grandpa he was handling it OK from the start. Your grandpa gave us free drinks the rest of the night.

"Henry asked your grandpa why he asked us. He said, 'Hell, I fought you guys before. You two hit real good. I figured if I was in a fight, I'd rather have you two on my side than against me.' Henry took that as real good compliment. He was proud of his fighting. I never was that proud. I was just at the wrong place when Henry wanted to fight.

"From that day on, your grandpa and Henry and I were on good terms. We never had an argument or a fight since that day at Old Joe's. Your grandpa gave us our first drink on the house and our last drink. He just said, 'Drive carefully. Any problem, call me first.' We never had a problem except one time.

"We witnessed a car wreck. We stopped and helped this old guy out of his car. The other cars, all of them, were out on their own. Henry did have too much to drink. The officer noticed his beer breath. He asked how much he had. Henry told him, 'Hell, we've seen the wreck and helped this old guy out. I did not plan on me being questioned.'

"The police officer thanked him for helping, but he smelled the beer. Henry asked, 'Are you going to arrest me?' The officer asked, 'Will you take the test?' Henry took a few seconds and told him, 'Do you not think the injured should be taken care of first? Wonder if one of them needs an ambulance. While you are messing with me, someone dies.' The officer told Henry, 'I have help coming.' At that moment, the old guy fated while we were getting out of the car. The cop told Henry, 'You do not leave.'

"I thought what your grandpa told us. I called him. I never used my phone that much. I am just glad I had Old Joe's on my memory list. I pushed the button. Your grandpa answered. I told him, 'This is Jake. We have a problem.' Your grandpa asked, 'Well, what is it?' I told him the situation. Your grandpa asked, 'What is the officer's name.' Hell, I did not know. Your grandpa told me, 'Let me speak to him when he comes back.'

"We stood there for five to ten minutes. Your grandpa never left the phone. Finally, the officer came back. I handed him the phone and told him, 'Here, this person wants to talk to you.' The officer took the phone. I do not know what your grandpa told him. The officer gave me back the phone and told us, 'Thanks for helping. Get the hell out of here.'"

Ciara asked, "You still do not know?"

"Well, several years later, Henry asked him about that. Your grandpa, with that smile of his, told Henry, 'It is not what you do. It is who you know.' At that time, it just so happened the mayor was a customer of his. He would get drunk, and your grandpa would take him home. Sometimes he took him to another house. He did not know who lived there. He just knew it was not his house. The mayor always said to your grandpa, 'For your not telling anyone, I will not forget it.'

"So your grandpa, with that smile, told that police office to call the mayor and tell him that Old Joe's needs this matter dropped. He did not give his name or nothing. Your grandpa told the officer, 'If you do not, I will make sure you are going to be on dog patrol.'

"Well, after that phone call, neither Henry nor I have ever been bothered by the police. Believe me, we should have been. They just took us home or told us to go straight home. I believe your grandpa knew whose house it was. He just did not let us or, for that matter, anyone now. Since then, naturally, the mayor died and your grandpa. The police still treats me nice until now."

Jake looked right at Charles, who said, "Well, I do not want no harm or trouble. I just want to find the truth about my son's murder."

Jake looked at Charles and Carlo with this big grin. "Hell, I am too old to fight anymore. So you do whatever is necessary. Mary and I can take care of ourselves. I believe Carlo and you are not stupid. Just be careful."

Ciara interrupted, "As long as I am on the team, I will do my best to make sure of that."

Charles did not realize, after all these stories, Mary brought the food. They were almost done eating. He looked at the big clock on the wall. He liked that kind of clock because he could see the numbers really well. Charles asked Ciara, "Would it be all right if we leave after we eat and have one more drink?"

Ciara smiled. "That will be fine with me. Maybe we can use your Jacuzzi one more time."

Carlo, with a big smile, asked Charles, "That sounds like fun. Can I come?"

Charles looked a Ciara. "Well, not this time but maybe some other time."

Ciara told Carlo. "Well, I agree with Charles. Three is a crowd this time."

Carlo was still laughing. "Well, I just thought I'd ask."

Charles told him, "Good try, my friend. I cannot wait till you meet my friend Tom. You two will definitely get along."

When they finished their drink, Charles and Ciara thanked everyone for a good time. Charles noticed there was no ticket yet. He asked Mary, "How much do I owe?"

"This is on us."

Charles told her, "Thanks but next time. I told all of you I was buying." He handed Carlo a hundred. "Here, you take care of this. Give me the change tomorrow."

"Hey, what time?"

Ciara told him, "Any time after seven thirty. I will be gone by then. Some of us has to work."

Carlo told Charles, "I will be there at eight o'clock. I want to check out your room. I have never seen a fancy hotel room."

"Sure, that will be great."

On the way to the hotel, Charles asked Ciara if she thought things would be all right for her tomorrow. Ciara assured him she probably would be in some kind of trouble but nothing she could not handle. Charles told her, "If there is anything I or Carlo can do, you make sure you get hold of us fast."

Ciara assured him she would. "Let's just have fun tonight. Worry about tomorrow when it comes." Charles reached over and gave her a light kiss on the cheek. "Just wait. We are almost there. I can hardly wait either."

As Ciara pulled up to the lobby, she parked her car. Charles noticed that a car was parked with two guys in it. Ciara had seen it. "Yes, they are the two guys we pulled over earlier. Do not worry about them. You are getting more observant. You might not get yourself killed as fast after all."

Charles told her, "Very funny."

As Charles opened the hotel door for Ciara, he noticed that nobody was around. This was strange to him. He had always seen someone at the desk or somewhere in the area. Charles started to tell Ciara, "Something is strange."

"Just keep going."

When they got right to the desk, a guy stood up. Ciara and Charles both were startled. He asked, "Can I help you, Mr. Appel?"

"No, we are just going to my room."

The guy told Charles, "I dropped a damn key on the floor. I could not find it."

Charles told Ciara, "Let's go."

As she walked around the counter toward the elevator, she noticed the key card just caught the edge of a manila folder. She stopped, took the key card out, and told the desk clerk, "Here is your key card." The clerk looked at it. He could not believe he could not see that.

Charles told Ciara, "Hurry up, the elevator door is open."

Ciara walked faster toward Charles. With her funny look, she asked, "Are you getting impatient?" He told her yes and then kissed her as they entered the elevator. They were still kissing as it reached the floor. Charles never felt this way for many years. He could tell he was rushing things. Ciara thought the same thing; she never felt this way over a person for so long.

Charles opened the room door for Ciara. The second she was in the room, she already had her blouse unbuttoned. Charles went right toward her. He reached out toward her, had his hand on her breast, and started to take off her bra. Ciara helped him take off his shirt. They were both naked in no time. Ciara told Charles she cannot wait to get in the Jacuzzi.

She made sure her naked body was rubbing against Charles's while she was getting in the Jacuzzi. Charles started to kiss her and rub her breasts. Ciara said with a big smile, "You are doing a lot better." They made love in the Jacuzzi.

When they were done, Ciara asked if he could get her a glass of wine. Charles was looking at her nice body as he was reaching for it. He told her, "I cannot believe how I feel toward you. I never felt this way in a long time."

Ciara said with a smile, "Me either." Then she gave him a nice long kiss.

They just sat in the Jacuzzi enjoying each other, not saying a word, just looking at each other. Ciara broke the silence. "I have to get some sleep for tomorrow." Charles agreed and went toward the bed. She spanked Charles's ass. He grabbed Ciara and pushed her on the bed. They made love one more time before they went to sleep.

When Charles woke up in the morning, Ciara was already dressed. She told Charles she had to be at her apartment so George can pick her up. Charles told her, "Good luck with your captain."

"Do not worry, just call me at around nine. Tell me where you and Carlo will be."

"Do not worry, I will make sure we get a hold of you." Charles then got out of bed and gave Ciara a kiss goodbye. They were both smiling like they never smiled before.

Charles proceeded to get dressed. By this time, he was waking up. He decided to call Tom and Kate to make sure everything was on time. Just before he picked up the phone, it rang. Charles answered it. It was Carlo down at the lobby. Charles thought Carlo was early, but instead, he was late. He told him, "Just come on up."

"That will be great. I love to see your room."

Charles started to dial the phone. After a few minutes, he had finally gotten through. By this time, Carlo was knocking on the door. Charles walked over and let him in. Carlo was checking out the rooms. Kate finally answered. Charles started to talk to her about picking him up at the airport. Kate told him, "We will be there."

"Will Tom be there?"

"What do you think?"

"No, he is playing cards uptown."

"You got that right." Kate went on. "You will never believe whom he will be with."

Charles asked in a surprised voice, "All right, who is he playing with?"

"Judge Hallway from New York."

Charles just about dropped the phone. Carlo noticed the look on Charles's face. He asked, "Are you all right?" Charles told him to just pour him a drink too.

Charles then asked Kate, "What brought him to Coal City?"

"Well, he called your house. He did not get an answer, so he called us. He knew about Jake. He wanted to tell you. Then I told him where you were and that you'd be back late today. He told me he is coming to Coal City. I told him that was not necessary. Well, here he is. He got here last night. You know, he knows something. He wants to wait to tell us when you get here."

"Do not say no more. Just tell Tom whatever the judge wants to do, just do it."

Kate told Charles, "Hell, after they play cards, they have a tee time."

"See you at the airport tonight."

"Oh wait, Nate called and told me he knows he will be there. The schedule should work out." Charles thanked Kate and then hung up.

Carlo handed Charles his drink. He told Charles, "Ciara is right. This is one hell of a suite."

"Yes. I have never seen this kind of room in my life until this week."

Carlo asked, "What is wrong?" Charles gave him a look. "Hey, I could tell you are surprised or something."

"Well, this Judge Hallway came to Coal City."

"Who is Judge Hallway?"

"Well, I will tell you on the way to the golf course."

Carlo and Charles left the room. Walking to the elevator, Charles had seen Isabel. He asked her how things were going. She told Charles, "Just fine. Thanks for asking."

They kept walking toward the elevator. Charles stopped and turned around. "Isabel, I have a favor to ask."

Isabel turned to her side. "What do you need?"

"Do you have any relation or friends that work in any nice hotel in New York?"

Isabel said with a big smile, "I sure do."

"Could you, by chance, try to get a couple of rooms, say, next week?"

"Well, I can try."

"I want the floors your friends work on."

Isabel told Charles, "I understand."

Charles took a napkin off her cart. "Here, call this number." Then he turned. "Hell, Carlo, what is your number?" Carlo walked up, took the pen, and wrote down his cell number. Charles told Isabel, "Keep this to ourselves."

"Do not worry, I will call you, say, by noon."

"That will be great."

Carlo and Charles then went to the elevator. Carlo told him, "Now you have to explain this too."

"Hell, I hope the golf course is a long ways."

"It is not, but we have eighteen holes to talk about this."

The elevator was on the main floor in no time. Charles walked by Susan and asked, "How is your morning?"

With a smile, she replied, "Just fine, Charles."

Carlo asked, "Is there anyone you do not know?"

Charles laughed. "Well, I just talk to people."

Carlo, in a quiet voice, said, "No shit."

Charles heard that and just tapped Carlo on the shoulder. "All right, you smart-ass." Then they were both laughing.

Carlo told Charles as they were walking to the car, "You notice that car over there?"

"Yes, they were here last night too."

"You must really have someone nervous."

"I hope not too nervous. I want to beat you in golf."

"Not today. This is my day."

As Carlo started toward the golf course, he asked, "All right, who is Judge Hallway?"

Charles looked at him. "Well, here is the story. A few years ago, Kate, Tom, his son and daughter, and I went to a New York golf tournament. Well, Kate—as a surprise to us—made a tee time at this good golf course. Then Kate and Bobby went shopping.

"Well, Tom and his boy, Bill, and I had this tee time. Well, Judge Hallway played with us. Like usual, we were drinking. For some reason, I was not feeling that good. So I thought I'd wait till supper. Well, Tom and this judge hit it off real good. By the time we were done, the judge had enough beer. The judge still beat all of us. Well, anyway, to settle up, we invited the judge to have one more drink with us. So he did. Then he left. Well, we left just not too long after that.

"Well, I was driving. We went down this road, trying to find our turn. Well, this car was in the ditch. You could tell he missed his turn by four to five feet. Well, I got out. Hell, it was the judge. Well, I told Tom, 'Let's try to get the car out.' Well, a car was coming at us. So I put the judge in the back seat. By this time, the car was getting close. I noticed it was a cop. He asked what I was doing. I told him I was making sure this guy was all right.

"The cop asked who was driving this car. The other cop told his partner, 'Hey, look who this is. This is Judge Hallway.' Then the cop asked, 'What is going on?' Then Tom was walking over. Hell, here, we have a drunk judge. Tom was not in too good of shape. Just glad young Bill and I were the only ones in good shape. So I told the cops I was driving the judge home, and young Bill was following us. Then I turned around and asked the judge, 'Where is the turn?' That was when I drove off the road.

"Well, I do not think the cops believed me, but here was the judge in the back seat. I was not drunk for once. Young Bill was not drunk, just the judge and Tom. So they helped get the car out of the ditch and even made sure we made it to the judge's house. You could not believe this house. Hell, it has to be two to three million.

"Anyway, we got the judge in his house. Bill made some coffee. Hell, he has a butler. He was off that day. So we made sure the judge was all right, and then we were going to leave. Well, Judge Hallway insisted we stay awhile. So young Bill called his mom and told him we'd be there in a few minutes. The judge told Bill, 'Hey, tell them to put on some good clothes. I am going to treat all of you.'

"Well, the judge got his phone. He had some numbers on speed dial. The first number was a restaurant. He made the reservations for all of us. Then he pressed another number. He told this person, 'Hey, pick up . . .' And then he asked us for their last name. Bill said Parkes. 'Pick up the Parkes family in twenty minutes.' Then he asked where we were staying at. Tom told him the Hilton down the road. The judge relayed the info. Then he hung up.

"Tom asked the judge what was going on. He said, 'Well, for helping me out, I made your group a reservation in this nice restaurant. I have a limo picking you up. This is all on me. I will have special tickets for you tomorrow at the tournament. They will be at the hotel desk by tomorrow morning.'

"Sure enough, we went to the lobby and asked the hotel clerk if anyone left us anything. The clerk told us yes and handed me this envelope. Sure enough, there were these golf passes. The clerk asked when we were leaving. Tom told him in about a half hour. The clerk told Tom, 'Good, that will give me time.' I asked, 'Time for what?' He said, 'I am to call Judge's limo service so the limo can pick you up.' I asked, 'Pick us up?' The clerk said with a smile, 'The judge is going to let you use his limo today. That is all I know.' The clerk started to dial this number. He talked to someone. Then after he hung up, the clerk told us, 'The limo will be here in a half hour. Just be at the main door.'

"Sure enough, in a half hour, here was this same limo that we had last night. Kate and Bobby could not believe it. For that matter, never could us guys. The limo took us right to the main gate. The driver opened the door for us. Then he walked with us. He talked to this person at the gate. From that moment on, we had people with us the rest of the day.

"Bill and Bobby had all the autographs they could get. Kate and Bobby had several autographs. Tom and I had drinks with the pros when they were done with the round. I will never forget that day as long as I live.

Well, anyway, from that day on, Judge Hallway gave us a Christmas card. He gave us golf tickets to several tournaments no matter where the tournaments are.

"Judge Hallway is in Coal City right now. Hell, I have not seen him for a year and half. He is going to stay there until Tuesday. Kate told me he is staying with them."

Carlo told Charles, "Hell, sounds like he wants to see you bad."

"It will be a very interesting time when I get back. Right now, though, I am going to beat you in golf."

"That will not happen today."

"Well, hell, I will bet you a meal at the airport."

Carlo told Charles, "You have a bet."

By this time, they were at the golf course. Ciara called using Carlo's cell phone number. Carlo handed the phone to Charles. He asked, "How are things going with the captain?"

"Hell, not real good. I am not fired yet. I am still off the case. How was the game going?"

"Hell, I am two strokes down, just teeing off on number 3."

Ciara laughed and then told him, "Good luck."

"Why not I call you, say, in three hours? You can meet us at the hotel or the airport." Ciara told Charles said it would most likely have to be at the airport. Charles asked, "You will make sure you see me, won't you?"

"Yes, I will. I love you."

Charles was looking at Carlo and then told Ciara, "I love you too. I will call in three hours." Then he hung up.

Carlo was laughing. "I love you too." Then he hit his drive right down the middle.

Charles told him to be quiet, and he hit his drive to the right, about ten yards in the rough. "I will still beat you."

"For a dinner before you leave."

"You have a bet."

At the end, Charles lost by five strokes. Carlo told him he was getting hungry. Charles told him, "After we go to the hotel and pack, we will call Ciara and then eat at the airport."

"That will be fine. You are buying."

"I know."

While they were lifting their clubs in the car, Carlo noticed they were still following them. He told Charles, "They are still with us."

"Hell, I am leaving today anyway. Who cares? We will go the hotel, make arrangements, and then call Ciara. We can all eat at the airport."

They went back to Charles's room. Carlo helped himself to a drink. Charles told him, "Do not forget me."

Charles noticed a note on the table. It just told him to talk to Isabel before he left. He told Carlo, "Isabel must have done me some good."

Carlo handed him his drink as Charles was going back to the door. Charles opened the door and did not see anyone. He told Carlo, "We have to find Isabel before I leave."

He then called Ciara on Carlo's cell, where Ciara's phone number was saved. Charles had to have Carlo dial. He told him, "I am going have to learn this shit." Carlo handed the phone to Charles. The phone was still ringing.

Ciara's voice answered, "Hello, Charles, Carlo."

Charles told her it was him. "Can you be at the airport in a half hour or so?"

"Yes, that will be great."

"Just meet us at the bar. Love you." Ciara told him she loved him.

As Charles hung up, Carlo told him, "You are hooked."

Charles laughed. "Hell, this is all a new experience for me."

Charles called down to the desk. He was hoping it was Susan. Sure enough, the voice from desk asked, "How can I help you, Charles?" He knew it was Susan.

"I am checking out in the next few minutes. Make sure my bill is ready."

"No problem."

Charles then asked Susan, "Is there any chance getting this same room or one like it in, say, three weeks or so?"

"I am sure I can figure a way. When you check out, I will give you some dates."

"That will be fine. One more thing, I need to talk to Isabel. I cannot find her."

Susan told him, "I will let her know. She will be there, say, in five minutes. She is probably on another floor. We had one call off today." Charles thanked Susan and then hung up.

Carlo was already on his second drink. He was getting one for Charles while he was packing. Carlo heard someone at the door and told Charles about it. He told Carlo, "Ask if it is Isabel. If so, let her in."

Carlo went to the door; it was Isabel. He let her in just as Charles asked. Isabel came walking in the room where Charles was packing. She told Charles, "Here, I will do that. You are wrinkling your clothes."

Charles asked, "Well, did you do me any good?"

"I have your reservations at the New York Express a week from today. The room is on the same floor as my cousin works on."

Charles thanked her and handed her two hundred dollars. "Here, take this, and split it up with all of you that helped me." Isabel thanked Charles.